★ ★ ★ THE ★ ★ ★

PRESIDENCY

IN HEADLINES
AND QUOTES

THE
PRESIDENCY
IN HEADLINES
AND QUOTES

A Satirical Exploration Of The Art Of
Literature By Irreverent Youth

Sponsored By:
The Cyrenaic Literary Society of America

Compiled and Edited By:
Ethelréd Pennämé

To the moon for its humanity, the sea for its honesty, the sky for its sincerity, the earth for its probity, the shore for its steadfastness, the stars for their tenderness, the forest for its candor, the tide for its faithfulness, the mountains for their affection, the plains for their constancy, the valleys for their harmony, the rain for its integrity, the snow for its loyalty, the sleet for its simplicity, the ice for its love, the slope for its bravery, the cliff for its determination, the earthquake for its wisdom, the tsunami for its frankness, the tornado for its devotion, the hurricane for its sagacity, the flood for its sensitivity, the mudslide for its allegiance, the meteor for its unfussiness, and the writer for his anthropomorphism.

CONTENTS

INTRODUCTION

The Cyrenaic Literary Society of America was created to foster a heightened interest in outstanding literary works by encouraging scholarly competition among irreverent youth: particularly literature majors. The goal was to create an alternative approach to the study of literature that would employ novel techniques to motivate supremely indifferent and congenitally unfit young people to plunge deeply into the pool of great works, thus fostering a primitive appreciation of symbolism, erudition, subtlety, structure and style separate and apart from social media.

This book represents one such technique. Randomly selected sweet but slow college students representing schools from around the world have been asked to enter into a two–year competition under which they are to match headlines from various news organizations about the Trump presidency with possibly-related quotations from historical and contemporary literature. To foster uniformity of expression and similarity of research, the first year would be dedicated to mellifluous headlines and quotes, and the second year would be dedicated to avuncular headlines and quotes. Each school would be assigned two topics to consider a year.

Presented here is a barely-conscious selection of the most imaginative satirical headlines and quotes relating to the president's first year in office. They have been selected for flavor, hue, buoyancy, alacrity, turbidity and proclivity. It is hoped the effort has fostered a greater appreciation of the art of literature. Alienated college students from around the world are encouraged to conduct similar competitions in their environs and on their quadrangles using the literary publications to hand.

Finally, if it serves no other purpose, let this tome be a history of incompetence and narcissism so profound it staggers the imagination.

CHAPTER 1

THE WALLY BALLOU LANGUAGE IMMERSION AND ORIENTAL PHONETICS COLLEGE

TOPICS:
POPULARITY AND REPUTATION

The Wally Ballou Language Immersion and Oriental Phonetics College

1 Trump Arrives, Set to Assume Power
— *New York Times, 1/20/17*

There is nothing more explosive than a skilled population condemned to inaction. Such a population is likely to become a hotbed of extremism and intolerance, and be receptive to any proselytizing ideology, however absurd and vicious, which promises vast action.
— *Eric Hoffer, "Automation, Leisure, And The Masses" (1967)*

2 Inauguration Protesters and Police Clash on Washington Streets
— *New York Times, 1/20/17*

If a house be divided against itself, that house cannot stand.
— *Bible, Mark 3:25*

3 Defiant Voices Flood U.S. Cities as Women Rally for Rights
— *New York Times, 1/21/17*

Mass movements can rise and spread without belief in a God, but never without belief in a devil.
— *Eric Hoffer, "The True Believer" (1951)*

4 Trump Takes to Twitter to Weigh in on Women's March
— *New York Times, 1/21/17*

More cranks take up unfashionable errors than unfashionable truths.
— *Bertrand Russell, "On An Outline Of Intellectual Rubbish" (1950)*

5 So Many Protests, So Little Space

— *New York Times, 1/27/17*

A little rebellion, now and then, is a good thing, and as necessary in the political world as storms in the physical.

— *Thomas Jefferson, Letter To James Madison (1787)*

---

6 Anarchists Respond to Trump's Inauguration, by Any Means Necessary

— *New York Times, 2/2/17*

Assent – and you are sane - / Demur – you're straightaway dangerous - / And handled with a chain.

— *Emily Dickenson, Poem (1862)*

---

7 Pro-Trump Rally in Berkeley, California, Turns Violent

— *Huffington Post, 3/5/17*

It is notorious that no war between countries elicits as much hate and cruelty as civil war, in which there is no lack of acquaintance between the two warring sides.

— *Erich Fromm, "The Anatomy Of Human Destructiveness" (1973)*

---

8 Judge: Trump Incited Violence Against Protestors at Kentucky Rally

— *Reddit, 4/2/17*

Hatred is the coward's revenge for being intimidated.

— *George Bernard Shaw, "Major Barbara" (1905)*

---

9 For Liberals, Is It Time to Move to Norway?

— *New York Times, 4/15/17*

He that fears you present will hate you absent.

— *Thomas Fuller, M. D., "Gnomologia" (1732)*

_____

10 'He's An Embarrassment': Hostile Welcome for Trump on Return to New York

— The Guardian, 5/5/17

There is no fate that cannot be surmounted by scorn.

— Albert Camus, Title Essay, "The Myth Of Sisyphus" (1942)

_____

11 Donald Trump Impeachment Probe Resolution Passed by Los Angeles Council

— Reddit, 5/8/17

Resistance to tyrants is obedience to God.

— Thomas Jefferson, Motto Found Among His Papers (1826)

_____

12 Anti-Protest Bills Would 'Attack Right to Speak Out' Under Donald Trump

— The Guardian 5/8/17

The dagger plunged in the name of Freedom is plunged into the breast of Freedom.

— Jose Marti, "Pensamientos Seleccionados En Las Obras" (1942)

_____

13 Disapproval of Trump at Its Highest Yet

— Washington Post, 5/11/17

Moral contempt is a far greater indignity and insult than any type of crime.

— Nietzsche, "The Will To Power" (1888)

_____

14 FBI Agents Change Their Facebook Profile Photos to James Comey - A Gesture Normally Reserved for Slain Colleagues

— Independent, 5/12/17

Praise makes good men better and bad men worse.
— *Thomas Fuller, M.D., "Gnomologia" (1732)*

---

15 The Head of the Census Just Resigned. It Could Be as Serious as James Comey
— *Time, 5/13/17*

Behind everything we feel, there is always a sense of fear.
— *Ugo Betti, "Struggle 'Till Dawn" (1949)*

---

16 'The Art of the Deal' Ghostwriter: Trump Will Find a Way to Resign
— *Washington Examiner, 5/17/17*

There is no good in arguing with the inevitable. The only argument available with an east wind is to put on your coat.
— *James Russell Lowell, "Democracy And Other Addresses" (1887)*

---

17 Donald Trump Impeachment Petition Passes One Million Signatures
— *Yahoo!, 5/19/17*

The instinct of the people is right.
— *Emerson, "Power," The Conduct Of Life (1860)*

---

18 Approval of Donald Trump Drops to Lowest Since Inauguration: Reuters/Ipsos Poll
— *Reuters, 5/19/17*

The function of wisdom is to discriminate between good and evil.
— *Cicero, "De Offichs" (44 BCE)*

---

19 Jerry Brown Defies Trump on World Stage
— *Politico, 6/1/17*

Opposition, n. In politics, the party that prevents the Government from running amuck by hamstringing it.
— Ambrose Bierce, "The Devil's Dictionary" (1181-1911)

---

20 Support for Donald Trump's Impeachment Is Now Higher Than His Approval Rating
— Newsweek, 6/5/17

Justice delayed is democracy denied.
— Robert F. Kennedy, "Secure These Rights," The Pursuit Of Justice (1964)

---

21 'Cloud' Over Trump Is Now a Full Blown Thunderstorm
— Boston Globe, 6/8/17

It was [his] fate always to know the disaster that was coming and be unable to avert it.
— Edith Hamilton, "Mythology" (1940)

---

22 Comey's Testimony Shows: the Impeachment Machine Is Warming Up
— The Guardian, 6/8/17

Plots, true or false, are necessary things, / to raise up commonwealths, and ruin kings.
— John Dryden, "Absalom And Achitophel" (1681)

---

23 D.C. and Maryland to Sue President Trump Alleging Breach of Constitutional Oath
— Washington Post, 6/12/17

No man is above the law and no man is below it; nor do we ask any man's permission when we ask him to obey it.
— Theodore Roosevelt, Address (1904)

---

24 Victories Against Trumpcare Mounting. Here's How We Deal the Final Blow
— *The Guardian, 6/18/17*

The problems of victory are more agreeable than those of defeat, but they are no less difficult.
— *Sir Winston Churchill, Speech, House of Commons (1942)*

25 Six Members of President Trump's Advisory Council on HIV/ AIDS Have Resigned
— *The Verge, 6/18/17*

Conscience is thoroughly well-bred and soon leaves off talking to those who do not wish to hear it.
— *Samuel Butler, "Note-Books" (1912)*

26 Massachusetts and California vs. Trump
— *Wall Street Journal, 6/19/17 (Misconstrued)*

What counts is not necessarily the size of the dog in the fight – it's the size of the fight in the dog.
— *Dwight D. Eisenhower, Address To Republican National Committee (1958)*

27 California, Virginia Refuse to Give Personal Data to Trump's Voter Fraud Commission
— *Time, 6/29/17*

Better a friendly denial than unwilling compliance.
— *German Proverb*

28 Justice Department Corporate Crime Watchdog Resigns Saying Trump Makes It Impossible to Do Job
— *IBT National, 7/2/17*

Discontent is the first step in the progress of a man or a nation.
— Oscar Wilde, "A Woman Of No Importance" (1893)

---

29 Most Americans Think Washington Is Less Civil Under Trump
— Huffington Post, 7/3/17

With malice toward none, with charity for all, with firmness in the right as God gives us to see the right, let us strive on to finish the work we are in, to bind up the nation's wounds.
— Abraham Lincoln, Second Inaugural Address (1865)

---

30 Democrats File No Confidence Resolution Against Trump, Listing 88 Reasons Why He Is Unfit to Serve as President
— Independent, 7/19/17

When the Presidential virus attacks the system there is a tendency for the patient in his fever to move from the Right or the Left to the Center where the curative votes are.
— Gore Vidal, "Rocking The Boat" (1962)

---

31 Billionaire Florida Donor Rails Against Trump
— Politico, 7/20/17

Anger may be foolish and absurd, and one may be irritated when in the wrong, but a man never feels outraged unless in some respect he is at bottom right.
— Victor Hugo, "Fantine," Les Miserables (1862)

---

32 Trump's Failed Boycott Leads to Most Watched Sunday Football in Seven Years
— Shareblue Media, 7/26/17

To make fun of a person to his face is a brutal way of amusing one self; be delicate and cunning, and keep your laugh in your sleeve, lest you frighten away your game.
— Gelett Burgess, "The Romance Of The Commonplace" (1916)

---

33 Obamacare / Huge Blow for Trump as Revolt by McCain Kills Off Repeal Bill
— The Guardian, 7/28/17

If the abuse be enormous, nature will rise up, and claiming her original rights, overturn a corrupt political system.
— Samuel Johnson, Quoted In Boswell's "Life of Samuel Johnson" (1763)

---

34 Giant Inflatable Chicken Appears Behind White House
— ABC 7, 8/9/17

Our aches and pains conform to opinion. A man's as miserable as he thinks he is.
— Seneca, Letters To Lucilius (1st C. CE)

---

35 Don't Just Impeach Trump. End the Imperial Presidency
— New Republic, 8/12/17

A king can stand people's fighting but he can't last long if people start thinkIng.
— Will Rogers, "The Autobiography Of Will Rogers" (1949)

---

36 Protestors Swarm Trump Tower After Charlottesville: 'No Trump, No KKK, No Fascist USA'
— Daily Beast, 8/13/17

I could not love thee, dear, so much, / Loved I not honour more.
— Richard Lovelace, "To Lucasta, On Going To The Wars" (1649)

---

37 Merck CEO Resigns From Trump Council After Charlottesville
— *New York Times, 8/14/17*

Men of integrity, by their very existence, rekindle the belief that as a people we can live above the level of moral squalor. We need that belief; a cynical community is a corrupt community.
— *John W. Gardner, "The Aims Of A Free People," Excellence (1961)*

38 Thousands Give Trump Bronx Cheers as He Returns to Manhattan Home
— *New York Times, 8/15/17*

While the people retain their virtue and vigilance, no administration, by any extreme of wickedness or folly, can very seriously injure the government in the short space of four years.
— *Abraham Lincoln, First Inaugural Address (March, 1861)*

39 Under Armour and Intel C.E.O.s Follow Merck Chief Quitting Panel in Rebuke to Trump
— *New York Times, 8/15/17*

The fate of America cannot depend on any one man. The greatness of America is grounded in principles and not on any single personality.
— *Franklin D. Roosevelt, Speech, New York City (Nov., 1932)*

40 CEOs Rethinking Ties With White House
— *Wall Street Journal, 8/16/17 (Misconstrued)*

Ignorance is a blank sheet, on which we may write; but error is a scribbled one, on which we must first erase.
— *Charles Caleb Colton, "Lacon" (1825)*

41 Trump's Arts Council Puts Hidden 'RESIST' Message in Resignation Letter

— *Vice News, 8/18/17*

Ignorance is always ready to admire itself, / Procure yourself critical friends.

— *Nicolas Boileau, "L'Art Poetique" (1674)*

---

42 Carl Icahn Drops Out of Presidential Advisory Role

— *CNBC, 8/18/17*

O that I had wings like a dove! For then would I fly away, and be at rest.

— *Bible, Psalms 15:6*

---

43 Apple's CEO Cook Joins Chorus of Business Leaders Criticizing Trump's Remarks

— *Wall Street Journal, 8/18/17 (Misconstrued)*

Better be wise by the misfortunes of others than by your own.

— *Aesop, "The Lion, The Ass And The Fox Hunting," Fables (6th C. BCE)*

---

44 Wave of Resignations Hits Commerce Department's Board of 'Digital Economy' Advisors

— *Politico, 8/18/17*

To serve an unintelligent man is like crying in the wilderness, massaging the body of a dead man, planting water lilies on dry land, whispering in the ear of the deaf.

— *Panchatantra, Indian Fables (300 BCE)*

---

45 Trump's Evangelical Panel Remains Intact as Others Disband. Here Are His Religious Cheerleaders

— *The Guardian, 8/18/17*

I never knew any man in my life who could not bear another's misfortunes perfectly like a Christian.
— Alexander Pope, "Thoughts On Various Subjects" (1727)

---

46 Some Liberty University Graduates Are Returning Their Diplomas to Protest Trump
— NPR, 8/20/17

A peace above all earthly dignities, a still and quiet conscience.
— Shakespeare, "Henry VIII" (1612)

---

47 Trump Cybersecurity Advisors Resign, Citing His 'Insufficient Attention' to Threats
— Fortune, 8/26/17

World War III will be triggered off not by suppressed nationalists seeking political independence, as happened the first time around when the Serbs at Sarajevo shot the heir to the Austrian throne, but by some semiliterate, whacked-out "loner" who lobs a rocket into a nuclear arsenal in order to impress Brook Shields.
— Philip Roth, "The Counterlife" (1987)

---

48 Most Americans Strongly Dislike Trump – But the Angry Minority That Adores Him Controls Our Politics
— Salon, 8/30/17

Behavior is a mirror in which everyone displays his own image.
— Goethe, "Elective Affinities" (1809)

---

49 Trump Becomes the Boogeyman: 'American Horror Story' [TV Show] Portrays a Post-Election World Gone Mad
— Washington Post, 9/3/17

Fear is an instructor of great sagacity and the herald of all revolutions.

— Emerson, "Compensation," Essays: First Series (1841

50 Ann Arbor Council Votes 11 – 0 to Join Fight Against Trump's Travel Ban

— MLive, 9/5/17

What country can preserve its liberties, if its rulers are not warned from time to time, that this people preserve the spirit of resistance?

— Thomas Jefferson, Letter To Col. William S. Smith (Nov., 1787)

51 Attorneys General From 15 States and D.C. Sue to Save DACA

— Washington Post, 9/6/17

It is not desirable to cultivate a respect for the law, so much as for the right.

— Thoreau, "Civil Disobedience" (1849)

52 Lin-Manuel Miranda Slams Trump For Puerto Rico Attacks: 'You're Going Straight to Hell'

— The Hill, 9/30/17

One is always wrong to open a conversation with the devil, for, however he goes about it, he always insists on having the last word.

— Andre Gide, "Journals" (1917)

53 US Defense Secretary Breaks With Trump in Backing Iran Nuclear Deal

— The Guardian, 10/3/17

There are people whom one [the Defense Secretary] should like very well to drop, but would not wish to be dropped by.

— Samuel Johnson, Quoted In Boswell's "Life Of Samuel Johnson" (1781)

---

54 'Tonight Show' Writer Fires Back at Trump: 'Stop Tweeting Nonsense and Go Do Your Job'

— Reddit, 10/7/17

When I think over what I have said, I envy dumb people.

— Seneca, "On A Happy Life," Moral Essays" (1st C. BCE)

---

55 Donald Trump Threatens to 'Change Tax Law' to Penalize NFL Over 'Take a Knee' Protests

— Independent, 10/10/17

Speaking generally, punishment hardens and numbs, it produces concentration, it sharpens the consciousness of alienation, it strengthens the power of resistance.

— Nietzsche, "The Genealogy Of Morals" (1887)

---

56 U.S. States Sue to Block Trump's Obamacare Subsidies Cut

— Huffington Post, 10/13/17

A stitch in time saves nine.

— Francis Bailey, Journal (1797)

---

57 Democrats in California Governor's Race Compete to Be the Most Anti-Trump

— News Source, 10/15/17

Virtue is more clearly shown in the performance of fine actions than in the nonperformance of base ones.

— Aristotle, "Nicomachean Ethics" (4th C. BCE)

---

58 Trump's Numbers are Really, Really Bad

— Bloomberg, 10/16/17

I think the bottom of the barrel is where the answers are.

— *Fred Eaglesmith, QUOTEMaster (2017)*

---

59 Donald Trump is Toxic and Inspiring a Democratic Surge in Virginia Governor's Race

— *Newsweek, 10/28/17*

God may still be in His Heaven, but there is more than sufficient evidence that all is not right with the world.

— *Irwin Edman, "Adam, The Baby, And The Man From Mars" (1929)*

---

60 Americans Will March in the Streets in 48 States If Trump Fires Robert Mueller

— *Newsweek, 10/30/17*

If there be fuel prepared, it is hard to tell whence the spark shall come that shall set it on fire.

— *Francis Bacon, "Of Seditions And Troubles," Essays (1625)*

---

61 Poll: Most Say This is the Lowest Point They Can Remember for US

— *The Hill, 11/1/17*

I do care for something; but in my conscience, sir, I do not care for you: if that be to care for nothing, sir, I would it would make you invisible.

— *Shakespeare, "Twelfth Night" (1601 - 1602)*

---

62 Donald Trump Mocked by Hawaiians Holding 'Welcome to Kenya' Signs

— *Independent, 11/4/17*

I to make thee mad do mock thee thus.

— *Shakespeare, "Henry VI, Part 3" (1591)*

63 Cyclist Lost Her Job After Raising Middle Finger at Trump's Motorcade

— *New York Times, 11/6/17*

If the shoe fits, wear it.

— *Daniel Defoe, "The Dyet Of Poland" (1705)*

64 Homeland Security Chief Resisted White House Pressure on Immigrant Program

— *Wall Street Journal, 11/9/17 (Misconstrued)*

The heart of a fool is in his mouth, but the mouth of a wise man is in his heart.

— *Benjamin Franklin, "Poor Richard's Almanack" (1732 - 1757)*

65 UK House Speaker Doubles Down on Trump Parliament Speech Ban

— *Huffington Post, 11/10/17*

People do not seem to talk for the sake of expressing their opinions, but to maintain an opinion for the sake of talking.

— *William Hazlitt, "On Coffee-House Politicians," Table Talk (1821)*

66 President Trump Wasn't Even on the Ballot: Nevertheless, He Lost [Recent Elections]

— *Huffington Post, 11/11/17*

No man can lose what he never had.

— *Izaak Walton, "The Compleat Angler" (1653)*

67 Jacinda Ardern [New Zealand Prime Minister] to Donald Trump, 'No One Marched When I Was Elected'

— *The Guardian, 11/17/17*

Irreverence is the champion of liberty and its only sure defense.
— *Mark Twain, Notebook (1935)*

---

68 MSNBC'S Tur: Democrats Are 'Reeling' in Fundraising
— *News Source, 11/21/17*

Good luck needs no explanation.
— *Shirley Temple Black, Child Star (1988)*

---

69 Van Tries to Cut Into Trump's Motorcade in Florida [Driver Makes Obscene Gestures]
— *News Source, 11/25/17*

Safe Despair is it that raves - / Agony is frugal. / Puts itself severe away / For its own perusal.
— *Emily Dickinson, Poem (1873)*

---

70 Retired General Launches Remarkable Attack on Donald Trump: 'I Have Wasted 40 Years of My Life'
— *Independent, 11/27/17*

Oh, seek, my love, your newer way; / I'll not be left in sorrow. / So long as I have yesterday, / Go take your damned tomorrow!
— *Dorothy Parker, "Godspeed," Enough Rope (1926)*

---

71 Pelosi-Schumer Tactics Won't Beat Trump. Take the Fight to Him, Democrats
— *USA Today, 12/4/17*

A Smith and Wesson always beats 4 aces.
— *Canada Bill Jones, Riverboat Gambler and Card Sharp (1837 - 1877)*

---

72 USA Today Bashes Trump as 'Not Fit to Clean the Toilets' in Obama's Presidential Library

— *CNN, 12/13/17*

Every man is entitled to be valued by his best moment.

— *Emerson, "Beauty," The Conduct Of Life (1860)*

---

73 US Outnumbered 14 to 1 as It Vetoes UN Vote on Status of Jerusalem

— *The Guardian, 12/19/17*

When people are fanatically dedicated to political or religious faiths or any other kinds of dogmas or goals, it is always because those dogmas or goals are in doubt.

— *Robert M. Pirsig, "Zen And The Art Of Motorcycle Maintenance" (1974)*

---

74 This Guy Sent Trump's Treasury Secretary a Pile of Manure for Christmas [Over Tax Bill]

— *BuzzFeed News, 12/24/17*

With all this manure around, there's got to be a pony someplace.

— *Lois McMaster Bujold, Science Fiction Author, PictureQuotes (B. 1949)*

---

75 'We Have Tapped Into Something': Impeachment Drive Builds Digital Army to Take on Trump

— *Politico, 12/27/17*

A good indignation brings out all one's powers.

— *Emerson, "Journals" (1841)*

---

76 Trump Backs Protestors – As Long as They're Not Protesting Him

— *Politico, 1/2/18*

There is nothing that makes more cowards and feeble men than public opinion.
— Henry Ward Beecher, "Proverbs From Plymouth Pulpit" (1887)

---

77 The Voters [Blue-Collar Whites] Abandoning Donald Trump
— The Atlantic, 1/11/18

Wisdom / comes alone through suffering.
— Aeschylus, "Agamemnon" (458 BCE)

---

78 Sadiq Khan: Donald Trump's 'Got the Message' That Londoners Don't Want Him Here, Says Mayor
— Independent, 1/12/18

O, he is as tedious as a tired horse, a railing wife, worse than a smokey house.
— Shakespeare, "Henry IV, Part 1" (1597)

---

79 [Rep.] Maxine Walters Tears Into Donald Trump: The 'Most Despicable Human Being'
— Huffington Post, 1/13/18

All persons are puzzles until at last we find some word ["shithole"] or act the key to the man, to the woman; straightaway all their past words and actions lie in sight before us.
— Emerson, "Journals" (1842)

---

80 Projector Lights Up Trump's D.C. Hotel With 'Shithole' and Poop Emojis
— Huffington Post, 1/13/18

What's good for the goose is good for the gander.
— Idiom, "What's Sauce For the Goose Is Sauce For the Gander" (1670s)

---

81 Trump's Presidency Sinks Below Rock Bottom
— *Spiegel Online, 1/16/18*

He may keep his own grace, but he's almost out of mine, I can assure him.
— *Shakespeare, "Henry IV, Part 2" (1596 - 1599)*

---

82 Majority of National Park Service Board Resigns, Citing Administration Indifference
— *NPR, 1/17/18*

Stupid people are like glow sticks. I want to snap them and shake the shit out of them until the light comes on.
— *Pin By Brandi Swindell, Pinterest (Launched 2010)*

CHAPTER 2

AURORA COLLEGE OF THE EPHEMERAL MOUNDS AND DUNES

TOPICS:
PATRIOTISM AND DEVOTION

Aurora College of the Ephemeral Mounds and Dunes

83 White House Grants Press Credentials to a Pro-Trump Blog
— *New York Times, 1/13/17*

The pleasure we derive from doing favors is partly in the feeling it gives us that we are not altogether worthless.
— *Eric Hoffer, "The Passionate State Of Mind" (1954)*

84 Building a Wall of Ignorance
— *New York Times, 1/30/17*

The spirit of our American radicalism is destructive and aimless: it is not loving, it has no ulterior and divine ends; but is destructive only out of hatred and selfishness.
— *Emerson, "Politics," Essays: Second Series (1844)*

85 Trump's Warm Words for Strongmen Set Off Alarms
— *Politico, 2/5/17*

Dictators ride to and fro upon tigers from which they dare not dismount.
— *Hindustani Proverb, From Winston Churchill's "While England Slept" (1936)*

86 Donald Trump Has Made the World a 'Darker, Unstable Place,' Says Amnesty International
— *Reddit, 2/22/17*

One kills a man, one is an assassin; one kills millions, one is a conqueror; one kills everybody, one is a God.
— *Jean Rostand, "Pensees D'Un Biologiste" (1939)*

87 Why Trump Loves to Hate the Media
— *Washington Post, 2/22/17*

The most violent passions sometimes leave us at rest, but vanity agitates us constantly.
— *La Rochefoucauld, "Maxims" (1665)*

---

88 Bannon and Trump Are Out For Revenge
— *Washington Post, 2/24/17*

Do not judge, and you will never be mistaken.
— *Rosseau, "Emile" (1762)*

---

89 President's Attack Follows a Game Plan for Disruption
— *New York Times, 2/25/17*

Where the laws are not supreme, there demagogues spring up.
— *Aristotle, "Politics" (4th C. BCE)*

---

90 As Trump Heads to Congress, Polarization Is Hardening
— *Wall Street Journal, 2/28/17 (Misconstrued)*

A sect or party is an inelegant incognito devised to save a man from the vexation of thinking.
— *Emerson, "Journals" (1831)*

---

91 Do Vigilantes See Trump Giving Them a Wink and a Nod?
— *Washington Post, 3/2/17*

Hatred which could destroy so much, never failed to destroy the man who hated and this was an immutable law.
— *James Baldwin, "Notes Of A Native Son" (1994)*

---

92 Voters See More Hatred in the Country Since Trump Was Elected

— *Washington Post, 3/10/17*

We know well enough we are being unjust and despicable. But we don't restrain ourselves because we experience a certain pleasure, a primitive sort of satisfaction in moments like that.

— *Ugo Betti, "Landslide" (1936)*

---

93 How Trump Has Already Hurt American Democracy – in Just 50 Days

— *Washington Post, 3/10/17*

It is extraordinary we go through life with eyes half shut, with dull ears, with dormant thoughts. Perhaps it's just as well; and it may be that it is this very dullness that makes life to the incalculable majority so supportable and so welcome.

— *Joseph Conrad, "Lord Jim" (1900)*

---

94 As Trump Embraces the Military, Some Officers Express Wariness About Their Commander in Chief

— *Washington Post, 3/15/17*

Idealism is the noble toga that political gentlemen drape over their will to power.

— *Aldous Huxley, New York Herald Tribune (1963)*

---

95 Trump's 100th-Day Speech May Have Been the Most Hate-Filled in Modern History

— *Washington Post, 5/2/17*

I love mankind - it's the people I can't stand.

— *Charles M. Schulz, "Go Fly A Kite, Charlie Brown" (1963)*

---

96 DOJ Official Dodges Questions on Trump's Role in Hate Crime Surge

— *Huffington Post, 5/4/17*

Flight is lawful, when one flees from tyrants.

— *Racine, "Phaedra" (1677)*

———

97 Clapper: U.S. Institutions Under Assault by Trump

— *CNN, 5/14/17*

Though those that are betrayed do feel the treason sharply, yet the traitor stands in worse case of woe.

— *Shakespeare, "Cymbeline" (1609)*

———

98 Congressman Threatened With Lynching After Calling for Trump Impeachment

— *CBS, 5/20/17*

Man, is, and was always, a block-head and dullard, much readier to feel and digest [and threaten], than to think and consider.

— *Thomas Carlyle, "Sartor Resartus" (1836)*

———

99 Tough Talk [by Trump] on Extremism Weakened by Backing of Autocracies

— *The Guardian, 5/21/17*

Above all, it behooves us to oppress, and if possible to extinguish once and for all, our inveterate tendency to judge others by the extent to which they contrive to be like ourselves.

— *George F. Kennan, "American Diplomacy 1900-1950" (1951)*

———

100 Trump Praises Philippines President Duarte for Drug War That Has Killed 9,000 People

— *Huffington Post, 5/23/17*

Praise to the undeserving is severe satire.

— Benjamin Franklin, "Poor Richard's Almanack" (1732-57)

---

101 Portland Attack: Donald Trump Called on to Make Statement About Double Murder

— The Guardian, 5/28/17

Peace dies when the framework is ripped apart. When there is no longer a place that is yours in the world. Where you know no longer know where your friend is to be found.

— Saint-Exupery, "Flight To Arras" (1942)

---

102 Clearly President Trump Hates His Voters

— Seattle Times, 5/29/17

Any man who hates dogs and babies can't be all bad.

— Leo Rosten, Speaking at A Masquers' Club Banquet for W. C. Fields (1939)

---

103 Donald Trump Has Unleashed a White Crime Wave

— Business Insider, 6/3/17

There are many humorous things in the world, among them the white man's notion that he is less savage than the other savages.

— Mark Twain, "The White Man's Notion," Following The Equator (1897)

---

104 Trump Doubles Down on Fear-Mongering Despite Pushback

— Huffington Post, 6/11/17

Neither a man nor a crowd nor a nation can be trusted to act humanely or to think sanely under the influence of great fear.

— Bertrand Russell, "Intellectual Rubbish Outline," Unpopular Essays (1950)

---

105 Trump Political Arm to GOP: Get in Line

— Politico, 6/25/17

Tyrants never perish from tyranny, but always from folly, – when their fantasies have built up a palace for which the earth has no foundation.
— *Walter Savage Landor, "Imaginary Conversations" (1824-53)*

---

106 Trump's 'Fake News' Crusade Is the Stuff of Dictators
— *Chicago Tribune, 6/28/17*

There is no nonsense so arrant that it cannot be made the creed of the vast majority by adequate governmental action.
— *Bertrand Russell, "An Outline Of Intellectual Rubbish" (1950)*

---

107 The Trump Administration Is Planning An Unprecedented Attack on Voting Rights
— *The Nation, 6/30/17*

I believe there are more instances of the abridgment of the freedom of the people by gradual and silent encroachments of those in power than by violent and sudden usurpation.
— *James Madison, Speech, Virginia Convention (1788)*

---

108 Trump Joins Fray Over Request for States' Voter Data
— *Wall Street Journal, 7/1/17 (Misconstrued)*

To whom you tell your secrets, to him you resign your liberty.
— *Spanish Proverb*

---

109 Trump's Voter Suppression Efforts Have Begun
— *New York Times, 7/3/17*

So long as men worship the Caesars and Napoleons, Caesars and Napoleons will duly rise and make them miserable.
— *Aldous Huxley, "Ends And Means" (1937)*

---

110 Trump's Deeply Worrisome New York Times Interview Reveals a Lawless President

— Washington Post, 7/20/17

When you choose the lesser of two evils, always remember that it is still an evil.

— Max Lerner, "Actions And Passions" (1949)

111 Duterte Rejects Trump's Invitation to White House: 'I've Seen America and it's Lousy'

— Newsweek, 7/21/17

Cruel is the strife of brothers.

— Aristotle, "Politics" (4th C. BCE)

112 Trump Request for Voter Details Rattles States

— Wall Street Journal, 7/23/17 (Misconstrued)

Our imagination and reasoning powers facilitate anxiety; the anxious feeling is precipitated not by an absolute pending threat - such as worry about an examination, a speech, travel - but rather by the symbolic and often unconscious representations.

— Willard Gaylin, "Feelings: Our Vital Signs" (1979)

113 'Irresponsible, Unprofessional': NYPD Slams Trumps Comments Urging Police Not to Be 'Too Nice' to Suspects

— Business Insider, 7/29/17

It's the admirer and the watcher who provoke us to all the insanities we commit.

— Seneca, Letters To Lucilius (1st C. CE)

114 Jeff Sessions Bows to Trump Pressure and Launches Crackdown on Leakers
— *The Guardian, 8/4/17*

The Moving Finger writes; and, having writ, / Moves On: Nor all your Piety nor Wit / Shall lure it back to cancel half a Line / Nor all your Tears wash out a Word of it.
— *Omar Khayyam, "Rubaiyat" (11th – 12th C. CE)*

---

115 Poison Once Flowed in America's [Polluted] Waters. With Trump, It Might Again
— *The Guardian, 8/14/17*

We lose the forest for the trees, forgetting, even so far as we think at all, that we are trustees for those who come after us, squandering the patrimony which we have received.
— *Learned Hand, "The Spirit Of Liberty" (1959)*

---

116 Massive Search Warrant Targets Anti-Trump Website in Clear Threat to the Constitution
— *ACLU, 8/15/17*

Fear is sharp-sighted, and can see things underground, and much more in the skies.
— *Cervantes, "Don Quixote" (1605)*

---

117 Donald Trump Is a Nazi Sympathizer
— *Foreign Policy, 8/17/17*

It all goes back to those German existentialists who tell you how good dread is for you, how it saves you from distraction and gives you your freedom and makes you authentic. God is no more. But Death is.
— *Saul Bellow, "Herzog" (1964)*

---

118 Trump Pressures Courts on Border Restrictions
— *Wall Street Journal, 8/19/17 (Misconstrued)*

Do not expect justice where might is right.
— *Phaedrus, "The Cow, the Goat, the Sheep…," Fables (1st C. CE)*

---

119 Where Does the Trump Presidency Go Now? After the Last Week, It Looks Like a Descent Into Barbarism
— *Salon, 8/22/17*

One of the evils of democracy is you have to put up with the man you elect whether you want him or not.
— *Will Rogers, "The Autobiography of Will Rogers" (1949)*

---

120 There Is No Other Way to Say It: Trump's Arpaio Pardon Is Fascist
— *Daily Beast, 8/26/17*

Nowhere are prejudices more mistaken for truth, passion for reason, and invective for documentation than in politics. That is a realm, peopled by only villains or heroes, in which everything is either black or white and gray is a forbidden color.
— *John Mason Brown, "Through These Men" (1956)*

---

121 Biden: Trump's Contempt for U.S. Constitution 'Knows No Bounds'
— *The Hill, 8/27/17*

Those who see and observe kings, heroes, and statesmen, discover that they have headaches, indigestion, humors and passions, just like other people; every one of which in their turns determine their wills in defiance of their reason.
— *Lord Chesterfield, Letters To His Son (Dec., 1749).*

---

122 Fox News Poll: Americans Think Donald Trump Is An Unstable, Dishonest, Immoral Bully

— *Huffington Post, 9/1/17*

Those whose cause is just will never lack / good arguments.

— *Euripides, "Hecuba" (425 BCE)*

---

123 U.S. Appeals Court Rules Against Trump's Efforts to Broadly Enforce Travel Ban

— *Huffington Post, 9/7/17*

Tyrants are but the spawn of Ignorance, / Begotten by the slaves they trample on.

— *James Russell Lowell, "Prometheus" (1843)*

---

124 White House Spokeswoman: Justice Department 'Should Certainly Look At' Prosecuting Comey

— *Washington Post, 9/12/17*

There's no need to hang about waiting for the Last Judgment – it takes place every day.

— *Albert Camus, "The Fall" (1956)*

---

125 Trump Lied About 'Voter Fraud'…Now He Wants to Steal People's Votes

— *The Guardian, 9/14/17*

In years divisible by two we expect the truth to be trashed and decency to be mugged.

— *George F. Will, "The Pollution Of Politics" (1990)*

---

126 Trump Casts a Shadow Over Malliotakis's NYC Mayoral Bid

— *Wall Street Journal, 9/18/17 (Misconstrued)*

He was horrible and fascinating all at once, like a scorpion prepared to strike, all angles and sharp lines and menace.
— *Kelly Creagh, "Nevermore" (2010)*

———————

127 Trump Goes Nuclear
— *Wall Street Journal, 9/21/17 (Misconstrued)*

It is in vain that we get upon stilts, for, once on them, it is still with our legs that we must walk and on the highest throne in the world we are still sitting on our own arses.
— *Montaigne, "Of Experience," Essays (1580)*

———————

128 Trump Says NFL Owners Should Fire Any 'Son Of A Bitch' Who Refuses to Stand for the National Anthem
— *BuzzFeed, 9/22/17*

With effervescing opinions, as with the not yet forgotten champagne, the quickest way to let them go flat is to let them get exposed to the air.
— *Oliver Wendell Holmes Jr., Opinion, U.S. Supreme Court (1920)*

———————

129 Trump Moves to Get Base 'Stirred Up' With NFL Attacks
— *Politico, 9/25/17*

A political leader must keep looking over his shoulder all the time to see if the boys are still there. If they aren't still there, he's no longer a political leader.
— *Bernard M. Baruch, Quoted In Obituary, The New York Times (June, 1965)*

———————

130 The Trump Administration Wants Being Gay to Be a Fireable Offense
— *Vice, 9/26/17*

Macho does not prove mucho.
— Zsa Zsa Gabor, Actress (1917-2016)

_____

131 The Trump Administration is Targeting Anti-Trump Facebook Users
— Fortune, 9/28/17

It is honorable to be accused by those who deserve to be accused.
— Latin Proverb

_____

132 Corker: Tillerson, Mattis and Kelly 'Separate Our Country From Chaos'
— CNN, 10/4/17

Human history if you read it right, is the record of the efforts to tame Father. Next to the striking of fire and the discovery of the wheel, the greatest triumph of what we call civilization was the domestication of the human male.
— Max Lerner, "The Unfinished Country" (1959)

_____

133 'We're Walking Down a Dark Path': Biden Hammers Trump in Scathing Speech
— The Guardian, 10/5/17

Alas for this mad melancholy beast man! What phantasies invade it, what paroxysms of perversity, hysterical senselessness, and mental bestiality break out immediately at the very slightest check on its being the beast of action.
— Nietzsche, "The Genealogy Of Morals" (1887)

_____

134 Donald Trump is Treating a Potential War Like a Reality Show Cliffhanger
— CNN, 10/6/17

Men play at tragedy because they do not believe in the reality of tragedy which is actually being staged in the civilized world.
— *Jose Ortega Y Gasset, "The Revolt Of The Masses" (1930).*

---

135 Donald Trump Threatens to Shut Down NBC and Other TV News Networks That Criticize Him

— *Independent, 10/11/17*

The liberty of the press is most generally approved when it takes liberties with the other fellow, and leaves us alone.
— *Edgar Watson Howe, "Country Town Sayings" (1911)*

---

136 Fox News Host to Trump: You're Running Out of Friends

— *The Hill, 10/11/17*

Abiding in the midst of ignorance, thinking themselves wise and learned, the fools go aimlessly hither and thither, like blind led by the blind.
— *Upanishads, Sacred Hindu Treatise (800 - 200 BCE)*

---

137 Donald Trump to Become First President to Speak at Anti-LGBT Hate Group's Annual Summit

— *Independent, 10/12/17*

Hate is the consequence of fear; we fear something before we hate it; a child who fears noises becomes a man who hates noises.
— *Cyril Connolly, "The Unquiet Grave" (1945)*

---

138 Donald Trump Warns John McCain: "At Some Point I Fight Back'

— *News Source, 10/17/17*

It is enough that one man hate another for hate to gain, little by little, all mankind
— *Jean-Paul Sartre, "The Devil And The Good Lord" (1916)*

————————

139 Rigged: How Voter Suppression Threw Wisconsin to Trump
— *Mother Jones, 10/19/17*

The dictator, in all his pride, is held in the grip of his party machine. He can go forward; he cannot go back. He must blood his hounds, and show them sport, or else, like Actaeon of old, be devoured by them. All-strong without, he is all-weak within.
— *Sir Winston Churchill, Radio Address To The United States, (Oct., 1938)*

————————

140 Newt Gingrich: Bannon's Strategy Will Undermine, Not Strengthen the Trump Agenda
— *News Source, 10/20/17*

Evil men by their own nature cannot ever prosper.
— *Euripdes, "Ion" (421 - 408 BCE)*

————————

141 Guardian: Trump 'Kowtows' to Xi With 'Extraordinary Elevation'
— *News Source, 10/26/17*

We adore, we invoke, we seek to appease, only that which we fear.
— *Voltaire, "Religion," Philosophical Dictionary (1764)*

————————

142 Schumer to Trump: Stop 'Politicizing and Dividing America' at Times of National Tragedy
— *News Source, 11/1/17*

Modern politics has become little more than shirking responsibility and blaming somebody else.
— *Ross Perot, "United We Stand: We Can Take Back Our Country" (1992)*

---

143 Twitter Employee on Last Day of Job Deactivated Trump's Account, Company Says

— *Washington Post, 11/3/17*

I only regret that I have but one life to lose for my country.

— *Nathan Hale, Quoted By British Captain John Montressor (1776)*

---

144 Pussy Riot Star Breaks Down the Similarities Between Trump and Putin

— *Huffington Post, 11/4/17*

From this day to the ending of the world, we in it shall be remembered, we few, we band of brothers...

— *Shakespeare, "Henry V" (1599)*

---

145 April Ryan: Trump Intentionally Galvanizing Uneducated White Males With Cultural Issues

— *News Source, 11/7/17*

Those who are incapable of committing great crimes, do not readily suspect them in others.

— *La Rochefoucauld, "Maxims" (1665)*

---

146 Trump in the Age of the Strongman

— *New York Times, 11/10/17*

Even though counting heads is not an ideal way to govern, at least it is better than breaking them.

— *Learned Hand, Speech, Federal Bar Association (Mar., 1932)*

---

147 Sanders: Trump Has Never Met An Authoritarian Leader He Hasn't Liked

— *The Hill, 11/11/17*

Whatever pretext we may give for our affections, often it is only interest and vanity which cause them.
— *La Rochefoucauld, "Maxims" (1665)*

---

148 President Trump Praises Philippine's Duterte - and Says Nothing About Thousands Killed in Drug Crackdown
— *Time, 11/13/17*

I'm not a teacher: only a fellow traveler of whom you asked the way. I pointed ahead - ahead of myself as well as you.
— *George Bernard Shaw, Author And Playwright (1856 - 1950)*

---

149 Trump Shatters Longstanding Norms [with "Banana Republic" Politics of Retribution] by Pressing for Clinton Investigation
— *New York Times, 11/14/17*

It is folly to punish your neighbor with fire when you live next door.
— *Publilius Syrus, "Moral Sayings" (1st C. BCE)*

---

150 How Did Pedophilia Become Part of Trump's War on the Establishment
— *Telegraph, 11/19/17*

War is like love. It always finds a way.
— *Berthold Brecht, "Mother Courage" (1939)*

---

151 Trump Signals That Competitive Elections May be Bad for America
— *Washington Post, 11/21/17*

When a nation has allowed itself to fall under a tyrannical regime, it cannot be absolved from the faults due to the guilt of that regime.
— *Sir Winston Churchill, Message After Visit To Italy (July, 1944)*

152 FCC Will Stop States From Passing Their Own Net Neutrality Laws
— *The Verge, 11/22/17*

Injustice in this world is not something comparative; the wrong is deep, clear, and absolute in each private fate.
— *George Santayana, "Little Essays" (1920)*

153 US Government Uses Project Veritas [Far-Right Group] Video in Trial of Anti-Trump Protesters
— *The Guardian, 11/28/17*

The propagandist's purpose is to make one set of people forget that certain other sets of people are human.
— *Aldous Huxley, "The Olive Tree" (1937)*

154 Trump White House Weighing Plans for Private Spies to Counter "Deep State" Enemies
— *The Intercept, 12/4/17*

I had rather take my chance that some traitors will escape detection than spread abroad a spirit of general suspicion and distrust, which accepts rumor and gossip in place of undismayed and unintimidated inquiry.
— *Learned Hand, Speech, New York State University (Oct., 1952)*

155 Trump's 'Fake News' Mantra a Hit With Despots
— *Politico, 12/8/17*

Birds of a feather flock together.
— *William Turner, "The Rescuing Of Romish Fox" (1545)*

156 Trump Responds to 'Lock Her Up' Chants, Cites 'Rigged System'

— *CNN, 12/9/17*

Though we [the people] love goodness and not stealing, yet also we love freedom and not preaching.

— *Emerson, "Journals" (1842)*

---

157 This Evangelical Leader Denounced Trump. Then the Death Threats Started

— *Politico, 12/17/17*

Take away the cause [the Evangelical Leader], and the effect ceases; what the eye ne'er sees, the heart ne'er rues.

— *Cervantes, "Don Quixote" (1605)*

---

158 When Does Political Discord Escalate to Incitement? Ask Donald Trump

— *The Guardian, 12/19/17*

The tools of their trade were simple, effective things; iron knuckles, saps and the like. But the iconic tool of the scuttler arsenal was a woven leather belt with a heavy iron brass buckle used to decrease intelligence one wallop at a time.

— *C. Barrus, "Discovering Aberration" (2014)*

---

159 Trump Asserts 'Absolute Right' to Do What He Wants With Justice [Department]

— *MSNBC, 12/28/17*

I am sorry for thy much misgovernment.

— *Shakespeare, "Much Ado About Nothing" (1598 - 1599)*

---

160 Trump Isn't 'King,' Can't Do Whatever He Wants, Bush Ethics Lawyer Warns
— *Newsweek, 12/30/17*

All kings is mostly rapscallions.
— *Mark Twain, "The Adventures Of Huckleberry Finn" (1884)*

---

161 Words Fail Trump, But for Supporters His Message Is Loud and Clear [Male Chauvinistic, Oddly Adolescent]
— *The Guardian, 12/31/17*

Smart like bull. Strong like fox.
— *Michael J. Weinstock, "Aphorisms" (1975)*

---

162 Trump Is Undermining the 2020 Census. Marginalized Communities Will Bear the Brunt.
— *ACLU, 1/5/18*

Away, thou tedious rogue, I am sorry I shall lose a stone by thee!
— *Shakespeare, "Timon Of Athens" (1605 - 1608)*

---

163 Trump Blasts Court's DACA Ruling, Which May Complicate Congressional Action to Help Dreamers
— *Los Angeles Times, 1/10/18*

Injustice is relatively easy to bear; what stings is justice.
— *H. L. Mencken, ""Prejudices: Third Series" (1922)*

---

164 Donald Trump Flushes Away America's Reputation
— *New York Times, 1/12/18*

In his sleep he does little harm, save to his bedclothes about him.
— *Shakespeare, "All's Well That Ends Well" (1604 - 1605)*

---

165 Republican Senator Calls Trump 'Repulsive,' Compares Him to Stalin
— Think Progress, 1/14/18

History repeats itself, but in such cunning disguise that we never detect the resemblance until the damage is done.
— Sydney J. Harris, "Clearing The Ground" (1986)

---

166 Trump's Presidency Has 'Accelerated' the Decline of Democracy – Report
— Fortune, 1/16/18

The blind lead the blind. It's the democratic way.
— Henry Miller, "The Air-Conditioned Nightmare" (1945)

---

167 Landmark Human Rights Report Singles Out Donald Trump for Encouraging Oppression Around the World
— Independent, 1/18/18

Death is a softer thing by far than tyranny.
— Aeschylus, ""Agamemnon" (458 BCE)

CHAPTER 3

HAMUL UNIVERSITY FOR SERIOUS STUDENTS AT PECKHAM POINT

TOPICS:
FORTHRIGHTNESS AND CONSISTENCY

Hamul University for Serious Students at Peckham Point

168 In Inaugural Address, Trump Continues to Shun Establishment

— *New York Times, 1/20/17*

If a man makes me keep my distance, the comfort is, he keeps his at the same time.

— *Jonathan Swift, Thoughts On Various Subjects" (1711)*

---

169 After Election, Trump's Professed Love for Leaks Quickly Faded

— *New York Times, 2/15/17*

Now that I've met you, would you object to never seeing me again?

— *Paul Thomas Anderson, "Magnolia," Film (1999)*

---

170 Trump's Congress Speech Was a Heroic Effort in Contradiction and Cliché

— *The Guardian, 3/1/17*

Remember that, however patiently you study, you will never in adult life learn any language perfectly; the best you can hope for is to be a bore.

— *Evelyn Waugh, "The Tourist's Manual," Vogue Magazine (1935)*

---

171 Trump on Track to Spend Enormous Amount of Taxpayer Dollars on Travels

— *The Guardian, 3/4/17*

People who are greedy have extraordinary capacities for waste – they must, they take in too much.

— *Norman Mailer, "Miami And The Siege Of Chicago" (1968)*

---

172 Trump Makes His First Visit to a School as President, and It's a Private, Religious One

— *Huffington Post, 3/4/17*

Hypocrisy is a fashionable vice, and all fashionable vices pass for virtues.

— *Moliere, "Don Juan" (1665)*

---

173 Trump Loved WikiLeaks as a Candidate. But as President He is Not a Fan of Leaks

— *Washington Post, 3/7/17*

Fate finds for every man / His Share of Misery.

— *Euripides, "Helen" (412 BCE)*

---

174 Donald Trump Could Reverse Cuts to Arts, Poor and Elderly If He Stopped Staying at Mar-a-Lago, Figures Show.

— *Reddit, 3/17/17*

If we had to tolerate in others all that we permit in ourselves, life would become completely unbearable.

— *Georges Courteline, "La Philosophie De G. Courteline" (1917)*

---

175 Donald Trump, Accused of More Than 10 Sexual Assaults, Declares April Sexual Assault Awareness Month

— *Reddit, 4/1/17*

It is easier to pretend to be what you are not than to hide what you really are; but he that can accomplish both has little to learn in hypocrisy.

— *Charles Caleb Colton, "Lacon" (1825)*

176 Trump Shifting Positions at a Breakneck Pace

— *Politico, 4/15/13*

He who is shipwrecked the second time cannot lay the blame on Neptune.

— *English Proverb*

177 Majority No Longer Thinks That Trump Keeps His Promises

— *Reddit, 4/17/17*

It is vain to find fault with those arts of deceiving wherein men find pleasure to be deceived.

— *John Locke, "An Essay Concerning Human Understanding" (1690)*

178 Will Trump Really 'Do a Big Number' on the Banks?

— *New York Times, 5/2/17*

The words of the double-tongued are as if they were harmless, but they reach even to the inner part of the bowels. Praise be to the Lord, who distinguishes our cause and delivers us from unjust and deceitful men.

— *Muriel Spark, "The Ballad Of Peckham Rye" (1960)*

179 Under Trump, Inconvenient Data That Was Previously Public Is Being Sidelined

— *Washington Post, 5/14/17*

Everyone is a moon and has a dark side which he never shows to anybody.
— *Mark Twain, Notebook (1935)*

---

180 Trump Wants to Defund Programs That Help Small Farmers Survive
— *Huffington Post, 5/28/17*

To try may be to die, but not to care is never to be born.
— *William Redfield, "One Might Have Played Hamlet, The Other Did" (1968)*

---

181 Funny How Trump Was Cool With Ted Nugent Joking About Killing the President
— *Huffington Post, 5/31/17*

Hypocrisy is the necessary burden of villainy, affectation part of the chosen trappings of folly; the one completes a villain, the other only finishes a fop.
— *Samuel Johnson, "The Rambler" (1750)*

---

182 After Calls to 'Get Down' to Business, Trump Goes on 23rd Trip to Golf Course
— *TPM Livewire, 6/4/17*

If your desires be endless, your care and fears will be so too.
— *Thomas Fuller, M.D., "Gnomologia" (1732)*

---

183 Trump Support Drops in Military Communities
— *NBC, 6/4/17*

The soldier, above all people, prays for peace, for he must suffer and bear the deepest wounds and scars of war.
— *Douglas MacArthur, Address, U. S. Military Academy, West Point (1962)*

---

184 Trump Said He 'Wants Approvals' of Nominees - But He Hasn't Nominated Anyone for 79% of Key Positions

— *Business Insider, 6/5/17*

There is no more miserable human being than one in whom nothing is habitual but indecision.

— *William James, "The Principles Of Psychology" (1892)*

---

185 Grassley Criticizes Trump Over Access to Information

— *Wall Street Journal, 6/10/17 (Misconstrued)*

No man, for any considerable period, can wear one face to himself, and another to the multitude, without finally getting bewildered as to which may be true.

— *Nathaniel Hawthorne, "The Scarlet Letter" (1850)*

---

186 The Trumps Are Complaining About the 'Viciousness' of Politics. Irony Is Dead

— *Washington Post, 6/12/17*

A sharp sense of the ironic can be the equivalent of the faith that moves mountains. Far more quickly than reason or logic, irony can penetrate rage and puncture self-pity.

— *Moss Hart, "Act One" (1959)*

---

187 Trump Seeks Sharp Cuts to Housing Aid, Except for Program That Brings Him Millions

— *Washington Post, 6/20/17*

I detest that man, who / hides one thing in the depths of his heart, and speaks forth another.

— *Homer, "Iliad" (9th C. BCE)*

---

188 Trump Plays Victim After Vicious Twitter Jag
— *The Guardian, 6/29/17*

By the time an actor knows how to play any sort of part he is often too old to act any but a few.
— *W. Somerset Maugham, "The Summing Up" (1938)*

---

189 Fox News Is Defending Donald Trump With Mystery Writers and Anonymous Sources
— *Newsweek, 7/1/17*

With so many roosters crowing, the sun never comes up.
— *Italian Proverb*

---

190 Lost Records of Lawsuit Claiming Trump Tower Exploited Undocumented Workers Have Been Found
— *Reddit, 7/5/17*

The image of myself which I try to create in my own mind in order that I may love myself is very different from the image which I try to create in the minds of others in order that they may love me.
— *W.H. Auden, "Hic Et Ille," The Dyer's Hand (1962)*

---

191 ACLU Sues Trump Over Election Integrity Commission
— *Politico, 7/10/17*

No man can climb out beyond the limitations of his own character.
— *John Morley, "Robespierre," Critical Miscellanies (1871-1908)*

---

192 Trump Sued for Blocking Twitter Users
— *Bloomberg, 7/11/17*

The greatest superstition now entertained by public men is that hypocrisy is the royal road to success.
— *Robert G. Ingersoll, Speech (Dec. 13, 1886)*

---

193 Remove Trump Children and Kushner From the White House, Texas Congressman Says
— *Newsweek, 7/13/17*

All men are tempted. There is no man that lives that can't be broken down, provided it is the right temptation, put in the right spot.
— *Henry Ward Beecher, "Proverbs From Plymouth Pulpit" (1887)*

---

194 Head of Trump Voter Fraud Probe Wanted to Change Law to Make Registering More Difficult
— *Huffington Post, 7/15/17*

Often a noble face hides filthy ways.
— *Euripides, "Electra" (413 BCE)*

---

195 Trump: 'In America We Don't Worship Government, We Worship God'
— *Washington Post, 7/26/17*

Everyman thinks God is on his side. The rich and powerful know He is.
— *Jean Anouilh, "The Lark" (1955)*

---

196 Trump's D.C. Hotel Sells Clothes Made in China, Vietnam, Peru During 'Made in America' Week
— *Daily Beast, 7/27/17*

The politician is an acrobat. He keeps his balance by saying the opposite of what he does.
— *Maurice Barres, "Mes Cahiers" (1896)*

---

197 As Trump Debases the Presidency, the Religious Right Looks Away
— *Washington Post, 7/28/17*

Morality turns on whether the pleasure precedes or follows the pain.
— *Samuel Butler, "Elementary Morality," Note-Books (1912)*

---

198 President Trump, Who Got Five Draft Deferments, Renews Attacks on Sen. Blumenthal's Military Record
— *Los Angeles Times, 8/7/17*

It is easy to be brave from a safe distance.
— *Aesop "The Wolf And The Kid," Fables (6th C. BCE))*

---

199 Trump Is Deporting Fewer Immigrants Than Obama
— *Washington Post, 8/10/17*

One of these days is none of these days.
— *English Proverb*

---

200 Trump Defends Confederate Statues In Wake of Charlottesville Violence
— *Wall Street Journal, 8/18/17 (Misconstrued)*

The frivolity with which all theatrical activity is conducted has one consoling feature – there are no rules of behavior that apply regularly to any part of the theatre.
— *Moss Hart, "Act One" (1959)*

---

201 Trump and CEO's: Behind the Collapse of An Alliance
— *Wall Street Journal, 8/21/17 (Misconstrued)*

If you pick up a starving dog and make him prosperous, he will not bite you. This is the principle difference between a dog and a man.
— *Mark Twain, "Pudd'nhead Wilson's Calendar," Pudd'nhead Wilson (1894)*

---

202 Trump Pick to Oversee Worker Protections Promoted Sweat Shops on Remote US Islands
— *Mother Jones, 8/22/17*

I never made a decision in my life that wasn't one hundred per cent selfish.
— *John Updike, "The Centaur" (1963)*

---

203 Trump Shifts Labor Policy Focus From Worker to Entrepreneur
— *New York Times, 9/3/17*

A man's word / Is believed just to the extent of the wealth in his coffers stored.
— *Juvenal, "Satires" (2nd C. CE)*

---

204 To Allies' Chagrin, Trump Swerves Left
— *New York Times, 9/6/17*

Sincerity that thinks it is the sole possessor of the truth is a deadlier sin than hypocrisy, which knows better.
— *Sidney J. Harris, "Clearing The Ground" (1986)*

---

205 Donald Trump Has Changed His Mind – A Heck of a Lot
— *New York Times, 9/14/17*

Half of the failures in life arise from pulling in one's horse as he is leaping.
— *Augustus William Hare, "Guesses At Truth" (1827)*

---

206 9 Lies About DACA Trump Is Buying Into
— *News Source, 9/14/17*

People can be induced to swallow anything, provided it is sufficiently seasoned with praise.
— Moliere, "The Miser" (1668)

---

207 'Step Right, Step Left': Mercurial Trump Leaves Supporters Reeling
— The Guardian, 9/16/17

Adolescence is the age of cosmic yearnings and private passions, of social concern and personal agony. It is the age of inconsistency and ambivalence.
— Haim G. Ginott, "Between Parent & Teenager" (1969)

---

208 Kushner Used Private Email to Conduct White House Business
— Politico, 9/24/17

We are not hypocrites in our sleep.
— William Hazlitt, "On Dreams," The Plain Speaker (1826)

---

209 President Trump: We'll Be Talking About Gun Laws
— News Source, 10/3/17

The most exhausting thing in life, I have discovered, is being insincere.
— Anne Morrow Lindbergh, "Channeled Whelk," Gift From The Sea (1955)

---

210 Trump's Strategy With Congress: Be More Like Obama
— New York Times, 10/14/17

Imitation is the sincerest form of flattery.
— Charles Caleb Colton, "Lacon" (1820)

---

211 Trump's Shifting Language on Payments to Health Insurers

— *Wall Street Journal, 10/18/17 (Misconstrued)*

That same purpose-changer, that sly divel, that broker, that still breaks the pate of faith, that daily break-vow!

— *Shakespeare, "King John" (1594 -1596)*

---

212 Trump's Support for Health Fix Tied to Conservatives' ACA Rollbacks

— *Wall Street Journal, 10/19/17 (Misconstrued)*

The distinction between 'bribery' and 'extortion' seems to be this: the former offense consists in the offering of a present, or receiving one, if offered; the latter, in demanding a fee or present, by color of office.

— *Black's Law Dictionary, "Extortion" (1951)*

---

213 Trump Attacks on Generals [in Old Tweets] Resurface After White House Said It's 'Inappropriate' to Question Generals

— *Reddit, 10/21/17*

You are a huge translation of hypocrisy, vilely compil'd, profound simplicity.

— *Shakespeare, "Love's Labour's Lost" (Mid -1590s)*

---

214 Under Trump, Made in America Is Losing Out to Russian Steel

— *Bloomberg, 10/25/17*

I hate false words, and seek with care, difficulty, and moroseness, those that fit the thing.

— *Walter Savage Landor, "Imaginary Conversations" (1824)*

---

215 Trump Wins Visas to Hire 70 Foreign Workers at Mar-a-Lago
— *The Hill, 11/4/17*

You undergo too strict a paradox, striving to make an ugly deed look fair.
— *Shakespeare, "Timon Of Athens" (1605 - 1608)*

———

216 Mitch McConnell Leads Establishment Republicans in Effort to Push Roy Moore Out of Alabama Race
— *News Source, 11/9/17*

You are a vane blown with all winds.
— *Shakespeare, "Much Ado About Nothing" (1598 - 1599)*

———

217 [GOP] Senate Plan Would Make Individual Tax Breaks Temporary While Corporate Cuts Would Be Permanent
— *Los Angeles Times, 11/15/17*

I think you the most pathetical break-promise, and the most hollow lover that may be chosen out of the gross band of the unfaithful.
— *Shakespeare, "As You Like It" (1599)*

———

218 Gretchen Carlson Rips Trump for Attacking Franken: What About Your [Sexual Misconduct] Accusers?
— *The Hill, 11/17/17*

The self-righteous scream judgments against others to hide the noise of skeletons hiding in their own closet.
— *John Mark Green, Goodreads.com (2007)*

———

219 Hillary Blasts Trump, Moore for Not Accepting Responsibility on Sexual Misconduct Allegations
— *News Source, 11/17/17*

You are essentially a natural coward without instinct.
— Shakespeare, "Henry IV, Part 1 (1597)

---

220 Archbishop Baffled by Christian Trump Backers
— News Source, 11/28/17

I came, I saw, I was confused.
— Breyten Breytenbach, "Return To Paradise" (1993)

---

221 Cory Booker: Why Isn't Trump Doing the 'Honorable Thing' Like Al Franken and Resign
— Washington Examiner, 12/10/17

Do as I say, not as I do.
— John Selden, "Table-Talk" (1654)

---

222 After Months of Withering Criticism, Trump Prepares to Visit FBI
— NPR, 12/15/17

Keep your friends close and your enemies closer.
— Mario Puzo and Francis Ford Cuppola, "The Godfather Part II" (1974)

---

223 After Tax Cuts, Republicans May Suddenly Find Trump Is More Trouble Than He's Worth
— USA Today, 12/20/17

Some people are like clouds. When they go away, it's a beautiful day.
— Bill Murray, Actor And Comedian, Tweet (June, 2015)

---

224 Trump Will Build a [Sea] Wall in Ireland to Protect His Golf Course From Climate Change
— Business Insider, 12/22/17

We ought to see far enough into a hypocrite to see even his sincerity.

— G. K. Chesterton, "Heretics" (1905)

---

225 Scarborough: Conservatives Would Have Raised 'Holy Hell' If Obama Attacked FBI Like Trump

— *The Hill, 12/23/17*

We don't live in a democracy; we live in a hypocrisy.

— Sarah Silverman, "What I've Learned: With Jimmy Kimmel" (2007)

---

226 Trump Scraps His Widely Denounced Commission on Voter Fraud

— *The Guardian, 1/4/18*

Oops!

— Exclamation, "To Blunder," Wicktionary (Used Since 1921)

---

227 Trump Reiterates He Wants DACA as Long as It Comes With Border Wall

— *CNN, 1/7/18*

At the very smallest wheel of our reasoning it is possible for a handful of questions to break the bank of our answers.

— Antonio Machado, "Juan De Mairena" (1943)

---

228 Trump to Open Floodgates on Selling US-Made Weapons to Previously Restricted Buyers

— *Newsweek, 1/8/18*

Man is, perhaps, no more prone to war than he used to be and no more inclined to commit other evil deeds. But a given amount of ill will or folly will go further than it used to.

— Joseph Wood Krutch, "The Measure Of The Man" (1954)

---

229 Donald Trump Mocked for Appearing to Stumble His Way Through National Anthem [at College Football Championship Game]

— *The Telegraph, 1/9/18*

Better a quiet death than a public misfortune.

— *Spanish Proverb*

---

230 Trump Administration Waives Punishment for Convicted Banks, Including Deutsche - Which Trump Owes Millions

— *IBT, 1/9/18*

Nothing emboldens sin so much as mercy.

— *Shakespeare, "Timon Of Athens" (1605 - 1608)*

---

231 Trump Hands Florida Governor a Win on [Offshore] Drilling but Leaves Other States Hanging

— *CNN, 1/10/18*

One will seldom go wrong if one attributes extreme actions to vanity, average ones to habit, and petty ones to fear.

— *Neitzsche, "Human, All Too Human" (1878)*

---

232 Trump's 'Shithole' Countries Are Worth $46.6 Billion in Trade to America

— *Newsweek, 1/12/18*

Thou art so leaky that we must leave thee to thy sinking.

— *Shakespeare, "Antony And Cleopatra" (1606)*

---

233 Trump - Trudeau Love-in Threatened as Canada Attacks US Over Trade

— *The Guardian, 1/13/18*

When you say you're done this time, mean it. Don't keep going back to someone who doesn't deserve you.
— *StephMc5, Twitter (June, 2017)*

---

234 Don Lemon: Watching Trump Honor Dr. King 'Kind Of Makes Your Skin Crawl'
— *Huffington Post, 1/13/18*

To show an unfelt sorrow is an office which the false man does easy.
— *Shakespeare, "Macbeth" (1606)*

---

235 [Director] Mulvaney Requests No Funding for Consumer Financial Protection Bureau [for Second Quarter]
— *Politico, 1/18/18*

Damn the torpedoes! Full speed ahead!
— *Adm. David Farragut, Order During the Battle Of Mobile Bay (1864)*

CHAPTER 4

THE GUADALUPE INSTITUTE FOR WAYWARD CO-EDS AND BESOTTED YOUTH

TOPICS:
THE BEST AND THE BRIGHTEST

The Guadalupe Institute for Wayward Co-Eds and Besotted Youth

236 Rocky First Weekend for Trump Troubles Top Aides
— *New York Times, 1/22/17*

A new broom is good for three days.
— *Italian Proverb*

---

237 Donald Trump and a Sea of Empty Desks
— *New York Times, 1/23/17*

There is nothing which we receive with so much reluctance as advice.
— *Joseph Addison, "The Spectator" (1711)*

---

238 Bannon Is Given Security Role Usually Held for Generals
— *New York Times, 1/29/17*

There is but one step from the sublime to the ridiculous.
— *Napoleon I, After The Retreat From Russia (1812)*

---

239 Trump Staffers Reportedly Removed Top-Secret Documents From a Secure Facility
— *Business Insider, 2/8/17*

Idiot, n. A member of a large and powerful tribe whose influence in human affairs has always been dominant and controlling.
— *Ambrose Bierce, "The Devil's Dictionary" (1881-1911)*

---

240 Steve Bannon Cited Italian Thinker Who Inspired Fascists
— *New York Times, 2/10/17*

What is objectionable, what is dangerous about extremists is not that they are extreme, but that they are intolerant. The evil is not what they say about their cause, but what they say about their opponents.
— *Robert F. Kennedy, "The Pursuit Of Justice" (1964)*

---

241 For Kushner, Israel Policy May Be Shaped by the Personal
— *New York Times, 2/11/17*

Man is not committed in detail by his biological constitution to any particular variety of behavior.
— *Ruth Benedict, "Patterns Of Culture" (1934)*

---

242 Turmoil At the National Security Council, From the Top Down
— *New York Times, 2/12/17*

I find war detestable but those who praise it without participating in it even more so.
— *Romain Rolland, "Inter Arma Caritas, Journal de Geneve" (1914)*

---

243 Michael Flynn Resigns as National Security Advisor
— *New York Times, 2/13/17*

All men [Trump] are liable to error; and most men are, in many points, by passion or interest, under temptation to it.
— *John Locke, "An Essay Concerning Human Understanding" (1690)*

---

244 A Look at Mar-a-Lago's Members With a Front Row Seat to History
— *New York Times, 2/18/17*

With what your friend you nobly share, / At least you rescue from your heir.
— *Horace, "Odes" (23 BCE-15 CE)*

---

245 Trump Chooses Army Strategist to Be National Security Advisor
— *New York Times, 2/21/17*

It is always a silly thing to give advice, but to give good advice is absolutely fatal.
— *Oscar Wilde, "The Critical Writings Of Oscar Wilde" (1969)*

246 How Trump's Campaign Staff Tried to Keep Him Off Twitter
— *Politico, 2/22/17*

It is a great misfortune not to possess sufficient wit to speak well, or sufficient judgment to keep silent.
— *La Bruyere, "Characters" (1688)*

247 Trump's Budget Ripped From Bannon's Nationalistic Playbook
— *Politico, 3/16/17*

Altogether, national hatred is something peculiar. You will always find it strongest and most violent where there is the lowest degree of culture.
— *Goethe, Quoted In Eckermann's, "Conversations with Goethe" (1830)*

248 Civil War Rages Throughout Trump Administration
— *Politico, 4/7/17*

Those who set out to serve both God and Mammon soon discover that there is no God.
— *Logan Pearsall Smith, "Afterthoughts" (1931)*

249 Brand Ivanka: Inside the Tangled Empire of the President's Closest Ally
— *The Guardian, 5/1/17*

He who serves two masters has to lie to one.
— *Portuguese Proverb*

---

250 Trump's Tweets Leave His Aides in An Awkward Spot
— *Wall Street Journal, 5/17/17 (Misconstrued)*

We never forgive those that make us blush.
— *Jean Francois De La Harpe, "Melanie" (1770)*

---

251 Trump Pushing Big Staff Changes as Russia Crises Grows
— *Wall Street Journal, 5/27/17 (Misconstrued)*

There is nothing we value and hunt and cultivate and strive to draw to us, but in some hour we turn and rend it.
— *Emerson, "Journals" (1836)*

---

252 White House Details Ethics Waivers for Ex-Lobbyists and Corporate Lawyers
— *New York Times, 6/1/17*

The moral sense enables one to perceive morality - and avoid it. The immoral sense enables one to perceive immorality and enjoy it.
— *Mark Twain, "Notebook" (1935)*

---

253 Special Counsel's Trump Campaign Investigation Includes Manafort Case. May Expand to Include Attorney General Sessions
— *Washington Post, 6/2/17*

A foolish consistency [in staff] is the hobgoblin of small minds, adored by little statesmen and philosophers and divines.
— *Emerson, "Self-Reliance," Essays (1841)*

---

254 Comey Forces Trump Defenders Into Extreme and Absurd Spin
— *Mother Jones, 6/7/17*

We do what we can, and then make a theory to prove our performance the best.
— *Emerson, "Journals" (1834)*

---

255 Behind Trump's Silence: Why the Counterpuncher Let Others Do the Punching
— *Washington Post, 6/8/17*

God! Is there anything uglier than a frightened man!
— *Jean Anouilh, "Antigone" (1942)*

---

256 Trump Team's Shifts Jolt Some Allies and Soothes Others
— *New York Times, 6/9/17*

It is best not to swap horses when crossing the river.
— *Abraham Lincoln, Reply To The National Union League (1864)*

---

257 Transactions by Kushner, Others Under Investigation
— *Washington Post, 6/16/17*

Comedy springs from the ludicrous; but the ludicrous is stuck in the muck of reality, resolutely hostile to what is impossible.
— *Cynthia Ozick, ""Cultural Impersonation," Art & Ardor (1983)*

---

258 Donald Trump Attorney Mark Kosowitz Hit With Ethics Complaints
— *Huffington Post, 6/17/17*

Ethics is in origin the art of recommending to others the sacrifices required for co-operation with oneself.
— *Bertrand Russell, "Mysticism And Logic" (1917)*

259 Trump Administration: Sheriff David Clarke Withdraws From Homeland Security Post

— *The Guardian, 6/17/17*

I fear the Greeks even when they bring gifts.

— *Virgil, "Aeneid" (30-19 BCE)*

260 White House Frustration Grows With Tillerson Over Jobs for Trump Allies

— *Washington Post, 6/23/17*

It is fit I should commit offense to my inferiors.

— *Shakespeare, "Cymbeline" (1611)*

261 Tillerson Blows Up at White House Aide

— *Politico, 6/28/17*

The worst pain a man can have is to know much and be impotent to act.

— *Herodutus, "The Histories" (5th C. BCE)*

262 18 States, Consumer Groups Sue Betty DeVos Over Delay of Student Loan Protections

— *Politico, 7/6/17*

Injustice, swift, erect and unconfined, / Sweeps the wide earth, and tramples o'er mankind.

— *Homer, "Illiad" (9th C. BCE)*

263 Politics Gets Personal as Harsh Glare Hits Trump Family

— *New York Times, 7/12/17*

Politics cannot stop to study psychology. Its methods are rough; its judgments rougher still.
— Henry Adams, "The Education Of Henry Adams" (1907)

———————

264 Trump Lawyer Marc Kasowitz Threatens Stranger in Emails: 'Watch Your Back, Bitch'
— ProPublica, 7/13/17

There is no better way of exercising the imagination than the study of law. No poet ever interpreted nature as freely as a lawyer interprets truth.
— Jean Giraudoux, "Tiger At The Gates" (1935)

———————

265 White House Releases Sensitive Personal Information of Voters Worried About Their Sensitive Personal Information
— Washington Post, 7/14/17

It is so pleasant to come across people more stupid than ourselves. We love them at once for being so.
— Jerome K. Jerome, "The Idle Thoughts Of An Idle Fellow" (1889)

———————

266 Steve Bannon Reportedly Attacked Paul Ryan as 'A Limp-D**k Motherf**ker'
— Huffington Post, 7/18/17

Too much Truth / Is uncouth.
— Franklin P. Adams, "Nods And Becks" (1944)

———————

267 Shifts in Staffing Highlight Divisions in the White House
— Wall Street Journal, 7/21/17 (Misconstrued)

Egotism is the anesthetic that dulls the pain of stupidity.
— Frank Leahy, Look (Jan., 1955)

———————

268 Betsy DeVos: Trump's Illiberal Ally Seen as Most Dangerous Education Chief Ever

— *The Guardian, 7/26/17*

If you live with a cripple, you will learn to limp.

— *Plutarch, "The Education of Children," Moralia (100 CE)*

---

269 White House Infighting Boils Over Into Public View

— *Washington Post, 7/27/17*

Family quarrels are bitter things. They don't go by any rules. They're not like aches or wounds; they're more like splits in the skin that won't heal because there is not enough material.

— *F. Scott Fitzgerald, "The Crack-Up" (1945)*

---

270 Anthony Scaramucci Out at White House After Whirlwind 10 Days

— *Huffington Post, 7/31/17*

The test of a real comedian is whether you laugh at him before he opens his mouth.

— *George Jean Nathan, "American Mercury" (Sept. 1929)*

---

271 Sam Clovis: Trump's Pick for Top Science Job Called Progressives 'Race Traitors'

— *The Guardian, 8/2/17*

It is certain, in any case, that ignorance, allied with power, is the most ferocious enemy justice can have.

— *James Baldwin, "No Name In The Street" (1972)*

---

272 Rumors of 'Purge List' Rattle White House Staff

— *BuzzFeed, 8/4/17*

Another good thing about gossip is that it is within / everybody's reach, / And it is much more interesting than any / other form of speech.

— Ogden Nash, "I'm A Stranger Here Myself" (1938)

---

273 Sessions' Broad Attack on Leaks Aimed at An Audience of One: Trump

— Politico, 8/4/17

No man gains credit for his cowardly courtesies.

— Emerson, "Journals" (1832)

---

274 Stephen Bannon Out at the White House After Turbulent Run

— New York Times, 8/18/17

Misery acquaints a man with strange bedfellows.

— Shakespeare, "The Tempest" (1611)

---

275 Trump Throws Tantrum, Spitefully Fires Loyal Aide Over Sparse Rally Crowd

— Shareblue Media, 8/29/17

We are all serving a life-sentence in the dungeon of self.

— Cyril Connolly, "The Unquiet Grave" (1945)

---

276 Report: Chafing Under Gen. Kelley's Control, Trump Continues to Call Close Friends and Advisers

— News Source, 9/2/17

Conversation, n. A fair for the display of the minor mental commodities, each exhibitor being too intent upon the arrangement of his own wares to observe those of his neighbor.

— Ambrose Bierce, "The Devil's Dictionary" (1881 – 1911)

---

277 Report: Robert Mueller Wants to Interview White House Staffers Over Trump Tower Meeting Statement

— News Source, 9/7//17

He who does not bellow the truth when he knows the truth makes himself the accomplice of liars and forgers.

— Charles Peguy, "The Honest People," Basic Verities (1943)

---

278 Trump Jr. Says He Wanted Russian Dirt to Determine Clinton's Fitness for Office

— New York Times, 9/8/17

Truth's fountains may be clear – her streams are muddy, / And cut through such canals of contradiction, / That she must often navigate o'er fiction.

— Byron, "Don Juan" (1819)

---

279 Trump Tortured Spicer and Priebus [White House Aides]. Now They Get to Tell Investigators About Trump

— Washington Post, 9/8/17

Revenge is a dish that should be eaten cold.

— English Proverb

---

280 Krikorian: Trump Moves Closer to Becoming 'Amnesty Don' Everyday He Doesn't Fire Javanka

— News Source, 9/10/17

It is thus with most of us; we are what other people say we are. We know ourselves chiefly by hearsay.

— Eric Hoffer, "The Passionate State Of Mind" (1954)

---

281 Report: Trump White House Officials Fear Their Colleagues May Be Wearing Wires for Mueller Investigation
— *News Source, 9/18/17*

Trust in God, but tie your camel.
— *Persian Proverb*

---

282 White House 'Exodus' Expected as Staffers Prepare to Bolt
— *Vanity Fair, 9/22/17*

Consider the little mouse, how sagacious an animal it is, which never entrusts its life to one hole only.
— *Plautus, "Truculentus" (191 BCE)*

---

283 Tom Price Resigns as HHS Chief After Criticism of Jet Use
— *Wall Street Journal, 9/30/17 (Misconstrued)*

A bad beginning makes a bad ending.
— *Euripides, "Aeolus" (423 BCE)*

---

284 Federal Watchdog Opens Probe Into Travel by Interior Secretary Ryan Zinke
— *Washington Post, 10/2/17*

Few secret undertakings ever did any nation any good.
— *Arthur M. Schlesinger, Jr., "The Imperial Presidency" (1973)*

---

285 E.P.A. Chief's Calendar: A Stream of Industry Meetings and Trips Home
— *New York Times, 10/3/17*

Where there's smoke, there's fire.
— *Widely Known Proverb*

---

286 Trump Put Ivanka and Jared in the White House After Past Presidents Were Told It Was Unlawful
— *Newsweek, 10/3/17*

The problem of power is how to achieve its responsible use rather than its irresponsible and indulgent use - of how to get men of power to live for the public rather than off the public.
— *Robert F. Kennedy, "I Remember, I Believe," The Pursuit Of Justice (1964)*

---

287 The Things People Say Right Before They Leave the Trump Administration
— *The Atlantic, 10/4/17*

Like rats abandoning a sinking ship.
— *Slang, Webster's New World Dictionary (1988)*

---

288 Bob Corker on Trump's Biggest Problem: The 'Castration' of Rex Tillerson
— *Washington Post, 10/13/17*

I would rather have a German division in front of me than a French one behind me.
— *Gen. George S. Patton, Reply To Message From Gen. Eisenhower (1945)*

---

289 Sinister Figures Lurk Around Our Careless President
— *Washington Post, 10/13/17*

A man is known by the company he keeps.
— *Aesop, "Fables" (Late To Mid - 6th C. BCE)*

---

290 John Kelly and the Dangerous Moral Calculus of Working for Donald Trump
— *New Yorker, 10/20/17*

With friends like this, who needs enemies?
— *English Proverb*

———————

291 Report: Kabul Embassy Staff Had Trump Pinata Set for Hillary Victory
— *News Source, 10/28/17*

To wisdom belongs the intellectual apprehension of eternal things; to knowledge, the rational knowledge of temporal things.
— *St. Augustine, "On The Trinity" (5th C. CE)*

———————

292 Papadopoulos Followed a Winding Path Into Trump's Orbit
— *Wall Street Journal, 11/1/17 (Misconstrued)*

I am a moth to his flame and it frightens me how willingly I'd burn my wings off for him. Destroy the world. Follow him to Hell. It's scary to feel you can't breathe without someone.
— *Karen Marie Moning, "Burned" (2015)*

———————

293 [Commerce Secretary] Wilbur Ross Didn't Disclose Business Ties to Putin Inner Circle
— *Wall Street Journal, 11/5/17 (Misconstrued)*

Whoso diggeth a pit shall fall therein.
— *Bible, Proverbs 26:27*

———————

294 Bar Association Dubs Fourth Trump Judicial Nominee Unqualified
— *The Hill, 11/7/17*

There is always a heavy demand for fresh mediocrity. In every generation the least cultivated taste has the largest appetite.
— *Thomas Bailey Aldrich, "Ponkapog Papers" (1903)*

———————

295 Swamp Deepens as Trump Names Former Drug Industry Exec to Be Health Secretary
— *Los Angeles Times, 11/15/17*

He has the greatest blind side who thinks he has none.
— *Dutch Proverb*

___

296 FCC to Outline Plan to Roll Back Net-Neutrality Rules
— *Wall Street Journal, 11/20/17 (Misconstrued)*

The hand that rules the press, the radio, the screen and the far-spread magazine, rules the country.
— *Learned Hand, Memorial Address For Justice Brandeis (Dec., 1942)*

___

297 Top Trump Staffers Failed to File [Required] Financial Reports On Their Way Out the Door
— *The Seattle Times, 11/24/17*

I would rather have them say, "There he goes" than "There he lies."
— *H. L. Mencken, "Proverb and Platitude" (1921)*

___

298 White House Must Now Respond to Petition Calling for FCC Chairman Ajit Pai's Resignation [for Plan to Kill Net Neutrality]
— *The Daily Dot, 11/29/17*

Those he commands move only in command, nothing in love.
— *Shakespeare, "Macbeth" (1606)*

___

299 Flynn Guilty Plea Brings Mueller Investigation Directly Into the White House
— *Los Angeles Times, 12/1/17*

The chickens are coming home to roost.
— *Robert Southey, Derived From His Poem "The Curse Of Kehama" (1810)*

___

300 Botched Damage Control Efforts Keep Making Russia Scandal Worse for Trump
— *Washington Post, 12/4/17*

Arrogance, ignorance, incompetence. Not a pretty cocktail of personality traits in the best of situations. No siree. Not a pretty cocktail in an office-mate and not a pretty cocktail in a head of state. In fact, in a leader, it's a lethal cocktail.
— *Graydon Carter, Editor Of Vanity Fair (1992)*

301 Trump Continues to Leave Key State Department Posts Empty
— *CNN, 12/7/17*

It is a bad plan that admits of no modification.
— *Publilius Syrus, ""Moral Sayings" (1st C. BCE)*

302 Omarosa's Exit Highlights 'Ridiculous' Lack of Diversity at Trump White House
— *The Guardian, 12/17/17*

Take up the White man's burden - / Have done with childish days - / The lightly proffered laurel, / The easy, ungrudged praise.
— *Rudyard Kipling, "The White Man's Burden," Poem (1899)*

303 Where is Trump's Cabinet? It's Anybody's Guess [Unusual Layer of Secrecy]
— *Politico, 12/26/17*

Much unhappiness has come into the world because of bewilderment and things left unsaid.
— *Dostoyevsky, "Critical Articles: Intro.," Complete Collected Works (1895)*

304 White House Aides Already Anxious About 2018

— *Politico, 1/1/18*

Even-handed fate / Hath but one law for small and great: / That ample urn holds all men's names.

— *Horace, "Odes" (65 BCE – 8 BCE)*

---

305 Trump Tower Meeting With Russians 'Treasonous', Bannon Says in Book [by Michael Wolff]

— *The Guardian, 1/3/18*

The treason pleases, but the traitors are odious.

— *Cervantes, "Don Quixote" (1605)*

---

306 Trump Seen as a Child by Staff, Says Fire and Fury Author Michael Wolff

— *BBC, 1/5/18*

Children need models rather than critics.

— *Joseph Joubert, "Pensees" (1842)*

---

307 Senior White House Advisor Denounces Wolff Book as 'Garbage', Calls Trump 'Political Genius'

— *Los Angeles Times, 1/7/18*

In modern military parlance, to take point, walk point, be on point, or be a point man means to assume the first and most exposed position in a combat military formation, that is, the leading soldier or unit advancing through hostile or unsecured territory.

— *Wikipedia, "Take Point" (Launched 2001)*

---

308 White House Staff Could Be in Trouble If They Help Trump With Fake News Awards, Says Former WH Lawyer

— *Newsweek, 1/8/18*

Almost all absurdity of conduct arises from the imitation of those whom we cannot resemble.

— *Samuel Johnson, "The Rambler" (1750)*

---

309 Pence Silent in Wake of 'Shithole' Remark

— *Politico, 1/13/18*

He will never have true friends who is afraid of making enemies.

— *William Hazlitt, "Characteristics" (1823)*

---

310 Trump Set a Record for White House Staff Turnover in the First Year

— *Washington Post, 1/16/18*

'Tis almost morning; I would have thee gone...

— *Shakespeare, "Romeo And Juliet" (1591 - 1595)*

CHAPTER 5

MASSACHUSETTS ANISOTROPY, LIGO AND PINCUS INSTITUTE FOR ADVANCED STUDIES

TOPICS:
FREE SPEECH AND FREE PRESS

Massachusetts Anisotropy, Ligo and Pincus Institute for Advanced Studies

311 Trump Calls the News Media the 'Enemy of the American People'
— *New York Times, 1/18/17*

It is with narrow-souled people as with narrow-necked bottles; the less they have in them the more noise they make in pouring it out.
— *Alexander Pope, "Thoughts On Various Subjects" (1727)*

312 News Media, Target of Trump's Declaration of War, Expresses Alarm
— *New York Times, 1/22/17*

No government ought to be without censors; and where the press is free no one ever will.
— *Thomas Jefferson, Letter To George Washington (1792)*

313 Trump White House Bars News Organizations From Press Briefing
— *New York Times, 1/24/17*

Where there is official censorship it is a sign that speech is serious. Where there is none, it is pretty certain that the official spokesmen have all the loudspeakers.
— *Paul Goodman, "Growing Up Absurd" (1960)*

314 Trump Strategist Stephen Bannon Says 'Media Should Keep Its Mouth Shut'
— *New York Times, 1/26/17*

A bluff taken seriously is more useful than a serious threat interpreted as a bluff.

— *Henry A. Kissinger, "American Foreign Policy" (1969)*

---

315 Trump News Conference Filters Out the Tough Questions
— *New York Times, 2/13/17*

Next in criminality to him who violates the laws of his country, is he who violates the language.

— *Walter Savage Landor, "Archdeacon Hare And Walter Landor" (1824)*

---

316 President Trump Will Not Attend the White House Correspondents Dinner
— *Reddit, 2/26/17*

He who denies his own vanity, usually possesses it in so brutal a form that he instinctively shuts his eyes to avoid the necessity of despising himself.

— *Nietzsche, "Miscellaneous Maxims and Opinions" (1879)*

---

317 'Phony,' 'Failing,' 'Worthless' – Here Are All the Names Trump Has Called This Year's Pulitzer Prize Winners
— *Reddit, 4/11/17*

Pure good soon grows insipid, wants variety and spirit. Pain is bitter-sweet, which never surfeits. Love turns, with a little indulgence, to indifference or disgust; hatred alone is immortal.

— *William Hazlitt, "On the Pleasures of Hating," The Plain Speaker (1826)*

---

318 Trump to Skip White House Correspondents' Dinner 'No Need for Him to Go in and Pretend'
— *Washington Post, 4/11/17*

Laughter tends to mock the pompous and the pretentious; all man's boastful gadding about, all his pretty pomps, his hoary customs, his worn out creeds, changing the glitter of them into the dullest hue of lead.

— *Sean O'Casey, "The Power Of Laughter: Weapon Against Evil" (1964)*

---

319 It's Not Just CNN: Now ABC, CBS and NBC All Refuse to Run Trump Re-Election Campaign Ad That Blasts Them as "FAKE NEWS'

— *Daily Mail, 5/6/17*

In order that all men may be taught to speak truth, it is necessary that all likewise should learn to hear it.

— *Samuel Johnson, "The Rambler" (1750)*

---

320 At FDA, TV's Now Turned to Fox News and Can't Be Switched

— *CBS News, 5/6/17*

The sound of tireless voices is the price we pay for the right to hear the music of our own opinions.

— *Adlai Stevenson, Speech, New York City (1952)*

---

321 Donald Trump Says He Wants to Do Press Briefings Instead of Sean Spicer

— *Independent, 5/13/17*

Half of the harm that is done in this world / Is due to people who want to feel important.

— *T. S. Eliot, "The Cocktail Party" (1949)*

---

322 The Trump News You Missed: He Asked Comey to Jail Journalists

— *The Guardian, 5/17/17*

The press exerts the pressure of dissent on officials otherwise inclined to rest content with the congratulations of their retainers.
— Lewis Lapham, "Imperial Masquerade" (1990)

———————

323 Roger Ailes' Greatest Legacy at Fox News? Donald Trump
— The Guardian, 5/19/17

Duty largely consists of pretending that the trivial is critical.
— John Fowler, "The Magus" (1965)

———————

324 New York Times Reporter Says They Have Received Fake News Tips From Trump Administration
— Independent, 5/22/17

Whoever has even once become notorious by base fraud, even if he speaks the truth, gains no belief.
— Phaedrus, "Fables" (1st C. BCE)

———————

325 Make No Mistake: Donald Trump Has Fueled Violence Against Journalists
— The Guardian, 5/25/17

Politics, as a practice, whatever its professions, has always been the systematic organization of hatreds.
— Henry Adams, "The Education Of Henry Adams" (1907)

———————

326 Germany's Top Magazine Just Called for Trump's Impeachment in a Blistering Editorial
— Washington Journal, 5/26/17

Scorn and defiance, slight regard, contempt, and any thing that may not misbecome the mighty sender, doth he prize you at.
— Shakespeare, "Henry V" (1599)

———————

327 Sean Spicer: White House Is No Longer Taking Questions on Trump and Russia
— *The Guardian, 6/1/17*

Since unhappiness excites interest, many, in order to render themselves interesting, feign unhappiness.
— *Joseph Roux, "Meditations Of A Parish Priest" (1886)*

---

328 'Collusion Is Not a Crime': Trump's Media Allies Have a Striking New Talking Point That Experts Say Is 'Flawed' and 'Absurd'
— *Business Insider, 6/27/17*

In a world where everything is ridiculous, nothing can be ridiculed. You cannot unmask a mask.
— *G. K. Chesterton, "On The Common Spirit," Generally Speaking (1928)*

---

329 Senators Rebuke Trump for Tweets Insulting Cable Host
— *Wall Street Journal, 6/29/17 (Misconstrued)*

Mockery is often the result of a poverty of wit.
— *La Bruyere, "Characters" (1688)*

---

330 'I'm President and They're Not': Trump Slams Media in Speech Honoring Veterans
— *Business Insider, 7/1/17*

I have never found, in a long experience of politics, that criticism is ever inhibited by ignorance.
— *Harold MacMillan, Wall Street Journal (1963)*

---

331 Trump Keeps Up Criticism of Media
— *Wall Street Journal, 7/3/17 (Misconstrued)*

I wonder how anyone can have the face to condemn others when he reflects upon his own thoughts.

— W. Somerset Maugham, "The Summing Up" (1938)

_____

332 In Battling the Media Trump Is Harming You

— Washington Post, 7/3/17

He that does you a very ill turn will never forgive you.

— English Proverb

_____

333 White House Warns CNN That Critical Coverage Could Cost Time Warner Its Merger

— New York Magazine, 7/6/17

Revenge is always the joy of narrow, / Sick, and petty minds.

— Juvenal, "Satires" (1st C. CE))

_____

334 Trump Trashes the United States on the World Stage

— Washington Monthly, 7/6/17

Folk whose own behavior is most ridiculous are always to the fore in slandering others.

— Moliere, "Tartuffe" (1664)

_____

335 Donald Trump Doesn't Want the Media to Be Fair. He Wants It to Be Subservient

— Reddit, 7/6/17

By giving us the opinions of the uneducated, [journalism] keeps us in touch with the ignorance of the community.

— Oscar Wilde, "The Artist as Critic," Writings of Oscar Wilde (Edited,1969)

_____

336 Trump Asserts His 'Complete Power to Pardon' as He Again Attacks 'Fake News'

— *Washington Post, 7/22/17*

Next to the joy of the egotist is the joy of the detractor.

— *Agnes Repplier, "Writing An Autobiography," Under Dispute (1924)*

---

337 Polls Show Trump, the Least Popular President Ever, Is Plunging Even Lower

— *Newsweek, 7/22/17*

The fires of hate, compressed within the heart, / Burn fiercer and will break at last in flame.

— *Corneille, "Le Cid" (1636)*

---

338 Harvard Law Professor: If the White House Threatened 'Morning Joe' Hosts with a National Enquirer Story, It's a Crime

— *Business Insider, 7/30/17*

There is scarcely any man sufficiently clever to appreciate all the evil he does.

— *La Rochefoucauld, "Maxims" (1665)*

---

339 Trump Lashes Out at 'Fake News' When Pressed About Failure to Hold News Conference

— *Politico, 8/14/17*

It is much easier to be critical than to be correct.

— *Benjamin Disraeli, Speech (Jan., 1860)*

---

340 Poll: 40 Percent Now Support Trump Impeachment

— *NBC, 8/17/17*

Abused patience turns to fury.

— *Thomas Fuller, M.D. "Gnomologia" (1732)*

———

341 For Murdoch Empire, Perhaps a Decisive Point In Relationship to Trump

— *New York Times, 8/18/17*

Fate has terrible power. / You cannot escape it by wealth or war. / No fort will keep it out, no ships out-run it.

— *Sophocles, "Antigone" (442 BCE)*

———

342 Total Eclipse of the White House: Zero Trump Officials Brave Enough to Appear on Sunday TV

— *Shareblue Media, 8/20/17*

Between two cowards, he has the advantage who first detects the other.

— *Italian Proverb*

———

343 Trump Staffer Responsible for Finding Positive News Stories Resigns

— *Huffington Post, 8/25/17*

The worst things: / To be in bed and sleep not, / To want for one who comes not, / To try to please and please not.

— *Egyptian Proverb*

———

344 Most Voters Think Trump Dislikes the Media More Than [He Dislikes] White Supremacists, Poll Finds

— *Huffington Post, 8/31/17*

Hatred is a feeling which leads to the extinction of values.

— *Jose Ortega Y Gasset, "To the Reader," Meditations On Quixote (1914)*

———

345 Donald Trump's 'Crooked' And 'Fake' Media Slurs Crumble as Reporters Excel Chronicling Hurricane Harvey
— *Independent, 9/2/17*

The privilege of absurdity; to which no living creature is subject but man only.
— *Thomas Hobbes, "Leviathan" (1651)*

346 Donald Trump Is Making Someone Else Face the Cameras to Announce DACA's Fate
— *Huffington Post, 9/4/17*

The ultimate measure of a man is not where he stands in moments of comfort and convenience, but where he stands at times of challenge and controversy.
— *Martin Luther King, Jr., "Strength To Love" (1963)*

347 Fox News Is Now Attacking Republicans While Praising Trump and Democrats
— *Newsweek, 9/7/17*

If men are only shrewd enough, they may even serve kings, eat poison, and dally with women.
— *Panchatantra (300 BCE)*

348 Miami Airport Busts Trump Social Media Director for Spreading Fake News in Midst of Storm
— *Shareblue Media, 9/10/17*

Some people take more care to hide their wisdom than their folly.
— *Jonathan Swift, "Thoughts On Various Subjects" (1711)*

349 The Wall Street Journal's Trump Problem [Normalizing the President]
— *The Guardian, 9/10/17*

A windmill is eternally at work to accomplish one end, although it shifts with every variation of the weathercock and assumes ten different positions in a day.
— *Charles Caleb Colton, "Lacon" (1825)*

———————

350 Trump Says 'Fake News' Won't Show Rally Crowd as CNN Splits Screen [Showing Rally Crowd]
— *The Hill, 9/22/17*

Wherein thou judgest another, thou condemnest thyself.
— *Bible, Romans 2:1*

———————

351 Fox Host Embarrasses White House Official for Lying About Pre-Existing Conditions
— *Shareblue Media, 9/25/17*

Liar, liar, pants on fire!
— *William Blake, "The Liar" (1810)*

———————

352 Nikita Khrushchev's Granddaughter: Trump Uses 'Fake News' Like Stalin Used "Enemies of the People"
— *Washington Examiner, 10/11/17*

The tyrant claims freedom to kill freedom / and yet to keep it for himself.
— *Rabindranath Tagore, "Fireflies" (1928)*

———————

353 Donald Trump Urges 'Fake News' to Keep Talking About 'Wacky' [Representative] Frederica Wilson
— *News Source, 10/20/17*

There never was a child so lovely but his mother was glad to get him asleep.
— Emerson, "Journals" (1836)

_____

354 The FCC Plans to Roll Back Some of Its Biggest Rules Against Media Consolidation
— Washington Post, 10/25/17

Great power constitutes its own argument, and it never has much trouble drumming up friends, applause, sympathetic exegesis, and a band.
— Lewis Lapham, "Imperial Masquerade" (1990)

_____

355 Fox News Revenues Nosedive Despite Trump's Constant Viewing
— Huffington Post, 10/27/17

Can a man take fire in his bosom, and his clothes not be burned?
— Bible, Proverbs 6:27

_____

356 Adviser Roger Stone Launches Tirade of Foul-Mouthed Abuse Against CNN Journalists Critical of Donald Trump
— Independent, 10/28/17

Wilt thou show the whole width of thy wit in an instant?
— Shakespeare, "The Merchant Of Venice" (1596 - 1599)

_____

357 Trump Praises [President] Carter, Slams Media
— Politico, 10/28/17

The impulse to mar and to destroy is as ancient and almost as nearly universal as the impulse to create. The one is an easier way than the other of demonstrating power.
— Joseph Wood Krutch, "The Best Of Two Worlds" (1950)

---

358 Juan Williams: Trump's War on Media Is Truly Dangerous
— *News Source, 10/30/17*

When distant and unfamiliar and complex things are communicated to great masses of people, the truth suffers a considerable and often radical distortion. The complex is made over into the simple, the hypothetical into the dogmatic, and the relative into an absolute.
— *Walter Lippman, "The Public Philosophy" (1955)*

---

359 Fox Cancels Airing Of Ad Saying Trump Should Be Impeached
— *Washington Post, 11/6/17*

Thou wilt be as valiant as the wrathful dove, or most magnanimous mouse.
— *Shakespeare, "Henry IV, Part 2" (1596 - 1599)*

---

360 President Is Losing Support in 'Trump Counties,' a WSJ/NBC News Poll Finds
— *Wall Street Journal, 11/7/17 (Misconstrued)*

Oft expectation fails and most oft there where most it promises, and oft hits where hope is coldest and despair most fits.
— *Shakespeare, ""All's Well That Ends Well" (1602 - 1603)*

---

361 Mainstream Media Casts Trump's Asia Trip in Negative Light
— *News Source, 11/10/17*

If clearness about things produces a fundamental despair, a fundamental despair in turn produces a remarkable clearness or even playfulness about ordinary matters.
— *George Santayana, "Persons/Places: The Background Of My Life" (1944)*

_____

362 Media Showing Bias Against Trump to Push Russian Narrative?

— *News Source, 11/13/17*

Duty then is the sublimest word in our language. Do your duty in all things. You cannot do more. You should never wish to do less.

— *Robert E. Lee, Inscription Beneath His Bust, New York University*

_____

363 Trump Returns [to U.S.] and Attacks a Favorite Foe: CNN

— *New York Times, 11/15/17*

Make men large and strong [CNN], and tyranny will bankrupt itself in making shackles for them.

— *Henry Ward Beecher, "Proverbs From Plymouth Pulpit" (1887)*

_____

364 Fox News Poll: Obama Has Higher Favorability in Alabama Than Trump

— *The Hill, 11/16/17*

Surprise is the greatest gift which life can grant us.

— *Boris Pasternak, Speech, Writers' Plenum, Minsk (Feb., 1936)*

_____

365 Former Bush Speechwriter: Trump's Tweets Are a 'Direct Attack' on the Safety of Journalists

— *The Hill, 11/25/17*

The use of force alone is temporary. It may subdue for a moment, but it does not remove the necessity of subduing again: and a nation is not governed which is perpetually to be conquered.

— *Edmund Burke, "On Conciliation With The American Colonies" (1775)*

_____

366 Trump Resumes Battle With CNN, MSNBC After Returning From Mar-a-Lago

— *News Source, 11/27/17*

Thin skin is the only kind of skin human beings come with.

— *Mary Ellen "Meg" Greenfield, Editorial Writer (1930 - 1999)*

----

367 The Media Still Doesn't Know How to Cover a Bankrupt GOP

— *New Republic, 11/29/17*

Catastrophes come when some dominant institution [GOP], swollen like a soap-bubble and still standing without foundations, suddenly crumbles at the touch of what may seem a word or an idea, but is really some stronger material force.

— *George Santayana, "Persons And Places: The Middle Span" (1945)*

----

368 Fox News Host Says Lindsey Vonn is 'Un-American' for Ripping Donald Trump

— *Huffington Post, 12/8/17*

To the reactionary ear every whispered criticism of the Elite classes has always sounded like the opening shot of an uprising.

— *Reichard Hofstadter, "The American Political Tradition" (1948)*

----

369 [Press Secretary] Sanders Says 2016 Victory 'Answered' [Groping] Allegations Against Trump

— *Politico, 12/11/17*

Perfect nonsense goes on in the world. Sometimes there is no plausibility at all.

— *Nikolai Gogol, "The Nose" (1835)*

----

370 Fox News is Worried Moore's Loss Means Trump Might Be Held Accountable for Sexual Assault
— *ThinkProgress, 12/12/17*

No shit, Sherlock!
— *David Bowie, BBC Interview, "Five Years" Documentary (1976)*

---

371 David Cameron [Former British Prime Minister] to Trump: Your 'Fake News' Act is 'Dangerous'
— *Politico, 12/13/17*

Men are much more unwilling to have their weaknesses and Imperfections known than their crimes.
— *Lord Chesterfield, Letters To His Son (Sept., 1748)*

---

372 Trump's Popularity Starts to Fall Among Loyal Fox News Fans
— *Independent, 12/14/17*

Admiration is a very short-lived passion that immediately decays upon growing familiar with its object, unless it be still fed with fresh discoveries, and kept alive by a new perpetual succession of miracles rising up to its view.
— *Joseph Addison, "The Spectator" (1711)*

---

373 White House Confirms: Trump Talked to Murdoch About Disney Deal
— *CNN, 12/15/17*

It's nice to have friends in high places.
— *Warren Buffet, Op Ed Piece In New York Times (Aug., 2011)*

---

374 Twitter Reacts After Trump Retweets Photo of Himself With Bloody CNN Logo [on Bottom of Shoe]
— *Huffington Post, 12/24/17*

The right to be heard does not automatically include the right to be taken seriously.
— Hubert Humphrey, Speech To National Student Association (Aug., 1965)

––––––––––

375 Trump's Attacks Against a Biased Liberal Media Obscure One Fact: It Doesn't Exist
— The Guardian, 1/1/18

…Through the woodland, through the valley, comes a horseman wild and free, tilting at the windmills passing, who can the brave young horseman be…
— Gordon Lightfoot, "Don Quixote" (1972)

––––––––––

376 Trump's Lawyers Try to Halt [Michael Wolff's] Book Release as White House Fights to Contain Firestorm
— The Guardian, 1/4/18

What devil art thou that dost torment me thus? This torture should be roar'd in dismal hell.
— Shakespeare, "Romeo And Juliet" (1591 – 1595)

––––––––––

377 A President Who Attempts to Ban Books About Him Should Be Impeached
— The Nation, 1/5/18

The greatest triumphs of propaganda have been accomplished, not by doing something, but by refraining from doing. Great is truth, but still greater, from a practical point of view, is silence about the truth.
— Aldous Huxley, "Foreword, Brave New World" (1932)

––––––––––

378 I've Studied the Trump – Fox Feedback Loop for Months. It's Crazier Than You Think [President Live-Tweets Fox]
— Politico, 1/6/18

The search for a personal identity is the life task of a teenager.
— Haim G. Ginott, "Between Parent & Teenager" (1969)

---

379 'This is the Netherlands, You Have to Answer Questions': U.S. Ambassador Offers Uncomfortable Silence
— Chicago Tribune, 1/10/18

Free speech is about as good a cause as the world has ever known. But, like the poor, it is always with us and gets shoved aside in favor of things which seem at some given moment more vital.
— Heywood Broun, "The Miracle Of Debs," New York World (Oct., 1926)

---

380 Trump Picks Fight With WSJ Over Interview
— Politico, 1/14/18

A good man should and must / Sit rather down with loss than rise unjust.
— Ben Johnson, "Sejanus His Fall" (1603)

---

381 The Fake News Awards Are Another Escalation in Trump's Assault on Press Freedoms
— Los Angeles Times, 1/17/18

He who cannot shine by thought, seeks to bring himself into notice by a witticism.
— Voltaire, "Wit, Spirit, Intellect," Philosophical Dictionary (1764)

---

382 Donald Trump's Fake News Awards Neatly Encapsulate Every Reason Why He's Not Fit to Be Leader of Free World
— Independent, 1/18/18

News is history shot on the wing. The huntsmen from the Fourth Estate seek to bag only the peacock or the eagle of the swifting day.
— Gene Fowler, "Skyline" (1961)

CHAPTER 6

LICHTENSTEIN INTERNATIONAL MILITARY ACADEMY

TOPICS:
RATIONAL AND REALISTIC

Lichenstein International Military Academy

383 Runner-Up Didn't Make It to Supreme Court, But He Did Get to Altoona
— *New York Times, 1/31/17*

Look for the ridiculous in everything and you will find it.
— *Jules Renard, "Journal" (1890)*

384 It's 'The Apprentice, Supreme Court Edition' as Trump Summons Finalists to White House
— *New York Times, 1/31/17*

To be happy, we must not be too concerned with others.
— *Albert Camus, "The Fall" (1956)*

385 Stephen King on Donald Trump: 'How Do Such Men Rise? First, as a Joke'
— *The Guardian, 4/1/17*

There is no need to fasten a bell to a fool.
— *Danish Proverb*

386 Trump to Ease Restrictions on Religious Groups
— *Wall Street Journal, 5/4/17 (Misconstrued)*

All religions united with the government are more or less inimical to liberty. All separated from government are compatible with liberty.
— *Henry Clay, Speech, U. S. House Of Representatives (1818)*

387 Obama Warned Trump Against Hiring Flynn
— *Wall Street Journal, 5/8/17 (Misconstrued)*

When a finger points at the moon, the imbecile looks at the finger.
— Chinese Proverb

---

388 Firing Comey Won't Save Trump From Flames of Scandal
— *The Guardian, 5/11/17*

A lie has no leg, but a scandal has wings.
— *Thomas Fuller, M. D. "Gnomologia" (1732)*

---

389 New Trump Web Page Asks Americans If They Want to Ax National Park Service, Other Key Land Services
— *The Wilderness Society, 5/18/17*

No sane society chooses to commit national suicide.
— *John F. Kennedy, "The Strategy Of Peace" (1960)*

---

390 European Allies Fear Trump's Political Chaos Is Undermining U.S. Power
— *Washington Post, 5/19/17*

We're all muddlers. The thing is to see when one's got to stop muddling.
— *Iris Murdoch, "A Word Child" (1975)*

---

391 Rollercoaster Washington Week Ends With Trump Exit - But He'll be Back
— *The Guardian, 5/20/17*

It is the wise man's part / to leave in darkness everything that is ugly.
— *Euripides, "Hippolytus" (428 BCE)*

---

392 Trump Discovers Dangers of Governing at Daredevil Speed
— *New York Times, 5/20/17*

You can't set a hen one morning and have chicken salad for lunch.

— George Humphrey, Time (Jan., 1953)

---

393 The Awkward Body Language of Donald Trump

— New York Times, 5/28/17

Man is a mind betrayed, not served, by his organs.

— Jules De Goncourt, Journal (1861)

---

394 Trump's War on Regulations

— Politico, 5/28/17

A fool sees not the same tree that a wise man sees.

— William Blake, "The Marriage Of Heaven and Hell" (1790)

---

395 As Merkel Knows, Trump's Rudeness and Arrogance Can Unite Europe

— The Guardian, 5/29/17

The qualities we have do not make us so ridiculous as those which we affect.

— La Rochefoucauld, "Maxims" (1665)

---

396 Trump Targets 'Negative Press Covfefe' in Garbled Midnight Tweet

— Washington Post, 5/31/17

Use what language you will, you can never say anything but what you are.

— Emerson, "Worship," The Conduct Of Life (1860)

---

397 Is Trump Trying to Provoke a Domestic Terror Attack?

— Newsweek, 6/4/17

Though the wisdom or virtue of one can very rarely make many happy, the folly or vice of one man often makes many miserable.
— *Samuel Johnson, "Rasselas" (1759)*

———————

398 Trump Administration Has Failed to Answer 275 Inquiries: Democrats
— *ABC, 6/5/17*

Your abilities are too infant-like for doing much alone.
— *Shakespeare, "Coriolanus" (1605 – 1608)*

———————

399 On World Stage, Trump Remains Disruptor-in-Chief
— *Wall Street Journal, 6/6/17 (Misconstrued)*

Circus, n. A place where horses, ponies and elephants are permitted to see men, women and children act the fool.
— *Ambrose Bierce, "The Devil's Dictionary" (1881-1911)*

———————

400 Late Night Hosts on Trump and Russia: 'Make Justice Obstructed Again'
— *The Guardian, 6/17/17*

The most effective way of attacking vice is to expose it to public ridicule. People can put up with rebukes but they cannot bear being laughed at: they are prepared to be wicked but they dislike appearing ridiculous.
— *Moliere, Preface To "Tartuffe" (1664)*

———————

401 Trump: 'Why Didn't Obama Do Anything About Something I Said Never Existed?'
— *Red State, 6/24/17*

Camouflage is a game we all like to play, but our secrets are as surely revealed by what we want to seem to be as by what we want to conceal.

— *Russell Lynes, "The Truth About Status," Architectural Digest (1977)*

---

402 Steel Yourself for Trump's Anti-Trade Moves

— *Wall Street Journal, 6/26/17 (Misconstrued)*

It takes no more actual sagacity to carry on the everyday hawking and haggling of the world, or to ladle out its normal doses of bad medicine and worse law, than it takes to operate a taxicab or fry a pan of fish.

— *H. L. Mencken, "The Feminine Mind," In Defense Of Women (1922)*

---

403 Bizarre, Absurd, Ridiculous, Embarrassing Trump

— *Washington Post, 7/4/17*

Life is a jest and all things show it; / I thought it so once, but now I know it.

— *John Gay, "My Own Epitaph," Fables (1727-38)*

---

404 'Unelected, unqualified': The Internet's Reaction to Ivanka Trump Taking Her Dad's Seat at G-20

— *Washington Post, 7/817*

Who offends writes on sand, who is offended on marble.

— *Italian Proverb*

---

405 Donald Trump and the Decline of the West: Ten Thousand Years of Civilization and We End Up With This Guy?

— *Salon, 7/8/17*

The test of civilization is not the census, nor the size of cities, nor the crops - no, but the kind of man the country turns out.

— Emerson, "Civilization," Society And Solitude (1870)

_____

406 Trump Teaches Western Civ
— Wall Street Journal, 7/12/17 (Misconstrued)

All over the world today, not just in the totalitarian countries, assiduous functionaries in Ministries of Truth are clubbing history dumb and rendering language insensible.

— E. L. Doctorow, "Jack London, Hemingway, And The Constitution" (1993)

_____

407 Trump Goes All In on the 'Collusion Is Normal Defense'
— The Atlantic, 7/17/17

People tend not to see that their opinion of the world is also a confession of character.

— Emerson, "Worship," The Conduct of Life (1860)

_____

408 Exit Spicey, Enter the Mooch: Another Day in Trump's Tragicomic America
— The Guardian, 7/22/17

Like dreams, farces show the disguised fulfillment of repressed wishes.

— Eric Bentley, "The Psychology Of Farce" (1958)

_____

409 Trump: Senate Let America Down With Its Healthcare Vote
— Huffington Post, 7/28/17

Safe upon the solid rock the ugly houses stand: / Come and see my shining palace built upon the sand!

— Edna St. Vincent Millay, "Second Fig," A Few Figs from Thistles (1921)

_____

410 Steven Colbert to Produce An Animated Trump Series
— *New York Times, 7/28/17*

Of all the griefs that harass the distressed, / Sure the most bitter is a scornful jest.
— *Samuel Johnson, "London" (1738)*

---

411 Amtrak's $630m Trump Budget Cut Could Derail Service in 220 US Cities
— *The Guardian, 7/30/17*

What need had the businessman to scribble or philosophize when he dominated the imagination of his time, and the frantic materialism that was his principle of existence had become the haunting central figure in contemporary life?
— *Alfred Karin, "On Native Grounds" (1942)*

---

412 Trump Has Fired Enough Staffers for An All-Trump Season of Dancing With the Stars
— *Vanity Fair, 7/31/17*

Behavior, n. Conduct, as determined, not by principle, but by breeding.
— *Ambrose Bierce, "The Devil's Dictionary" (1881-1911)*

---

413 Trump Is Woody Allen Without the Humor
— *Wall Street Journal, 8/1/17 (Misconstrued)*

What things are sure this side of paradise: / Death, taxes, and the counsel of the Bore. / Though we outwit the tlthe, make death our friend, / Bores we have with us even to the end.
— *Phyllis McGinley, "Love Letters of Phyllis McGinley" (1954)*

---

414 The Best Quotes From Trump's Embarrassing Unpublished WSJ Interview

— New York Magazine, 8/1/17

Man is the only animal that blushes. Or needs to.

— Mark Twain, "Following The Equator" (1897)

———————

415 Shock Reports: Trump Winged It on N.K. [North Korea] Threat

— Huffington Post, 8/9/17

Tragedy and comedy are simply questions of value; a little misfit in life makes us laugh; a great one is tragedy and cause for expression of grief.

— Elbert Hubbard, "The Note Book" (1927)

———————

416 'God Has Given Trump Authority to Take Out Kim Jong Un,' Evangelical Advisor Says

— Washington Post, 8/9/17

It's a good thing God doesn't let you look a year or two into the future, or you might be sorely tempted to shoot yourself.

— Lee Iacocca, "Iacocca: An Autobiography" (1984)

———————

417 Trump Threatens 'Military Option' in Venezuela as Crisis Escalates

— The Guardian, 8/11/17

Glory is largely a theatrical concept. There is no striving for glory without a vivid awareness of an audience.

— Eric Hoffer, "The True Believer" (1951)

———————

418 Trump Tells Guam Governor Nuclear Tensions Will Mean More Tourism

— *Huffington Post, 8/12/17*

Almost any man may like the spider spin from his own inwards his own airy citadel.

— *Keats, Letter To John Hamilton Reynolds (Feb., 1818)*

---

419 Trump: Graham Telling 'Disgusting Lie' About My Charlottesville Remarks

— *The Hill, 8/17/17*

Other people are quite dreadful. The only possible society is one's self.

— *Oscar Wilde, "An Ideal Husband" (1895)*

---

420 Failing All Tests of the Presidency

— *New York Times, 8/21/17*

Shall I be remembered after death? I sometimes think and hope so but I trust I may not be found out before my death.

— *Samuel Butler, "The Life Of The World To Come," Note-Books (1912)*

---

421 Most Americans Think Trump Is a Bad President, Say No to Wall and War With North Korea

— *Newsweek, 8/26/17*

A scarecrow in a garden of cucumbers keepeth nothing.

— *"Apocrypha," Baruch 6:70*

---

422 Forceful Chief of Staff Grates on Trump, and the Feeling Is Mutual

— *New York Times, 9/1/17*

I think there is a danger in overexposure. Just think what happened to Lady Godiva – she became a chocolate.
— Kenneth Jay Lane, The New York Times (Dec., 1993)

_____

423 Under Child-King Trump, America Is a Runaway Train – And Derailment Is Imminent
— Salon, 9/3/17

Death hath a thousand doors to let out life.
— Philip Massinger, "A Very Woman" (1655)

_____

424 As North Korea Flexes Nuclear Muscles, U.S. Picks Fight With South
— Wall Street Journal, 9/4/17 (Misconstrued)

The only treaties that ought to count are those which would effect a settlement between ulterior motives.
— Paul Valery, "Reflections On The World Today" (1931)

_____

425 Does Trump Want a Nuclear Japan?
— Wall Street Journal, 9/5/17 (Misconstrued)

I will not excuse you, you shall not be excused, excuses shall not be admitted, there is no excuse shall serve, you shall not be excused.
— Shakespeare, "Henry IV, Part 2" (1596 – 1599)

_____

426 The Dreamer Debacle
— Wall Street Journal, 9/6/17 (Misconstrued)

Believe me, all evil comes from the old. They grow fat on ideas, and young men die of them.
— Jean Anouilh, "Catch As Catch Can" (1960)

_____

427 Tracking Trump: A Blow for 'Dreamers' and a Deal With Democrats

— *The Guardian, 9/8/17*

There is in the human race some dark spirit of recalcitrance, always pulling us in the direction contrary to that in which we are reasonably expected to go.

— *Max Beerbohm, "A Christmas Garland" (1895)*

———————

428 Trump Tells Cabinet Hurricane Irma Means Wealthy Need Their [Tax] Cuts Faster

— *Shareblue Media, 9/10/17*

To hazard much to get much has more of avarice than wisdom.

— *William Penn, "Some Fruits Of Solitude" (1693)*

———————

429 John Oliver Exposes Trump's Tell for When He Has No Plan Whatsoever

— *Daily Beast, 9/11/17*

Anyone who has looked deeply into the world may guess how much wisdom lies in the superficiality of men. The instinct that preserves them teaches them to be flighty, light, and false.

— *Nietzsche, "Beyond Good And Evil" (1886)*

———————

430 Congress Rejects Trump's Proposals to Cut Health Research Funds

— *New York Times, 9/12/17*

Life is full of absurdities which, strangely enough, do not even need to appear plausible since they are true.

— *Luigi Pirandello, "Six Characters In Search Of An Author" (1921)*

———————

431 Trump Aims to Rally His Base by Retweeting Memes

— *Washington Post, 9/17/17*

People are more slanderous from vanity than from malice.

— *La Rochefoucauld, "Maxims" (1665)*

---

432 Trump and Netanyahu Ready United Assault Against Iran Nuclear Deal

— *The Guardian, 9/18/17*

Alliance, n. In international politics, the union of two thieves who have their hands so deeply inserted in each other's pocket that they cannot separately plunder a third.

— *Ambrose Bierce, "The Devil's Dictionary" (1881-1911)*

---

433 Trump Bypasses Congress to Open Up World Markets to U.S. Gun Makers

— *News Source, 9/20/17*

Must we kill to prevent there being any wicked? This is to make both parties wicked instead of one.

— *Pascal, "Pensees" (1617)*

---

434 'Dotard' Trump? The Story of 'Rocket Man' Kim's Insult

— *BBC, 9/22/17*

We every day and every hour say things of another that we might more properly say of ourselves could we but apply our observations to our own concerns.

— *Montaigne, "The Affections Of Fathers To Their Children," Essays (1580)*

---

435 Donald Trump Is a Threat to Survival of Life on Earth; If Nuclear War Doesn't Get Us, Falling Oxygen Levels Will

— *Newsweek, 9/24/17*

Will no one [Congress] rid me of this meddlesome priest?
— *Henry II, Referring to Thomas Becket, Archbishop Of Canterbury (1170)*

---

436 Naomi Klein: Trump's Like the Fatberg – Horrible, Noxious, Hard to Dislodge
— *The Guardian, 9/27/17*

Only in men's imagination does every truth find an effective and undeniable existence. Imagination, not invention, is the supreme master of art as of life.
— *Joseph Conrad, "A Personal Record" (1912)*

---

437 Trump: NFL Owners Are Scared of Their Players
— *Politico, 9/28/17*

Everyone is more or less mad on one point.
— *Rudyard Kipling, "Plain Tales From The Hills" (1888)*

---

438 Donald Trump's Fed Choice: Continuity Or Disruption?
— *Wall Street Journal, 10/4/17 (Misconstrued)*

If the audience never understands the plot, it can be counted on to be attentive to the very end.
— *Benedict Marcello, "Il Teatro Alla Moda" (1720)*

---

439 Trump Expected to Refuse to Certify Iran's Compliance With Nuclear Deal
— *Wall Street Journal, 10/5/17 (Misconstrued)*

Bore, n. A person who talks when you want him to listen.
— *Ambrose Bierce, "The Devil's Dictionary" (1881-1911)*

---

440 Tillerson Chaos Lays Bare Kelly's Struggle to Manage White House

— *CNN, 10/6/17*

One of the most visible effects of a child's presence in the household is to turn the worthy parents into complete idiots when, without him, they would perhaps have remained mere imbeciles.

— *Georges Courteline, "La Philosophie De G. Courteline" (1917)*

---

441 Diplomats Fear Trump Is Tweeting the United States Into War

— *Vanity Fair, 10/9/17*

First learn the meaning of what you say, then speak.

— *Epictetus, "Discourses" (2nd C. CE)*

---

442 Trump Mocks Bob Corker's Height, Escalating Feud With a Key Republican

— *New York Times, 10/10/17*

Sticks and stones may break my bones, but names will never hurt me.

— *Children's Adage, The Christian Recorder (Mar., 1862)*

---

443 GOP Senators 'Laughed Out Loud' at Notion Border Wall Would Get Built

— *News Source, 10/11/17*

The pot calling the kettle black.

— *Thomas Shelton, Translation Of "Don Quixote" (1620)*

---

444 Man Rescued From Taliban: I Thought My Captors Were Kidding When They Said Trump Was President

— *The Hill, 10/16/17*

His addiction was to courses vain; his companies unletter'd, rude, shallow; his hours fill'd up with riots, banquets, sports. And never noted in him any study, any retirement, any sequestration from open haunts and popularity.
— *Shakespeare, "Henry V" (1599)*

---

445 Rush Limbaugh: 'Twitter is a Cacophony of Crap'
— *News Source, 10/16/17*

An 'extremely credible source' has called my office and told me that Barak Obama's birth certificate is a fraud.
— *Donald Trump, Twitter (Aug. 6, 2012)*

---

446 The Donald Trump Doctrine: 'Obama Built It. I Broke It. You Fix It.'
— *Independent, 10/18/17*

That's villainous, and shows a most pitiful ambition in the fool that uses it.
— *Shakespeare, "Hamlet" (1601)*

---

447 Former Presidents Obama and Bush Decry Trump Era Politics
— *BBC, 10/20/17*

He serves his party best who serves the country best.
— *Rutherford B. Hayes, Inaugural Address (Mar., 1877)*

---

448 Tom Hanks: Trump's Call to Soldier's Family 'One of the Biggest Cock-Ups on the Planet Earth'
— *The Hill, 10/22/17*

Great blunders are often made, like large ropes, of a multitude of fibres.
— *Victor Hugo, "Cosette," Les Miserables (1862)*

_____

449 The Power of the Presidential Tweet
— *Wall Street Journal, 10/22/17 (Misconstrued)*

You speak an infinite deal of nothing.
— *Shakespeare, "The Merchant Of Venice" (1596 - 1599)*

_____

450 GOP Senator Says It's Not His Job to Speak Up When Trump Lies
— *TPM, 10/25/17*

There is no more valour in you than in a wild duck.
— *Shakespeare, "Henry IV, Part 1" (1597)*

_____

451 'It's Just Messed Up': Most Think Political Divisions as Bad as Vietnam Era, New Poll Shows.
— *Washington Post, 10/28/17*

As democracy is perfected, the office [of the president] represents, more and more closely, the inner soul of the people. We move toward a lofty Ideal. On some great and glorious day, the plain folks of the land will reach their heart's desire at last, and the White House will be adorned by a moron.
— *H. L. Mencken, The Baltimore Evening Sun (July, 1920)*

_____

452 The Trump Deregulatory Juggernaut Is Rolling
— *Wall Street Journal, 10/30/17 (Misconstrued)*

115

Some scientists claim that hydrogen, because it is so plentiful, is the basic building block of the universe. I dispute that. I say there is more stupidity than hydrogen, and that is the basic building block of the universe.
— Frank Zappa, "The Real Frank Zappa Book" (1989)

_____

453 Sam Clovis, Trump's Nominee for USDA's Top Scientist, Confirms He Has No Hard Science Credentials
— Washington Post, 11/2/17

Every error has its consequences and venges itself unto the seventh generation.
— Arthur Koestler, ""Darkness At Noon" (1940)

_____

454 Trump USDA Nominee [Sam Clovis] Withdraws After Link to Russia Probe
— Bloomberg, 11/2/17

Beauty is in the eye of the beholder.
— Margaret Wolfe Hungerford, "Molly Bawn" (1878)

_____

455 Donald Trump Accused of Obstructing Satellite Research Into Climate Change
— The Guardian, 11/5/17

If life's a joke, then suicide's a bad punch line.
— Louise Erdrich, "Religious Wars," The Bingo Palace (1994)

_____

456 Steve Bannon: Trump Will Win Re-Election With 400 Electoral Votes
— News Source, 11/10/17

The most imaginative people are the most credulous, for to them everything is possible.

— Alexander Chase, "Perspectives" (1966)

---

457 The Clown Goes Abroad

— *Washington Post, 11/13/17*

A traveller without knowledge is a bird without wings.

— Sa'di, "Gulistan" (1258)

---

458 Trump to Lift Ban on Importing Elephant Trophies From Africa

— *News Source, 11/15/17*

Among all creatures that breathe on earth and crawl on it / there is not anywhere a thing more dismal than man is.

— Homer, "Iliad" (9th C. BCE)

---

459 A Year Into Trump's Presidency, Christians Are Facing a Spiritual Reckoning

— *Washington Post, 11/17/17*

No kingdom has ever suffered as many civil wars as Christ's.

— Montesquieu, "Letters Persanes" (1721)

---

460 Trump Voter: If Jesus Christ Told Me Trump Colluded With Russia, I'd Check With Trump

— *The Hill, 11/20/17*

As they say of the blind, / Sounds are the things I see.

— Sophocles, "Oedipus At Colonus" (401 BCE)

---

461 Trump Plays Down Roy Moore Allegations, Blasts 'Liberal' Rival in Alabama Race

— *News Source, 11/22/17*

Here's an equivocator that could swear in both scales against either scale.

— *Shakespeare, "Macbeth" (1606)*

———————

462 Trump Blasts NFL Chief for Ceding 'Control' to Players

— *Washington Post, 11/24/17*

'Tis strange, 'tis very strange; that is the brief and the tedious of it.

— *Shakespeare, "All's Well That Ends Well" (1604 - 1605)*

———————

463 Trump Calls CFPB [Consumer Financial Protection Bureau] 'a Total Disaster' on a Tweet Following Cordray's Resignation

— *News Source, 11/25/17*

Shall I compare thee to a summer's day? Thou art more lovely and more temperate…but thy eternal summer shall not fade…nor shall death brag thou wander'st in his shade…

— *Shakespeare, Sonnet 18, Fair Youth Sequence (1609)*

———————

464 Casting Wall Street as Victim, Trump Leads Deregulatory Charge

— *New York Times, 11/27/17*

Unextinguished laughter shakes the skies.

— *Homer, "Iliad" (9th C. BCE)*

———————

465 Ex-Clinton Staffer: If Obama Cured Cancer, Trump Would Try to Bring It Back

— *The Hill, 12/5/17*

Revenge is sweeter than life itself. So think fools.
— *Juvenal, Roman Poet And Satirist (1st - 2nd C. CE)*

—————

466 Trump's Border Wall: Climbing Tests Begin on Prototypes
— *BBC, 12/8/17*

One has to be a lowbrow, a bit of a murderer, to be a politician, ready and willing to see people sacrificed, slaughtered, for the sake of an idea, whether a good one or a bad one.
— *Henry Miller, Interview, "Writers At Work: Second Series" (1963)*

—————

467 The Trump Administration's Tax Report Reads Like Fan Fiction
— *Washington Post, 12/11/17*

Reports that say something hasn't happened are always interesting to me, because as we know, there are known knowns; there are things we know we know. We also know there are known unknowns; that is to say we know there are some things we do not know. But there are also unknown unknowns - the one's we don't know we don't know.
— *Donald Rumsfeld, Department Of Defense News Briefing (Feb., 2002)*

—————

468 Trump Daily Intel Updates Structured to Avoid Upsetting Him: Report
— *The Hill, 12/14/17*

The first step in wisdom, as well as in morality, is to open the windows of the ego as wide as possible.
— *Bertrand Russell, "Fortitude," New Hopes For A Changing World (1951)*

—————

469 Trump Administration Bans CDC [Center for Disease Control] From Using the Word 'Transgender'
— *Advocate.com, 12/16/17*

I am not so concerned with the right of everyone to say whatever he pleases as I am about our need as a self-governing people to hear everything relevant.
— *John F. Kennedy, Address, National Civil Liberties Conference (April, 1959)*

---

470 US 'Will Take Names' at UN Jerusalem Vote
— *BBC, 12/20/17*

My Dad is meaner than your Dad.
— *H. Clark, On DeviantArt (2013)*

---

471 America Is on the Brink of a Historic Break With Europe, Thanks to Trump
— *USA Today, 12/26/17*

To withdraw is not to run away, and to stay is no wise action, when there's more reason to fear than to hope.
— *Cervantes, "Don Quixote" (1605)*

---

472 Bernstein: Trump Presidency Is Tainted, Not FBI
— *CNN, 12/26/17*

Let none presume to wear an undeserved dignity. O that estates, degrees, and offices were not derived corruptly, and that clear honor were purchased by the merit of the wearer!
— *Shakespeare, "The Merchant Of Venice" (1596 - 1597)*

---

473 The World According to Trump: 2017 Was a Busy Year of Hurling Insults Globally
— *The Guardian, 12/28/17*

Surely human affairs would be far happier if the power in men to be silent were the same as that to speak. But experience more than sufficiently teaches that men govern nothing with more difficulty than their tongues, and can moderate their desires more easily than their words.

— *Spinoza, "Ethics" (1677)*

---

474 Trump Suggests Huma Abedin [Hillary Clinton Aide] Be Jailed After State Department Email Release

— *Politico, 1/2/18*

If all you have is a hammer, everything looks like a nail.

— *Abraham Maslow, "The Psychology Of Science" (1966)*

---

475 Stephen Colbert Blasts Trump for Twitter Feud With Kim Jong-un

— *New York Times, 1/3/18*

There is no end to the violations committed by children on children, quietly talking alone [or not].

— *Elizabeth Bowen, "The House In Paris" (1935)*

---

476 Trump Calls on Republicans to 'Finally Take Control' of the Russia Investigation

— *Business Insider, 1/10/18*

There can be no whitewash in the White House.

— *Richard M. Nixon, Televised Speech On Watergate (May 1, 1973)*

---

477 Trump Suggests Surveillance Law Could Have Been Used [by Obama Administration] to Abuse His Campaign.

— *The Guardian, 1/11/18*

He whose mouth is out of taste says the wine is flat.

— Montaigne, "Apology For Raimond De Sebonde," Essays (1580)

———————

478 Trump is a Dangerous 'Asteroid of Awfulness That Has Fallen on This World': British Politician

— Newsweek, 1/15/18

The universe does not jest with us, but is in earnest.

— Emerson, "Journals" (1841)

———————

479 In a Bizarre Reversal Under Trump, Consumer Agency Reveals Moves to Protect Payday Lenders

— Los Angeles Times, 1/19/18

The absurd is essentially a divorce. It lies in neither of the elements compared; it is born of their confrontation.

— Albert Camus, "The Myth Of Sisyphus" (1955)

CHAPTER 7

AMBROSE BIERCE INSTITUTE FOR BAGPIPING AND ADVENTURE STUDIES

TOPICS:
BEST ALLY AND LOYAL FRIEND

Ambrose Bierce Institute for Bagpiping and Adventure Studies

480 Trump and Putin Connect, But Avoid Talk of Lifting U.S. Sanctions
— *New York Times, 1/28/17*

Jealousy, which serves the struggle for survival, can deteriorate into the envy which draws defeat even from victory.
— *Willard Gaylin, "Feelings: Our Vital Signs" (1979)*

481 Russia Deploys Missile, Violating Treaty and Challenging Trump
— *New York Times, 2/14/17*

What difference does it make to the dead, the orphans and the homeless, whether the mad destruction is wrought under the name of totalitarianism, or the holy name of liberty or democracy?
— *Mohandas K. Gandhi, "Non-Violence In Peace and War" (1948)*

482 Blackwater Founder Held Secret Seychelles Meeting to Establish Trump-Putin Back Channel
— *Reddit, 4/4/17*

We do not feel grateful toward those who make our dreams come true [Putin]; they ruin our dreams.
— *Eric Hoffer, "The Passionate State Of Mind" (1954)*

483 British Spies Warned of Trump Team's Links With Russia in 2015
— *The Guardian, 4/13/17*

They talk of a man betraying his country, his friends, his sweetheart. There must be a moral bond first. All a man can betray is his conscience.

— Joseph Conrad, "Under Western Eyes" (1911)

———————

484 Trump Campaign Officials Questioned Over Russia Ties

— *Wall Street Journal, 5/6/17 (Misconstrued)*

It is a matter of regret that many low, mean suspicions turn out to be well founded.

— Edgar Watson Howe, "Ventures In Common Sense" (1919)

———————

485 Trump Dismisses Hearing on Campaign's Ties to Russia as 'Charade'

— *Huffington Post, 5/8/17*

Into each life some rain must fall, / Some days must be dark and gloomy.

— Longfellow, "The Rainy Day" (1842)

———————

486 White House Staff Deny Comey Sacking Linked to Russia

— *The Guardian, 5/10/17*

A clean glove often hides a dirty hand.

— English Proverb

———————

487 Abrupt Termination [of Comey] Upends Probe of Trump Campaign Ties to Russia

— *Wall Street Journal, 5/10/17 (Misconstrued)*

He who conceals his disease cannot expect to be cured.

— Ethiopian Proverb

———————

488 Trump Bars U.S. Press, But Not Russia's, at Meeting With Russian Officials

— *New York Times, 5/11/17*

He who boasts of a favor bestowed, would like it back again.

— *Publilius Syrus, "Moral Sayings" (1st C. BCE)*

---

489 Trump: Russia Laughing as U.S. 'Tears Itself Apart'

— *Politico, 5/12/17*

We often give our enemies the means for our own destruction.

— *Aesop, "The Eagle And The Arrow," Fables (6th C. BCE)*

---

490 Political Chaos in Washington Is a Return on Investment in Russia

— *Washington Post, 5/15/17*

There are two fools in every market: one asks too little, one asks too much.

— *Russian Proverb*

---

491 Trump Shared Intelligence Secrets With Russians

— *Wall Street Journal, 5/16/17 (Misconstrued)*

Weep for the dead for he lacks the light; and weep for the fool, for he lacks intelligence; weep less bitterly for the dead, for he has attained rest; but the life of the fool is worse than death.

— *"Apocrypha," Ecclesiasticus 22:11*

---

492 Russian State-Run Bank Financed Deal Involving Trump Hotel Partner

— *Wall Street Journal, 5/18/17 (Misconstrued)*

If the camel gets its nose in the tent, his body will soon follow.

— *Arabic Proverb*

493 Special Counsel Appointed to Oversee Inquiry of Russia, Trump

— *Washington Post, 5/18/17*

When you grow suspicious of a person and begin a system of espionage upon him, your punishment will be that you will find your suspicions true.

— *Elbert Hubbard, "The Note Book" (1927)*

494 Russian Probe Heats Up as Trump Tries to Limit Damage

— *Wall Street Journal, 5/19/17 (Misconstrued)*

Who shrinks from knowledge of his calamities but aggravates his fear; troubles half seen do torture all the more.

— *Seneca, "Agamemnon" (1st C. CE)*

495 Russians Are Laughing at the U.S., Not Just at Trump

— *Bloomberg, 5/19/17*

He who laughs best to-day, will also laugh last.

— *Nietzsche, ""Twilight Of The Idols" (1888)*

496 Jared Kushner Now Under FBI Scrutiny in Russia Probe, Say Officials

— *NBC, 5/25/17*

I think the family is the place where the most ridiculous and least respectable things in the world go on.

— *Ugo Betti, "The Inquiry" (1944)*

497 Russian Ambassador Told Moscow That Kushner Wanted Secret Communications Channel With Kremlin

— *Washington Post, 5/26/17*

I cannot forecast to you the action of Russia. It is a riddle wrapped in a mystery inside an enigma.

— *Sir Winston Churchill, Radio Broadcast (1939)*

---

498 Trump Faces Instability as Russia Probe Expands to Inner Circle

— *Wall Street Journal, 5/31/17 (Misconstrued)*

Almost all of our relationships begin and most of them continue as forms of mutual exploitation, a mental or physical barter, to be terminated when one or both parties run out of goods.

— *W. H. Auden, "Hlc Et Ille," The Dyer's Hand (1962)*

---

499 Former Diplomats: Trump Team Sought to Lift Sanctions on Russia

— *NBC, 6/1/17*

It is worse than a crime: it is a blunder.

— *Joseph Fouche, Comment On The Execution of Duc D'Enghien (1804)*

---

500 How Seven Trump Associates Have Been Linked to Russia

— *New York Times, 6/11/17*

The very madness of the scheme protects it.

— *Iris Murdoch, "A Word Child" (1975)*

---

501 Mr. Trump's Dangerous Indifference to Russia

— *New York Times, 6/17/17*

Man is a credulous animal, and must believe 'something;' in the absence of good grounds for belief, he will be satisfied with bad ones.

— *Bertrand Russell, "Outline: Intellectual Rubbish," Unpopular Essays 1950)*

---

502 Russia Renewed Unused Trump Trademarks in 2016
— *New York Times, 6/18/17*

In the majority of men gratitude is only a veiled desire of receiving greater benefaction.

— *La Rochefoucauld, "Maxims" (1665)*

---

503 White House Tries to Get G.O.P. to Water Down Russia Sanctions Bill
— *New York Times, 6/21/17*

He would sell even his share of the sun.

— *Italian Proverb*

---

504 Trump Says 'We'll Have to See' If Mueller Should Step Down From Russia Probe
— *Washington Post, 6/23/17*

Only individuals with an aberrant temperament can in the long run retain their self-esteem in the face of the disesteem of their fellows.

— *Thorstein Veblin, "The Theory Of The Leisure Class" (1899)*

---

505 NSA Director Frustrated Trump Won't Accept Russia Interfered in Election: Report
— *The Hill, 6/28/17*

Smallness of mind is the cause of stubbornness, and we do not credit readily what is beyond our view.

— *La Rochefoucauld, "Maxims" (1665)*

---

506 Stop Assuming Trump Is Innocent of Russian Collusion
— *New York Magazine, 6/29/17*

We are all exceptional cases.... Each man insists on being innocent, even if it means accusing the whole human race, and heaven.
— *Albert Camus, "The Fall" (1956)*

———

507 Russian Foreign Minister Says Trump Accepted Putin's Assurances That Russia Didn't Meddle in the U.S. Election
— *Washington Post, 7/7/17*

The folly of one man is the fortune of another.
— *Francis Bacon, "Of Fortune," Essays (1625)*

———

508 Trump's Son Met With Russian Lawyer After Being Promised Damaging Information on Clinton
— *New York Times, 7/9/17*

Children have never been good at listening to their elders, but they have never failed to imitate them.
— *James Baldwin, "Fifth Avenue Uptown," Nobody Knows My Name (1961)*

———

509 Graham Unloads on Trump: Blind Spot on Russia 'Undermining His Entire Presidency'
— *The Hill, 7/9/17*

People everywhere enjoy believing things that they know are not true. It spares them the ordeal of thinking for themselves, and taking responsibility for what they know.
— *Brooks Atkinson, "February 2," Once Around The Sun (1951)*

———

510 Donald Trump Claims Vladimir Putin Would Have Preferred a Hillary Clinton Victory
— *Huffington Post, 7/12/17*

Men endowed with a wild imagination should have, in addition, the great poetic faculty of denying our universe and its values so that they may act upon it with sovereign ease.

— Jean Genet, "Our Lady Of The Flowers" (1949)

———————

511 Trump Allies Pushing RNC to Cover Legal Fees of Russia Investigations

— The Hill, 7/13/17

Sometimes I feel something akin to rage, / At the corrupted morals of this age!

— Moliere, The School For Husbands" (1663)

———————

512 Dear Red-State Friends: Embracing Russia Is Not An Act of Patriotism

— Washington Post, 7/14/17

With respect to wit, I learned that there was not much difference between the half and the whole.

— Thoreau, "Visitors," Walden (1854)

———————

513 Trump Ends Covert CIA Program to Arm Anti-Assad Rebels in Syria, a Move Sought by Moscow

— Washington Post, 7/19/17

Every great mistake has a halfway moment, a split second when it can be recalled and perhaps remedied.

— Pearl S. Buck, "What America Means To Me" (1943)

———————

514 Russian Prime Minister Dimitri Medvedev: Trump Is An 'Incompetent Player' Who Will Be 'Liquidated by the US Establishment"

— Washington Examiner, 8/2/17

The sooner the better.

— *Idiom, Collins English Dictionary (1979)*

---

515 'I Want To Thank Him' [For Expelling U.S. Staff]: Trump's Message to Putin Leaves State Department Officials 'Horrified And Rattled'

— *Salon, 8/11/17*

In darkness one may be / ashamed of what one does, without the shame of disgrace.

— *Sophocles, "The Women Of Trachis" (413 BCE)*

---

516 Exclusive: Mueller Enlists the IRS For His Trump-Russia Investigation

— *Daily Beast, 8/31/17*

It is well to moor your bark with two anchors.

— *Publilius Syrus, "Moral Sayings" (1st C. BCE)*

---

517 Top House Intelligence Committee Member: Trump Is Being 'Dishonest' About Russia Ties

— *Business Insider, 9/4/17*

To be mistaken is a misfortune to be pitied; but to know the truth and not to conform one's actions to it is a crime which Heaven and Earth condemn.

— *Giuseppe Mazzini, "The Duties Of Man And Other Essays" (1910)*

---

518 Report: Trump Lawyers Wanted Jared Kushner Out of the White House Over Russia 'Complications'

— *News Source, 9/11/17*

No one tests the depth of a river with both feet.

— *Ashanti Proverb*

---

519 Dem's To Mueller: Flynn Failed to Disclose Trip to Broker Saudi-Russian Business Deal [With U.S. Companies]
— *CNN, 9/13/17*

You will only injure yourself if you take notice of despicable enemies.
— *Aesop, "The Bald Man And The Fly," Fables (6th C. BCE)*

---

520 Russian Trolls Promoted Trump While Trashing Black Lives Matter on Twitter
— *TPM, 9/13/17*

Evil enters like a needle and spreads like an oak tree.
— *Ethiopian Proverb*

---

521 Trump Using Campaign, RNC Funds to Pay Russia Probe Legal Bills: Reuters, Citing Sources
— *CNBC, 9/19/17*

God looks at the clean hands, not the full ones.
— *Publilius Syrus, "Moral Sayings" (1st C. BCE)*

---

522 Trump Says Russians Didn't Help Him Win. His Intelligence Agencies Say Yes They Did
— *Huffington Post, 9/25/17*

If we ever pass out as a great nation we ought to put on our tombstone "America died from a delusion that she had moral leadership."
— *Will Rogers, "The Autobiography Of Will Rogers" (1949)*

---

523 Special Counsel Probing Flow of Russian-American Money to Trump Political Funds
— *ABC, 9/26/17*

Ours is not so much an age of vulgarity as of vulgarization; everything is tampered with or touched up, or adulterated or watered down, in an effort to make it palatable, in an effort to make it pay.

— *Louis Kronenberger, "The Spirit Of The Age," Company Manners (1954)*

524 Trump Slow to Implement Russia, Iran, North Korea Sanctions Law: Senators

— *Reuters, 9/29/17*

There is a slowness in affairs which ripens them, and a slowness which rots them.

— *Joseph Roux, "Meditations Of A Parish Priest" (1886)*

525 Trump's Company Had More [Previously Unreported] Contact With Russia During Campaign, According to Documents Turned Over to Investigators

— *Washington Post, 10/2/17*

Honesty is for the most part less profitable than dishonesty.

— *Plato, "The Republic" (4th C. BCE)*

526 Donald Trump Suggests Russia, FBI and Democrats Colluded to Pay for Dossier on His Kremlin Links - But Provides No Evidence

— *Independent, 10/19/17*

A cynic is not merely one who reads bitter lessons from the past; he is one who is prematurely disappointed in the future.

— *Sydney J. Harris, "On The Contrary" (1962)*

527 Russia Update: [Another] Trump Campaign Official Under Investigation

— *Newsweek, 10/20/17*

There aren't any embarrassing questions - just embarrassing answers.
— Carl Rowan, New Yorker (Dec., 1963)

---

528 Trump Officials Suddenly Revoke Visa of Hero Being Hunted by Putin
— Shareblue Media, 10/23/17

The Russians train. They do not dare educate.
— Max Lerner, "The Unfinished Country" (1959)

---

529 Russia Inquiry: Trump Sends Barrage of Angry Tweets as Charges Reported
— The Guardian, 10/29/17

Much fool may you find in you, even to the world's pleasure and the increase of laughter.
— Shakespeare, "All's Well That Ends Well" (1604 - 1605)

---

530 The Trump Administration Is Up to Its Neck in Russians
— Washington Post, 11/6/17

Friendship needs a certain parallelism of life, a community of thought, a rivalry of aim.
— Henry Adams, "The Education Of Henry Adams" (1907)

---

531 Donald Trump: Putin's Manchurian Idiot
— Macleans, 11/11/17

It is possible to be a puppet on a string without realizing it.
— Steven Redhead, "Life Is A Cocktail" (2017)

---

532 Special Counsel Mueller Issued Subpoena for Russia-Related Documents From Trump Campaign Officials
— *Wall Street Journal, 11/16/17 (Misconstrued)*

There's a hot breath at the keyhole / And a tearing as of teeth! / Well do I know the bloodshot eyes / And the dripping jaws beneath! / There's a whining at the threshold - / There's a scratching at the floor - / To work! To work! In Heaven's Name! / The wolf is at the door!
— *Charlotte Perkins Gilman, "Anthology: Literature Of Social Justice" (1915)*

---

533 'A Long Winter': White House Aides Divided Over Scope, Risks of Russia Probe
— *Washington Post, 11/19/17*

No passion so effectually robs the mind of all its powers of acting and reasoning as fear.
— *Edmund Burke, "The Sublime And Beautiful" (1756)*

---

534 Trump and Russia Seem to Find Common Foe: The American Press
— *New York Times, 11/27/17*

Between friends there is no need of justice.
— *Aristotle, "Nicomachean Ethics" (4th C. BCE)*

---

535 Russia Investigation 'Wearing' on White House, Despite Spin
— *CNN, 12/1/17*

The guilty think all talk is of themselves.
— *Chaucer, "The Canterbury Tales" (1387 – 1400)*

---

536 Russia-Trump: President Criticized for Attacking FBI
— *BBC, 12/4/17*

All that we do is done with an eye to something else.
— *Aristotle, "Nicomachean Ethics" (4th C. BCE)*

———————

537 Doubting the Intelligence, Trump Pursues Putin and Leaves Russian Threat Unchecked
— *Washington Post, 12/14/17*

It is curious how often one prefers his enemies to his friends.
— *Gore Vidal, "Reflections Upon A Sinking Ship" (1969)*

———————

538 AP Poll: Most Americans Believe Trump Did Something Illegal Or Unethical with Russia
— *Chicago Tribune, 12/15/17*

To a vision so apparent rumour cannot be mute.
— *Shakespeare, "The Winter's Tale" (1609 - 1611)*

———————

539 Trump Allies Flip Out After Mueller Lands Tens of Thousands of Emails
— *Huffington Post, 12/16/17*

It is a painful thing / To look at your own trouble and know / That you yourself and no one else has made it.
— *Sophocles, "Ajax" (447 BCE)*

———————

540 Americans Are Allowing Trump to Turn U.S. Into Russia, Gary Kasporov Warns
— *Huffington Post, 12/19/17*

A thousand years scarce serve to form a state; / An hour may lay it in the dust.
— *Byron, "Childe Harold's Pilgrimage" (1812)*

———————

137

541 Putin's First Year in the White House
— *New York Magazine, 12/22/17*

Men are of no importance. What counts is who commands.
— *Charles DeGualle, Quoted In New York Times Magazine (May, 1968)*

---

542 [Senator] Blumenthal: Trump's Denial of Russian Collusion is Rotten to the Core
— *The Hill, 12/30/17*

It's never what you say, but how / You make it sound sincere.
— *Marya Mannes, "Controverse," But Will It Sell? (1955)*

---

543 Initial Talks Underway About Trump Interview in Mueller Probe
— *NBC, 1/8/18*

Circle the wagons. [Circle the wagons!]
— *American Idiom, The Free Dictionary By Fairlex (Launched 2003)*

---

544 WH Instructs Bannon to Avoid Answering Hill Queries in Russia Probe
— *CNN, 1/17/18*

Gather ye rosebuds [supporters] while ye may, / Old Time is still a-flying; / And this same flower that smiles today / Tomorrow will be dying.
— *Robert Herrick, "To The Virgins, To Make Much Of Time" (1591 - 1674)*

CHAPTER 8

SVALBARD COLLEGE OF ENGINEERING AND MIDDLE EAST STUDIES

TOPICS:
PRAGMATISM AND REALISM

Svalbard College of Engineering and Middle East Studies

545 'Up Is Down,' Trump's Unreality Show Echoes His Business Past
— *New York Times, 1/28/17*

God made everything out of the void, but the void shows through.
— *Paul Valery, "Mauvaises Pensees Et Autre" (1941)*

546 To Reject Trump the Perverse, Poets Wage a Battle in Verse
— *New York Times, 2/9/17*

A vain man may become proud and imagine himself pleasing to all when he is in reality a universal nuisance.
— *Spinoza, "Ethics" (1677)*

547 'Unbelievable Turmoil': Trump's First Month Leaves Washington Reeling
— *New York Times, 2/14/17*

The chief business of the nation, as a nation, is the setting up of heroes, mainly bogus.
— *H. L. Mencken, "Prejudices: Third Series"(1922)*

548 President Returns to Comfort Zone With Election-Style Rallies
— *New York Times, 2/19/17*

The anxiety for the figure we cut, for our personage, is constantly cropping out. We are showing off and are often more concerned with making a display than with living. Whoever feels observed, observes himself.
— *Andre Gide, "Journals" (1938)*

549 Trump's Call for Millions to Rally Fizzles
— *Huffington Post, 2/28/17*

Fools take to themselves the respect that is given to their office.
— *Alsop, "The Jackass In Office," Fables (6th C. BCE)*

550 He's a Performance Artist Pretending to Be a Great Manager
— *Politico, 2/28/17*

There are just times when you can't let the right thing stand in your way.
— *Winston Groom, "Forrest Gump" (1986)*

551 Trump Reprises His Bleak Vision of America – But Offers Few Ideas for Fixing It
— *Washington Post, 3/1/17*

All artists today are expected to cultivate a little fashionable unhappiness.
— *Lawrence Durrell, "Justine" (1957)*

552 Trump Offers Miracles But No Details
— *New York Times, 3/1/17*

There is in every miracle a slight chiding of the world, and a tacit reprehension of them who require, or who need miracles.
— *John Donne, Sermons, No. 47 (1627)*

553 Trump Promises Big on Middle East Peace: 'We Will Get It Done'
— *Politico, 3/5/17*

Why do men seek honour? Surely in order to confirm the favorable opinion they have of themselves.
— Aristotle, "Nicomachean Ethics" (4th C. BCE)

---

554 Analysts Scratch Their Heads Over Trump's Drug Price Tweet
— Wall Street Journal, 3/7/17 (Misconstrued)

To a teacher of language there comes a time when the world is but a place of many words and man appears a mere talking animal not much more wonderful than a parrot.
— Joseph Conrad, Prologue To Part I, "Under Western Eyes" (1911)

---

555 Donald Trump's Fictional America
— Politico, 4/3/17

All nations have present, or past, or future reasons for thinking themselves incomparable.
— Paul Valery, "Extraneous Remarks," Selected Writings (1964)

---

556 Trump: US 'Needs a Good Shutdown'
— The Hill, 5/2/17

The first duty in life is to be as artificial as possible. What the second duty is no one has yet discovered.
— Oscar Wilde, "Phrases/Philosophies For The Use Of The Young" (1891)

---

557 Trump's Fiscal Plans, Fed's Asset Unwinding Could Fuel Rate Rise
— Wall Street Journal, 5/8/17 (Misconstrued)

Put not your trust in money, but put your money in trust.
— Oliver Wendell Holmes, Sr., "The Autocrat Of The Breakfast Table" (1858)

---

558 Trump's Scandals Stoke Fear for 2018 Midterms Among Republicans Nationwide

— *Washington Post, 5/19/17*

Grief has limits, whereas apprehension has none. For we grieve only for what we know has happened, but we fear all that possibly may happen.

— *Pliny the Younger, "Letters" (1st C. 97-110 CE)*

———————

559 Trump's 3% Growth Target Looks Out of Reach

— *Wall Street Journal, 5/23/17 (Misconstrued)*

Life is the art of being well deceived; and in order that the deception may succeed it must be habitual and uninterrupted.

— *William Hazlitt, "On Pedantry," The Round Table (1817)*

———————

560 White House Officials 'Convinced They May Be Victims of Deep State Conspiracy'

— *Independent, 5/29/17*

Fine worries, like fine wines, are at their best only after they have been properly mellowed.

— *Dan Greenberg/Marcia Jacobs, "How To Make Yourself Miserable" (1966)*

———————

561 Nearly Half of Donald Trump's Twitter Followers Are Fake Accounts and Bots

— *Newsweek, 5/30/17*

There are some frauds so well conducted it would be stupidity not to be deceived by them.

— *Charles Caleb Colton, "Lacon" (1825)*

———————

562 Schumer to Trump: Play Comey Tapes Or Admit They Don't Exist

— *The Hill, 6/8/17*

Our greatest pretenses are built up not to hide the evil and ugliness in us, but our emptiness. The hardest thing to hide is something that is not there.

— *Eric Hoffer, "The Passionate State Of Mind" (1954)*

---

563 It's the Olympics for Trump Apologists

— *New York Times, 6/11/17*

You can bend it and twist it. You can misuse it and abuse it. But even God cannot change the truth.

— *Michael Levy, Author, Poet, Philosopher, PRWEB (Feb., 2005)*

---

564 Twitter is Having Fun With Trump's Odd Statement About Panama Canal

— *Huffington Post, 6/19/17*

Why do you necessarily have to be wrong just because a few million people think you are?

— *Frank Zappa, 'The Real Frank Zappa Book" (1989)*

---

565 Donald Trump: 'I Did Not Make and Do Not Have' Tapes of Comey Conversations

— *The Guardian, 6/22/17*

A liar will not be believed, even when he speaks the truth.

— *Aesop, "The Shepherd's Boy", Fables (6th C. BCE)*

---

566 Trump Thinks GOP Senate Critics Will Back Health Bill

— *Wall Street Journal, 6/24/17 (Misconstrued)*

Man has always sacrificed truth to his vanity, comfort and advantage. He lives not by truth but by make-believe.
— W. Somerset Maugham, "The Summing Up" (1938)

———

567 Trump Twists in the Wind as North Korea's Nuclear Capability Grows
— Huffington Post, 7/5/17

It is to escape the responsibility for failure that the weak so eagerly throw themselves into grandiose undertakings.
— Eric Hoffer, "The Ordeal Of Change" (1964)

———

568 Trump's Romance With China's Xi Has Cooled, "Ass-Kicking Ahead"
— The Guardian, 7/6/17

He who killeth a lion when absent feareth a mouse when present.
— English Proverb

———

569 White House Confuses Taiwan and China in Painful G20 Press Release Blunder
— TPM, 7/8/17

We couldn't live without comedy.
— Sean O'Casey, "The Power Of Laughter," Fifty Famous Essays (1964)

———

570 Donald Trump Is Dragging Down America
— The New Yorker, 7/10/17

When even despair ceases to serve any creative purpose, then surely we are justified in suicide.
— Cyril Connolly, "The Unquiet Grave" (1945)

———

571 This Presidency Can't Be Saved. It's All Downhill From Here

— *Washington Post, 7/21/17*

The flowers of life are but illusions. How many fade away and leave no trace; how few yield any fruit; and the fruit itself, how rarely does it ripen!

— *Goethe, "The Sorrows Of Young Werther" (1774)*

572 Trump Says Apple Will Build Three U.S. Plants. It won't.

— *Bloomberg, 7/26/17*

Lying is the only art form that the public sanctions and instinctively prefers to reality.

— *Jean Cocteau, "Diary Of An Unknown" (1952)*

573 Vincente Fox [Former Mexican President] Trolls Trump: White House Is Like 'Survivor' With Low Ratings

— *The Hill, 7/31/17*

Situation comedy on television has thrived for years on "canned" laughter grafted to gaglines by technicians using records of guffawing audiences that have been dead for years.

— *Russell Baker, "The Invisible Artist," All Things Considered (1962)*

574 Trump Worst Week Since Last Week

— *Daily Beast, 8/4/17*

If the fools do not control the world, it isn't because they are not in the majority.

— *Edgar Watson Howe, "Country Town Sayings" (1911)*

575 Greed Is Not Good: Will the Trump Team Disasters Put An End to the Businessman Myth?

— *Salon, 8/5/17*

Want is a growing giant whom the coat of Have was never large enough to cover.

— *Emerson, "Wealth, The Conduct Of Life" (1860)*

———————

576 Twitter Users Are Reporting Trump's Account for 'Threatening Violence' Against North Korea

— *The Denver Post, 8/11/17*

Language is in decline. Not only has eloquence departed but simple, direct speech as well, though pomposity and banality have not.

— *Edwin Newman, "Strictly Speaking" (1974)*

———————

577 Rare Look At Trump's Bookkeeping: 'Extraordinary Flimflammery'

— *MSNBC, 8/11/17*

The corruption of the age is made up by the particular contribution of every individual man; some contribute treachery, others injustice, irreligion, tyranny, avarice, cruelty, according to their power.

— *Montaigne, "Of Vanity," Essays (1580)*

———————

578 Trump's Business Councils Disbanded [by Trump]

— *Wall Street Journal, 8/17/17 (Misconstrued)*

God will have life to be real; we will be damned, but it shall be theatrical.

— *Emerson, "Journals" (1843)*

———————

579 Trump Responds to Barcelona Attack by Reviving Debunked Myth [Dip Bullets in Pig's Blood to Defeat Terrorists]

— *The Guardian, 8/17/17*

The man who never alters his opinion is like standing water, and breeds reptiles of the mind.
— William Blake, "The Marriage of Heaven And Hell" (1790)

---

580 Donald Trump Has Less Influence Every Day and Politicians Are 'Already Looking Beyond Him,' Former White House Advisor Says
— Independent, 8/19/17

It astounds us to come upon other egoists, as though we alone had the right to be selfish, and be filled with eagerness to live.
— Jules Renard, Journal (Nov., 1887)

---

581 'I Alone Can Fix It' Becomes 'It's Not My Fault'
— New York Magazine, 8/25/17

We wake from one dream into another dream.
— Emerson, "Illusions," The Conduct Of Life (1860)

---

582 Are Trump's August Controversies Careless – Or Calculated?
— Wall Street Journal, 8/29/17 (Misconstrued)

That is the consolation of a little mind; you have the fun of changing it without impeding the progress of mankind.
— Frank Moore Colby, "Simple Simon," The Colby Essays (1926)

---

583 Trump Threatens Insurer Payments to Push Congress on Health-Law Repeal
— Wall Street Journal, 7/31/17 (Misconstrued)

A tart temper never mellows with age, and a sharp tongue is the only edged tool that grows keener with constant use.
— Washington Irving, "The Sketch Book of Geoffrey Crayon, Gent." (1819)

---

584 Trump and Mnuchin Threaten China With Trade Sanctions After North Korea Nuke Test

— *News Source, 9/3/17*

There is a mortal breed most full of futility. / In contempt of what is at hand, they strain into the future, / hunting possibilities on the wings of ineffectual hopes.

— *Pindar, "Odes" (5th C. BCE)*

———————

585 Trump's [South] Korean Trade Folly

— *Wall Street Journal, 9/5/17 (Misconstrued)*

Profound ignorance makes a man dogmatic. The man who knows nothing thinks he is teaching others what he has just learned himself; the man who knows a great deal can't imagine that what he is saying is not common knowledge, and speaks more indifferently.

— *La Bruyere, "Characters" (1688)*

———————

586 When Trump Aides Admit He Has No Idea What He's Talking About

— *New York Magazine, 9/7/17*

All ignorance toboggans into know / and trudges up to ignorance again.

— *E. E. Cummings, "All Ignorance Toboggans…" 100 Selected Poems (1959)*

———————

587 Trump Faith Advisor Regrets Saying the President Was Anointed by God, Insists He Isn't Racist

— *ThinkProgress, 9/9/17*

How strange it is to see with how much passion / People see things only in their own fashion!

— *Moliere, "The School For Wives" (1662)*

———————

588 Alex Jones [Conspiracy Theorist] Claims Trump Is Being 'Covertly Drugged'

— *Washington Examiner, 9/12/17*

You ride astride the imaginary in order to hunt down the real.

— *Breyten Breytenbach, "Return To Paradise" (1993)*

---

589 Donald Trump: 'The Wall Will Come Later' After DACA Amnesty Deal

— *News Source, 9/14/17*

To believe in one's dreams is to spend all of one's life asleep.

— *Chinese Proverb*

---

590 Trump Threatens to Exterminate 25 Million People on the Floor of UN

— *ThinkProgress, 9/19/17*

The great proof of madness is the disproportion of one's designs to one's means.

— *Napoleon I, "Maxims" (1804)*

---

591 Is Trump All Talk on North Korea? The Uncertainty Sends a Shiver

— *New York Times, 9/24/17*

The bigger a man's head, the worse his headache.

— *Persian Proverb*

---

592 The Philosophical Assault on Trumpism

— *New York Times, 10/3/17*

His humour is lofty, his discourse peremptory, his tongue filed, his eye ambitious, his gait majestical, and his general behavior vain, ridiculous and thrasonical [vainglorious]. He it too picked, too spruce, too affected, too odd, as it were, too peregrinate, as I may call it.

— Shakespeare, "Love's Labour's Lost" (Mid 1590s)

---

593 Trump Says the Hurricane That Crushed Puerto Rico Wasn't a 'Real Catastrophe' Like Katrina

— BuzzFeed News, 10/3/17

Blind and naked Ignorance / Delivers brawling judgments, unashamed, / On all things all day long.

— Lord Tennyson, "Merlin And Vivien," Idylls Of The King (1859)

---

594 Trump Supporters Eager to 'Drain the Swamp' Help Fill GOP Coffers

— Washington Post, 10/6/17

I never could believe that Providence had sent a few men into the world, ready booted and spurred to ride, and millions ready saddled and bridled to be ridden.

— Richard Rumbold, "On The Scaffold" (1685)

---

595 The Trump Administration's Tax Plan Is An Atrocity

— Washington Post, 10/8/17

There is one difference between a tax collector and a taxidermist - the taxidermist leaves the hide.

— Mortimer Caplan, Time (Feb., 1963)

---

596 The Republican's Guide to Presidential Etiquette

— New York Times, 10/9/17

Etiquette is what you are doing and saying when people are looking and listening. What you are thinking is your business.

— *Virginia Cary Hudson, "O Ye Jigs & Juleps!" (1962)*

---

597 What Trump Bump? Businesses Aren't Borrowing From Banks

— *Wall Street Journal, 10/10/17 (Misconstrued)*

It is a capital mistake to theorize before one has data.

— *Sir Arthur Conan Doyle, "The Adventures Of Sherlock Holmes" (1891)*

---

598 Trump Takes Credit for Success in Fight Against ISIS

— *News Source, 10/18/17*

They are the children of an idle brain. Begot of nothing but vain fantasy, which is as thin of substance as the air and more inconstant than the wind.

— *Shakespeare, "Romeo And Juliet" (1591 - 1595)*

---

599 Trump Meets With Governor of Puerto Rico; Gives Himself a '10' for Hurricane Response

— *News Source, 10/19/17*

He draweth out the thread of his verbosity finer than the staple of his argument.

— *Shakespeare, "Love's Labour's Lost" (Mid 1590s)*

---

600 Trump May Be Following Palin's Trajectory

— *Wall Street Journal, 10/19/17 (Misconstrued)*

All hope abandon ye who enter here.

— *Dante Aligheri, "Inferno," Divine Comedy (1306 - 1321)*

---

601 Trump Plans to Bring 'Biggest Tax Cuts' Ever in US History, Praises Kelly
— *News Source, 10/22/17*

Modesty is the only sure bait when you angle for praise.
— *Lord Chesterfield, Letters To His Son (May, 1750)*

---

602 Trump Tweets His Administration Has Been Busiest in History
— *News Source, 10/22/17*

The advantage of doing one's praising to oneself is that one can lay it on so thick and exactly in the right places.
— *Samuel Butler, "The Way Of All Flesh" (1903)*

---

603 Michael Bloomberg: Brexit Is the Stupidest Thing Any Country Has Done Besides Trump
— *The Guardian, 10/24/17*

Two wrongs don't make a right, but they make a good excuse.
— *Thomas Szasz, "The Second Sin" (1973)*

---

604 Health Experts Say Trump's Opioid Response Relies on Magical Thinking
— *The Guardian, 10/27/17*

Imagination is more robust in proportion as reasoning power is weak.
— *Giambattista Vico, "The New Science" (1725)*

---

605 Donald Trump: We Will Hit Islamic State 'Ten Times Harder'
— *News Source, 11/3/17*

You must not count overmuch on your reality as you feel it today, since like that of yesterday, it may prove an illusion for you tomorrow.
— *Luigi Pirandello, "Six Characters In Search Of An Author" (1921)*

---

606 Donald Trump Talks Tough on Trade With Japan
— *News Source, 11/6/17*

The practice of fiction can be dangerous: it puts ideas into the head of the world.
— *Anthony Burgess, "You've Had Your Time" (1990)*

---

607 Paradise Papers Show How Misguided the G.O.P. Is on Taxes
— *New York Times, 11/12/17*

It is in the uncompromisingness with which dogma is held and not in the dogma or want of dogma that the danger lies.
— *Samuel Butler, "The Way Of All Flesh" (1903)*

---

608 Mark Cuban: Trump Cutting the Corporate Tax Rate Will Have Zero Impact on Investment
— *Business Insider, 11/16/17*

The best-laid schemes o' mice an' men / Gang aft agley, / An' lea'e us nought but grief an' pain, / For promis'd joy!
— *Robert Burns, "To A Mouse" (1785)*

---

609 'It's a Ponzi Scheme': Wall Street Fears Trump's Deranged Tax Plan Could Kick Off Economic Euthanasia
— *Vanity Fair, 11/17/17*

The folly which we might ourselves have committed is the one we are least ready to pardon in another.
— *Joseph Roux, "Meditations Of A Parish Priest" (1886)*

610 Trump's Dubious Trust-Busting

— *Wall Street Journal, 11/21/17 (Misconstrued)*

To appreciate nonsense requires a serious interest in life.
— *Gelett Burgess, "The Romance Of The Commonplace" (1916)*

611 37 of 38 Economists Said the GOP Tax Plan Would Grow the Debt. The 39th Misread the Question

— *Washington Post, 11/22/17*

I can see through almost any scam, especially one perpetrated by the federal government. I can see through it...they can't pull the wool over my eyes. It's absolutely freakin' impossible to pull the wool over my eyes.
— *Gary Coleman, Quotes And Sayings, SearchQuotes (1968 -2010)*

612 Trump Says He Will Achieve Middle East Peace - After a Quick Round of Golf

— *The Guardian, 11/24/17*

If wishes were horses, beggars would ride.
— *Scottish Proverb (1628)*

613 Trump's Menacing Talk on North Korea Is Leaving the US Isolated

— *The Guardian, 11/30/17*

Brevity is the soul of wit, and tediousness the limbs and outward flourishes.
— *Shakespeare, "Hamlet" (1601)*

614 Trump, Twitter and His 'Filter Bubble' [Follows Just 45 Like-Minded People]
— *BBC, 11/30/17*

Trumpet in a herd of elephants; / Crow in the company of cocks; / Bleat in a flock of goats.
— *Malay Proverb*

---

615 Trump Says Opposing Tax Cuts Will Cost Democrats 'Very Big' in Midterms
— *The Guardian, 12/2/17*

He who is not a bird should not build his nest over abysses.
— *Nietzsche, "On The Famous Wise Men," Thus Spoke Zarathustra (1883)*

---

616 In Florida, Trump Banks on Economy Outweighing His Many Woes in Campaign-Style Speech
— *Washington Post, 12/9/17*

Dreams are the subtle Dower / That make us rich an Hour - / Then fling us poor / Out of the Purple door.
— *Emily Dickenson, Poem (1876)*

---

617 A Capital Scorekeeper [Joint Committee on Taxation] Eviscerates the GOP's Tax Math [on the Size of the Deficit]
— *New Yorker, 12/12/17*

Straight To Hell: True Tales of Deviance, Debauchery and Billion-Dollar Deals
— *John LeFevre, Book Title (2015)*

---

618 AP FACT CHECK: Trump Considers Ambitions to Be Achievements
— *Reddit, 12/13/17*

All sins have their origin in a sense of inferiority, otherwise called ambition.

— Cesare Pavese, "The Burning Brand" (1961)

---

619 Trump and China: 2018 Could Get Nasty

— CNN, 12/19/17

If you place your head in a lion's mouth, then you cannot complain if one day he bites it off.

— Agatha Christie, "The Mysterious Affair At Styles" (1920)

---

620 To Infinity and Beyond: Trump Has Big Plans for NASA - But Is it Just a Fantasy?

— The Guardian, 12/26/17

Were it not for imagination a man would be as happy in the arms of a chambermaid as of a duchess.

— Samuel Johnson, Quoted In Boswell's "Life Of Samuel Johnson" (1778)

---

621 Robert Reich: Trump Voters He's Taking You for Suckers

— Newsweek, 12/30/17

In a society like ours, politics is improvisation. To the artful dodger rather than the true believer goes the prize.

— Gore Vidal, "Rocking The Boat" (1962)

---

622 Trump's 'America First' Security Strategy Imperils the U.S.

— Huffington Post, 12/31/17

There is no terror in your threats; for I am arm'd so strong in honesty that they pass by me as the idle wind, which I respect not.

— Shakespeare, "Julius Caesar" (1599)

---

623 Trump Hopes to Steady the Ship at Camp David Retreat After Bruising Start to Year
— *The Guardian, 1/6/18*

A man trying to escape never thinks himself sufficiently concealed.
— *Victor Hugo, "Cosette," Les Miserables (1862)*

---

624 Trump Mocked For Tweet Calling His Presidency 'Consensual'
— *Washington Examiner, 1/7/18*

This babble shall not henceforth trouble me.
— *Shakespeare, "The Two Gentlemen Of Verona" (1589 - 1593)*

---

625 Hawaii Missile Alert: Donald Trump Has Not Responded to False Alarm but Has Tweeted About Michael Wolff's Book
— *Independent, 1/14/18*

We do not have a money problem in America. We have a values and priorities problem.
— *Marian Wright Edelman, Remarks, Martin Luther King Celebration (2008)*

---

626 Trump's Approval Rating is the Lowest for Any President One Year Into His Term, NBC/WSJ Poll Says
— *Yahoo!, 1/19/18*

It is folly to sing twice to a deaf man.
— *English Proverb*

CHAPTER 9

CRAPSTONE INSTITUTE OF TECHNOLOGY

TOPICS:
BIRTH CONTROL
AND FAMILY PLANNING

Crapstone Institute of Technology

627 Pence Tells Anti-Abortion Marchers That 'Life Is Winning'
— *New York Times, 1/27/17*

Zeal will do more than knowledge.
— *William Hazlitt, "On The Difference Between Writing And Speaking" (1826)*

---

628 The Threat of Overpopulation Doesn't Faze Trump
— *Care2, 4/6/17*

There is no overpopulation problem; there is only a burial problem.
— *Michael J. Weinstock, "Aphorisms" (1975)*

---

629 Trump Drastically Expands Global Gag Rule on Abortion
— *Huffington Post, 5/17/17*

It is obvious that the best qualities in man must atrophy in a standing-room-only environment.
— *Stuart L. Udall, "The Quiet Crises" (1963)*

---

630 Trump's Budget Would Cut Planned Parenthood Out of All Federal Programs
— *Huffington Post, 5/22/17*

At Vatican Council II, one dissenting Roman Catholic theologian declared: "Yes, the Bible says 'Be fruitful and multiply,' but that was when the population was two per square world."
— *Israel Shanker, "Coat Of Many Colors" (1985)*

---

631 States Lead the Fight Against Trump's Birth Control Rollback
— *New York Times, 6/9/17*

We have been God-like in our planned breeding of our domesticated plants and animals, but we have been rabbit-like in our unplanned breeding of ourselves.
— *Arnold Toynbee, National Observer (1963)*

---

632 Dear Donald Trump: Letting Big Business Deny Birth Control Coverage Is Not a Valid Religious Liberty Concern
— *Vox, 6/20/17*

Men never do evil so completely and cheerfully as when they do it from a religious conviction.
— *Pascal, "Pensees" (1670)*

---

633 Trump Be Damned: States Are Fighting to Make Birth Control Over-the-Counter (Finally)
— *Mother Jones, 6/20/17*

The sky is not less blue because the blind man does not see it.
— *Danish Proverb*

---

634 Science Division of White House Office Left Empty as Last Staffers Depart
— *CBS, 6/30/17*

A man should keep his little brain attic stocked with all the furniture he is likely to use, and the rest he can put away in the lumber-room of his library, where he can get it if he wants it.
— *Sir Arthur Conan Doyle, "The Adventures Of Sherlock Holmes" (1891)*

---

635 Melinda Gates 'Deeply Troubled' by Donald Trump's Planned Budget Cuts [for Family Planning]
— *The Guardian, 7/11/17*

[He] can't see the forest for the trees.
— Expression, The New Dictionary Of Cultural Literacy, Third Edition (2005)

---

636 After 6 Months, Donald Trump's Presidency Is Stillborn
— Huffington Post, 7/20/17

Death cancels everything but truth.
— Anonymous

---

637 Trump Cuts Funding for Obama's Teen Pregnancy Program
— Axios, 8/19/17

It is admirable to consider how many millions of people come into, and go out of, the world, ignorant of themselves and of the world they have lived in.
— William Penn, "Some Fruits Of Solitude" (1693)

---

638 Trump Moves [to Cut Funds for Abortion Providers] Cheer Abortion Foes
— Wall Street Journal, 9/16/17 (Misconstrued)

Give me chastity and continence, but not just now.
— St. Augustine, "Confessions" (5th C. CE)

---

639 Planned Parenthood: New Bill [Blocking Birth Control] Is 'Worst ObamaCare Repeal Proposal Yet'
— The Hill, 9/18/17

The road to wisdom? – Well, it's plain / and simple to express: / Err / and err / and err again / but less / and less / and less.
— Piet Hein, "The Road To Wisdom," Grooks (1966)

---

640 Trump Administration Set to Roll Back Birth Control Mandate
— *New York Times, 10/5/17*

Creation destroys as it grows, throws down one tree for the rise of another. But ideal mankind would abolish death, multiply itself million upon million, rear up city upon city, save every parasite alive, until the accumulation of mere existence is swollen to a horror.
— *D. H. Lawrence, "St. Mawr" (1925)*

———————

641 California Suing Trump Administration Over Rollback of Birth Control Rule
— *Huffington Post, 10/6/17*

People who shut their eyes to reality simply invite their own destruction, and anyone who insists on remaining in a state of innocence long after that innocence is dead turns himself into a monster.
— *James Baldwin, "Notes Of A Native Son" (1955)*

———————

642 Trump is Being Sued on Behalf of 46 Million People [by Two State Attorneys General] to Keep His Hands Off Birth Control
— *Shareblue Media, 10/7/17*

A soft refusal is not always taken, but a rude one is immediately believed.
— *Alexander Chase, "Perspectives" (1966)*

———————

643 Donald Trump: 'We Are Stopping Cold the Attacks on Judeo-Christian Values'
— *News Source, 10/13/17*

There is a sort of transcendental ventriloquy through which men can be made to believe that something which was said on earth came from heaven.

— *Georg Christoph Lichenberg, "Aphorisms" (1764)*

———————

644 One Hundred 'Handmaids' Greet Mike Pence to Protest GOP's Anti-Choice Agenda

— *Common Dreams, 10/28/17*

Christ beats his drum, but he does not press men; Christ is served with voluntaries.

— *John Donne, Sermons, No. 39 (1626)*

———————

645 Notre Dame [Taking Advantage of New Trump Administration Rules] Will Drop Birth Control Coverage for Students, Faculty, and Staff

— *Vox, 10/31/17*

Twenty-five hundred years ago it might have been said that man understands himself as well as any other part of the world. Today he is the thing he understands least.

— *F. Skinner, "Beyond Freedom And Dignity" (1971)*

———————

646 Trump Team Wants Supreme Court to Discipline ACLU for Helping 17-Year-Old Illegal Immigrant Get Abortion

— *News Source, 11/4/1*

Under crowded conditions the friendly social interactions between members of a group become reduced, and the destructive and aggressive patterns show a marked rise in frequency and intensity.

— *Desmond Morris, "The Naked Ape" (1967)*

———————

647 [GOP] Tax Bill Offers Recognition of Unborn

— *New York Times, 11/5/17*

O, what a tangled web we weave, When first we practise to deceive!

— Sir Walter Scott, "Marmion: A Tale Of Flodden Field" (1808)

———————

648 Hidden in GOP Tax Bill: A Plan to Turn Churches Into Dark-Money Spigots [Allowing Endorsement of Candidates Without Losing Tax-Exempt Status]

— Salon, 11/23/17

Intellectually, religious emotions are not creative but conservative. They attach themselves readily to the current view of the world and consecrate it.

— John Dewey, "The Influence Of Darwinism On Philosophy" (1909)

———————

649 Judge Blocks Trump Rollback of Obamacare Contraception Mandate

— Politico, 12/15/17

Say, Not So, and you will outcircle the philosophers.

— Thoreau, Journal (June, 1840)

———————

650 Secret Pro-Life Meeting With Mike Pence Killed [Bipartisan] Obamacare Fix - For Now

— Daily Beast, 1/9/18

I tremble for my country when I reflect that God is just.

— Thomas Jefferson, "Notes On The State Of Virginia" (1784)

CHAPTER 10

SHOTTING COLLEGE OF LITERATURE AND SOPHISTRY

TOPICS:
INTEGRATION AND ASSIMILATION

Shotting Collge of Literature and Sophistry

651 Trump's Immigration Order Expands the Definition of 'Criminal'
— *New York Times, 1/26/17*

The plague of racism is insidious, entering into our minds as smoothly and quietly and invisibly as floating airborne microbes enter into our bodies to find lifelong purchase in our bloodstream.
— *Maya Angelou, "Wouldn't Take Nothing For My Journey Now" (1993)*

652 Trump Bars Refugees and Citizens of 7 Muslim Countries
— *New York Times, 1/27/17*

Since barbarism has its pleasures it naturally has its apologists.
— *George Santayana, "The Life Of Reason, Reason In Society" (1905)*

653 Judge Blocks Trump Order on Refugees Amid Chaos and Outcry Worldwide
— *New York Times, 1/28/17*

Smallness of mind is the cause of stubbornness, and we do not credit readily what is beyond our view.
— *La Rochefoucauld, "Maxims" (1665)*

654 Trump's Immigration Ban Draws Deep Anger and Muted Praise
— *New York Times, 1/28/17*

To spare oneself from grief at all cost can be achieved only at the price of total detachment, which excludes the ability to experience happiness.
— *Erich Fromm, "Man for Himself" (1947)*

655 Trump's Executive Order on Immigration: What We Know and What We Don't

— *New York Times, 1/29/17*

A mask tells us more than a face.

— *Oscar Wilde, "Pen, Pencil And Poison," Intentions (1891)*

—————

656 Trump Pushes Dark View of Islam to Center of U.S. Policy-Making

— *New York Times, 2/1/17*

It is not materialism that is the chief curse of the world, as pastors teach, but idealism. Men get into trouble by taking their visions and hallucinations too seriously.

— *H. L. Mencken, "Minority Report" (1956)*

—————

657 The Travel Ban and An Authoritarian 'Ladder of Violence'

— *New York Times, 2/2/17*

Savagery is necessary every four or five hundred years in order to bring the world back to life.

— *Edmond And Jules De Goncourt, Journal (1855)*

—————

658 Court Refuses to Reinstate Travel Ban, Dealing Trump Another Legal Loss

— *New York Times, 2/9/17*

Obstinacy and dogmatism are the surest signs of stupidity. Is there anything more confident, resolute, disdainful, grave and serious then an ass?

— *Montaigne, "On the Art Of Conference," Essays (1877)*

—————

659 Trump Suggests Financing for Historically Black Colleges May Be Unconstitutional

— *Politico, 5/7/17*

It is a measure of the Negro's circumstance that, in America, the smallest things usually take him so very long, and that, by the time he wins them, they are no longer little things; they are miracles.

— *Murray Kempton, "George," Part Of Our Time (1955)*

---

660 Trump's Remarks About Muslims Could Be What Ends Travel Ban, Testimony Suggests

— *The Guardian, 5/8/17*

Those who know the least of others think the highest of themselves.

— *Charles Caleb Colton, "Lacon" (1825)*

---

661 Despite Court Losses, Trump Has Found a Back Door to Continue the Muslim Ban

— *Huffington Post, 6/2/17*

When men are inhuman, take care not to feel towards them as they do towards other humans.

— *Marcus Aurelius, "Meditations" (2nd C. CE)*

---

662 Trump Is Appointing Racist Fake-News Purveyors to the Federal Bench

— *The Nation, 6/17/17*

Bigotry tries to keep truth safe in its hand / with a grip that kills it.

— *Rabindranath Tagore, "Fireflies" (1928)*

---

663 Trump: 'I Just Don't Want a Poor Person' in Cabinet Economic Jobs

— *CNN, 6/22/17*

(Snobbery) is not merely a silly human weakness but something basic in the mentality of modern man – a symptom which reflects the general sickness, the dislocation of social and cultural values in contemporary civilization.

— *Arthur Koestler, "The Anatomy of Snobbery," The Anchor Review (1955)*

---

664 Trump White House Continues to Neglect Spanish Speakers

— *The Guardian, 7/3/17*

Sometimes, it's [prejudice] like a hair across your cheek. You can't see it, you can't find it with your fingers, but you keep brushing at it because the feel of it is irritating.

— *Marian Anderson, Ladies' Home Journal (1960)*

---

665 Journalist Who Exposed the Racist Creator of Trump's CNN Tweets Gets Death Threats

— *Huffington Post, 7/4/17*

Rabble-Rouser – a person who tries to arouse people to anger, hatred or violent action by appeals to emotions, prejudices, etc.; demagogue.

— *Definition, Webster's New World Dictionary (1988)*

---

666 Trump Plans New Limits on Travel [to US], Appeals Ruling

— *Wall Street Journal, 7/15/17 (Misconstrued)*

We believe what we want to believe, what we like to believe, what suits our prejudices and fuels our passions.

— *Sydney J. Harris, "Clearing The Ground" (1986)*

---

667 Trump Administration to Bar Transgender Individuals From Serving In Military

— *Wall Street Journal, 7/26/17 (Misconstrued)*

As in political so in literary action a man wins friends for himself mostly by the passion of his prejudices and by the consistent narrowness of his outlook.

— *Joseph Conrad, "A Familiar Preface," A Personal Record (1912)*

---

668 The Emptiness of Trump's Promises of Tolerance

— *New York Times, 7/28/17*

All human beings have gray little souls / and they all want to rouge them up.

— *Maxim Gorky, "The Lower Depths" (1903)*

---

669 Trump-Backed Bill Would Cut Immigration Levels

— *Washington Post, 8/2/17*

Man is subject to innumerable pains and sorrows by the very condition of humanity, and yet, as if nature had not sown evils enough in life, we are continually adding grief to grief and aggravating the common calamity by our cruel treatment of one another.

— *Joseph Addison, "The Spectator" (1711)*

---

670 Trump Babbles in the Face of Tragedy [Charlottesville]

— *Washington Post, 8/12/17*

I wish to say what I think and feel today, with the proviso that tomorrow perhaps I shall contradict it all.

— *Emerson, "Journals" (1839)*

---

671 Neo-Nazi Site Daily Stormer Praises Trump's Charlottesville Reaction: 'He Loves Us All'

— *Huffington Post, 8/13/17*

I am convinced that we have a degree of delight and that no small one, in the real misfortunes and pains of others.

— *Edmund Burke, "Philosophical Inquiry Into…Origin Of Our Ideas…" (1756)*

---

672 Charlottesville Mayor on Trump: 'Look at The Campaign He Ran' [Emboldening Organized Racists]

— *CNN, 8/13/17*

No democracy can long survive which does not accept as fundamental to its very existence the recognition of the rights of minorities.

— *Franklin D. Roosevelt, Letter To The NAACP (June, 1938)*

---

673 We Need to Stop Acting Like Trump Isn't Pandering to White Supremacists

— *Vox, 8/13/17*

The pleasure of hating, like a poisonous mineral, eats into the heart of religion, and turns it to rankling spleen and bigotry; it makes patriotism an excuse for carrying fire, pestilence, and famine into other lands: it leaves to virtue nothing but the spirit of censoriousness.

— *William Hazlitt, "On The Pleasures Of Hating," The Plain Speaker (1826)*

---

674 'I Haven't Heard You Say "I Condemn White Supremacists"': Jake Tapper Confronts White House Advisor Over Trump's Refusal to Explicitly Call Out Neo-Nazis

— *Business Insider, 8/13/17*

Nothing is more conducive to peace of mind than not having any opinion at all.

— *Georg Christoph Lichtenberg, "Aphorisms" (1764)*

---

675 Fox News Host: Trump Is 'All Too Happy to Reap the Benefits' of Racism

— *Huffington Post, 8/14/17*

Never can true courage dwell with them, / Who, playing tricks with conscience, dare not look / At their own vices.

— *Samuel Taylor Coleridge, "Fears In Solitude" (1798)*

---

676 No, Mr. Trump, We're Not the Same as the Neo-Nazis

— *The Guardian, 8/15/17*

Precision of communication is important, more important than ever, in our era of hair-trigger balances, when a false, or misunderstood word may create as much disaster as a sudden thoughtless act.

— *James Thurber, "Lanterns And Lances" (1961)*

---

677 'Trump's Delivering Exactly What They Wanted: White Male Supremacy'

— *The Guardian, 8/16/17*

There is no strong performance without a little fanaticism in the performer.

— *Emerson, "Journals CE" (1859)*

---

678 Charlottesville Violence: Rabbis Cancel Trump Call Over Remarks

— *BBC, 8/24/17*

The worse evil of all is to leave the ranks of the living before one dies.

— *Seneca, "On Peace Of Mind," Moral Essays (1st C. CE)*

---

679 Trump Pardons Former Maricopa County Sheriff Joe Arpaio
— *Wall Street Journal, 8/26/17 (Misconstrued)*

One's worst enormities remain within, and it is only one's vulgar commonplaces of error and folly that turn into murders and suicides, treasons, infidelities, and betrayals.
— *Lewis Mumford, "Findings/Keepings. Analects For Autobiography" (1975)*

---

680 First Trump Came for Mexicans, Then Muslims, and Now Transgender People
— *Haaretz, 8/28/17*

Prejudice, n. A vagrant opinion without visible means of support.
— *Ambrose Bierce, "The Devils Dictionary" (1881-1911)*

---

681 Federal Judge Blocks Texas Ban on Sanctuary Cities In Blow For Trump
— *The Guardian, 8/30/17*

Prejudice is the child of ignorance.
— *William Hazlitt, "On Prejudice," Sketches And Essays (1839)*

---

682 Kamala Harris on 'Cruel' DACA Repeal: Trump's Siding With 'Derision' and 'Hate'
— *News Source, 9/5/17*

To judge a man means nothing more than to ask: What content does he give to the form of humanity? What concept should we have of humanity if he were its only representative?
— *Wilhelm Von Humboldt, "Uber Den Geist Der Menschheit" (1797)*

---

683 Trump Didn't Have 'The Balls' to End DACA Himself, Former Mexican President Says
— *Newsweek, 9/6/17*

O! / How vain and vile a passion is this fear! / What base uncomely things it makes men do.

— Ben Jonson, "Sejanus His Fall" (1603)

---

684 White House Says Jamele Hill Calling Trump a Racist Is a 'Fireable Offence.' Trump Once Called Obama a Racist

— Washington Post, 9/13/17

He threatens many that hath injured one.

— Ben Jonson, "Sejanus His Fall" (1603)

---

685 California Asks Congress to Officially Censure Trump Over Charlottesville

— The Hill, 9/16/17

Better a little chiding than a great deal of heartbreak.

— Shakespeare, "The Merry Wives Of Windsor" (1597)

---

686 The Dark Racial Sentiment in Trump's NBA and NFL Criticism

— CNN, 9/23/17

Little-minded people's thoughts move in such small circles that five minutes conversation gives you an arc long enough to determine their whole curve. An arc in the movement of a large intellect does not sensibly differ from a straight line.

— Oliver Wendell Holmes Sr., "The Autocrat Of The Breakfast Table" (1858)

---

687 Trump Can't Accept Brown People and Women Calling Him Out

— CNN, 10/1/17

Of all the cants which are canted in this canting world, though the cant of hypocrites may be the worst, the cant of criticism is the most tormenting.

— *Laurence Stern, "Tristam Shandy" (1759)*

---

688 Donald Trump is a 'Textbook Racist', Claims Duke University Professor

— *Independent, 10/7/17*

Opinions which justify cruelty are inspired by cruel impulses.

— *Bertrand Russell, "Ideas That Have Harmed Mankind," Essays (1950)*

---

689 Second Judge Rules Against Travel Ban, Saying Trump's Own Words Show It Was Aimed at Muslims

— *Washington Post, 10/18/17*

The world is white no longer, and it will never be white again.

— *James Baldwin, "Stranger In The Village" (1955)*

---

690 Anger Over Donald Trump's UK Crime Tweet [Linking Rise in Crime to Radical Islamic Terror]

— *BBC, 10/20/17*

How fiery and forward our pedant is!

— *Shakespeare, "The Taming Of The Shrew" (1590 - 1592)*

---

691 Trump Targets 11 Nations in New Refugee Order

— *News Source, 10/25/17*

We feel and weigh soon enough what we suffer from others: but how much others suffer from us, of this we take no heed.

— *Thomas A. Kempis, "The Imitation Of Christ" (1426)*

---

692 America is Being Run by Racists

— *The Boston Globe, 10/31/17*

Race prejudice is not only a shadow over the colored - it is a shadow over all of us, and the shadow is darkest over those who feel it least and allow its evil effects to go on.

— *Pearl S. Buck, "What America Means To Me" (1943)*

---

693 Trevor Noah: 'When It Was a Nazi, Trump Needed More Facts. When it Was a Muslim, That Was the Only Fact He Needed'

— *Washington Examiner, 11/2/17*

Men use thought only as authority for their injustice, and employ speech only to conceal their thoughts.

— *Voltaire, Dialogue 14, ""Le Chapon Et La Poularde" (1763)*

---

694 Majority of Californians Disagree With President Trump's Handling of NFL Protests

— *Los Angeles Times, 11/12/17*

The best way I know of to win an argument is to start by being in the right.

— *Lord Hailsham, The New York Times (Oct., 1960)*

---

695 President Trump Seems Keen on Picking Fights With Athletes. Or Is It With Black Athletes?

— *Los Angeles Times, 11/14/17*

We cannot all hope to combine the pleasing qualities of good looks, brains and eloquence.

— *Homer, "Odyssey" (9th C. BCE)*

---

696 Trump-Bashing Cardinals Hailed as Peacemakers and Bridge-Builders

— *News Source, 11/18/17*

The wolf shall dwell with the lamb, and the leopard shall lie down with the young goat, and the calf and the lion and the fattened calf together; and a little child shall lead them.

— *Bible, Isaiah 11:6*

---

697 Donald Trump Criticizes Marshawn Lynch for Anthem Protest in Mexico

— *ESPN, 11/20/17*

In politics as in religion, it so happens we have less charity for those who believe in half our creed [Lynch], than for those that deny the whole of it [Russia].

— *Charles Caleb Colton, "Lacon" (1825)*

---

698 Dem Rep Garamendi: 'Trump Has Been Going After African-Americans in Many, Many Ways'

— *News Source, 11/23/17*

Cannot the nation that has absorbed ten million foreigners into its political life without catastrophe absorb ten million Negro Americans into that same political life at less cost than their unjust and illegal exclusion will involve?

— *W. E. B. DuBois, "In Their Own Words" (1865-1916)*

---

699 Trump Retweets British Far-Right Leader's Anti-Muslim Videos

— *The Guardian, 11/29/17*

The tendency of the casual mind is to pick out or stumble upon a sample which supports or defies its prejudices, and then to make it the representative of the whole class.
— *Walter Lippman, "Public Opinion" (1929)*

---

700 Donald Trump is Testing How Much Open Racism He Can Get Away With
— *GQ, 11/29/17*

There's not en eye but is a-weary of thy common sight.
— *Shakespeare, "Henry IV, Part 1" (1597)*

---

701 How Trump Made Kathryn Steinle's Slaying a Center of Illegal Immigration Crusade
— *Los Angeles Times, 12/1/17*

While we allow the inhabitants of imaginary remote corners the authenticity of savages or sufferers, we rarely suppose them to possess the authenticity of complex, sophisticated perceptions.
— *Eva Hoffman, "Exit Into History" (1993)*

---

702 Removing Any Qualifications, Trump Endorses Roy Moore
— *NPR, 12/4/17*

There is nothing to winning, really. That is, if you happen to be blessed with a keen eye, an agile mind, and no scruples whatsoever.
— *Alfred Hitchcock, English Film Director And Producer (1899 - 1980)*

---

703 Trump is 'Racist' and 'Ungodly,' Says Republican Pastor as He Quits Party
— *Newsweek, 12/5/17*

We may not pay Satan reverence, for that would be indiscreet, but at least we can respect his talents.

— *Mark Twain, "Concerning The Jews," Harper's Magazine (Sept., 1899)*

---

704 Kareem Abdul-Jabbar: 'Trump is Where He Is Because of His Appeal to Racism'

— *The Guardian, 12/8/17*

It is not healthy when a nation lives within a nation, as colored Americans are living inside America. A nation cannot live confident of tomorrow if its refugees are among its own citizens.

— *Pearl S. Buck, "What America Means to Me" (1943)*

---

705 Pitts: Trump Needs to Take Rosa Park's Name 'Out of His Lying Mouth'

— *The Baltimore Sun, 12/10/17*

Intentions often melt in the face of unexpected opportunity.

— *Shirley Temple Black, Child Star (1988)*

---

706 Alabama Upset: What Jones Victory Over Moore Means for Trump

— *BBC, 12/13/17*

The fall of an ass is no great hurt.

— *Shakespeare, "Cymbeline" (1611)*

---

707 Trump Tweets 'Thank You' to Head of Group Accused of Illegal Political Activities, Racial Bias

— *Yahoo!, 12/22/17*

A new friend is like new wine; when it has aged you will drink it with pleasure.

— *"Apocrypha," Ecclesiasticus 9:10*

708 Trump Uses Derogatory, Racist Language to Describe Immigrants [at June Meeting]
— *Think Progress, 12/23/17*

Our sympathy is cold to the relation of distant misery.
— *Edward Gibbon, "Decline And Fall Of The Roman Empire" (1776)*

709 As Trump Rages About Immigrants [Job Stealing, Criminals, Rapists, People With AIDS], They Go to the Ivy League
— *New York Times, 12/24/17*

Your reasons are as two grains of wheat hid in two bushels of chaff: you shall seek all day ere you find them, and when you have them, they are not worth the search.
— *Shakespeare, "The Merchant Of Venice" (1596 -1599)*

710 Anti-Sharia Laws Proliferate as Trump Strikes Hostile Tone Toward Muslims
— *The Guardian, 12/30/17*

No man is much pleased with a companion who does not increase, in some respect, his fondness of himself.
— *Samuel Johnson, "The Rambler" (1750)*

711 Some Trump Supporters Think Mueller's Grand Jury Has Too Many Black People
— *Huffington Post, 1/3/18*

Treat us like men, and there is no danger but we will live in peace and happiness together. For we are not like you, hard-hearted, unmerciful, and unforgiving. What a happy country this will be, if the whites will listen.
— *David Walker, "Walker's Appeal" (Sept., 1829)*

712 Trump ICE [Immigration and Customs Enforcement] Chief Wants to Prosecute Politicians Who Won't Lock Up More Immigrants

— *Huffington Post, 1/3/18*

They that sow the wind shall reap the whirlwind.
— *Hebrew Bible, Hosea 8-7*

713 'Executive Time' and White Privilege: Our Laziest President and an Ugly Stereotype

— *Salon, 1/11/18*

The crab instructs its young, "Walk straight ahead - like me."
— *Hindustani Proverb*

714 [Rep.] Gutierrez: We Have Someone in the White House 'Who Could Lead the KKK'

— *The Hill, 1/12/18*

You are now, sir, muddied in Fortune's mood, and smell somewhat strong of her displeasure.
— *Shakespeare, "All's Well That Ends Well" (1604 - 1605)*

715 Donald Trump's Racism: The Definitive List

— *New York Times, 1/15/18*

The more we know of History, the less shall we esteem the subjects of it, and to despise [a symbol of] our species is the price we must pay for our knowledge of it.
— *Charles Caleb Colton, "Lacon" (1825)*

716 Reporters Shouting 'Are You a Rascist' Becomes C-Span's Most-Viewed Video of President Trump

— *Washington Examiner, 1/15/18*

How often have I said to you that when you have eliminated the impossible, whatever remains, however improbable, must be the truth?

— *John D. Barrow, "The Origin Of The Universe" (1994)*

CHAPTER 11

KENTUCKY COLLEGE OF THE HATFIELDS AND McCOYS, WEST VIRGINIA CAMPUS

TOPICS:
MODESTY AND HUMILITY

Kentucky College of the Hatfields and McCoys, West Virginia Campus

717 The President Who Buried Humility
— *New York Times, 1/21/17*

Heroes don't need to talk about what they did.
— *W.P. Kinsella, "Shoeless Joe" (1982)*

718 Donald the Menace
— *New York Times, 2/3/17*

Boys are capital fellows in their own way, among their mates; but they are unwholesome companions for grown people.
— *Charles Lamb, "The Old And The New Schoolmaster," Essays Of Elia (1823)*

719 Campaign Over, President Trump Will Hold (What Else?) Campaign Rally
— *New York Times, 2/16/17*

Actors should be overheard, not listened to, and the audience is fifty percent of the performance.
— *Shirley Booth, News Summaries (Dec., 1954)*

720 Democrats Laugh at Trump's Claim That He Is Draining the Swamp
— *Reddit, 3/1/17*

O, merry is the Optimist, / With the troops of courage leaguing. / But a dour trend / In any friend / Is somehow less fatiguing.
— *Phyllis McGinley, "A Pocketful Of Wry" (1940)*

721 Trump's Many Shades of Contempt
— *New York Times, 3/3/17*

We might define an eccentric as a man who is a law unto himself, and a crank as one who, having determined what the law is, insists on laying it down to others.
— *Louis Kronenberger, "Company Manners" (1954)*

---

722 Late-Night Hosts on Trump: 'How to Lose Friends and Influence No One'
— *The Guardian, 3/28/17*

Of all the countless folk who have lived before our time on this planet not one is known in history or in legend as having died of [another's] laughter.
— *Max Beerbohm, "Laughter," In The Art Of The Personal Essay (1994)*

---

723 The Offender of the Free World
— *New York Times, 3/28/17*

Rudeness is the weak man's imitation of strength.
— *Eric Hoffer, "The Passionate State Of Mind" (1954)*

---

724 Trump Can't Stop Obsessing About the Clintons
— *Politico, 3/29/17*

Fanaticism consists in redoubling your effort when you have forgotten your aim.
— *George Santayana "The Life Of Reason: In Common Sense" (1905)*

---

725 Donald Trump Suggests He Will Change Libel Laws Due to Negative Coverage of His Presidency
— *Huffington Post, 3/30/17*

He is not laughed at that laughs at himself first.
— Thomas Fuller, M.D., "Gnomologia" (1732)

---

726 Trump and the Plutocrat's Hubris
— Wall Street Journal, 4/3/17 (Misconstrued)

Openness as currently conceived, is a way of making surrender to whatever is most powerful, or worship of vulgar success, look principled.
— Allan Bloom, "Introduction: Our Virtue" (1987)

---

727 Trump Seeks to Mute Comey Outcry
— Wall Street Journal, 5/11/17 (Misconstrued)

Self-preservation is the first principal of our nature.
— Alexander Hamilton, "A Full Vindication" (1774)

---

728 'A No-Talent Guy': Angry Trump Attacks Colbert Over Late-Night Takedowns
— The Guardian, 5/12/17

There is no fate more distressing for an artist than to have to show himself off before fools, to see his work exposed to the criticism of the vulgar and ignorant.
— Moliere, "The Would-Be Gentleman" (1670)

---

729 'People Here Think Trump Is a Laughingstock'
— Politico, 5/19/17

Wit has a deadly aim and it is possible to prick a large pretense with a small pin.
— Marya Mannes, "Controverse," But Will It Sell? (1995-64)

---

730 Trump's Behavior at NATO a National Embarrassment

— *Washington Post, 5/25/17*

Give your friend cause to blush, and you will be likely to lose him.

— *Publilius Syrus, "Moral Sayings" (1st C. BCE)*

---

731 'Out of Step' Trump Takes Golf Cart While Rest of G-7 Leaders Walk

— *Huffington Post, 5/27/17*

We all wish to be of importance in one way or another. The child coughs with might and main, since it has no other claim on the company.

— *Emerson, "Journals" (1836)*

---

732 Nonprofits Brace for Cuts With Trump and Make Political Pitch to Donors

— *Washington Post, 6/2/17*

Every man takes the limits of his own field of vision for the limits of the world.

— *Schopenhauer, "Parega And Paralipomena" (1851)*

---

733 Trump Is Finding It Easier to Tear Down Old Policies Than to Build His Own

— *Washington Post, 6/4/17*

When smashing monuments, save the pedestals - they always come in handy.

— *Stanislaw Lee, "Unkempt Thoughts" (1962)*

---

734 Trump Invites His Employees to Praise Him During Cabinet Meeting

— *Huffington Post, 6/12/17*

Roughness may turn one's humour, but flattery one's stomach.

— *Thomas Fuller, M.D. "Gnomologia" (1732)*

---

735 Trump's Cabinet of Worship Is a Scary Sign of America's Collapse

— *Time, 6/13/17*

Admiration, n. Our polite recognition of another's resemblance to ourselves.

— *Ambrose Bierce, "The Devil's Dictionary" (1881-1911)*

---

736 Donald Trump Is Still Holding Campaign Rallies Because No One Else Will Validate Him

— *GQ, 6/22/17*

The most vulnerable and yet most unconquerable of things is human vanity; nay, through being wounded its strength increases and can grow to giant proportions.

— *Nietzsche, "Miscellaneous Maxims And Opinions" (1879)*

---

737 The Greatest Threat Facing the United States Is Its Own President

— *Washington Post, 7/4/17*

Love of fame, fear of disgrace, schemes for advancement, desire to make life comfortable and pleasant, and the urge to humiliate others are often at the root of the valour men hold in such high esteem.

— *La Rochefoucauld, "Maxims" (1665)*

---

738 Trump's Behavior Is the Biggest Threat to U.S. National Security

— *Washington Post, 7/9/17*

Children are completely egoistic; they feel their needs intensely and strive ruthlessly to satisfy them.

— Sigmund Freud, "The Interpretation Of Dreams" (1899)

———————

739 Trump and Putin: Where the Mutual Admiration Began

— *New York Times, 7/10/17*

Now and then, his look of commendation would rest particularly on you; whenever this happened it was as if, in his delight, he had reached over and squeezed you.

— Mary McCarthy, "The Company She Keeps" (1942)

———————

740 Donald Trump Isn't Happy About New Poll Showing He Is the President With the Lowest Approval Rating in 70 Years

— *Newsweek, 7/16/17*

We tolerate differences of opinion in people who are familiar to us. But differences of opinion in people we do not know sound like heresy or plots.

— Brooks Atkinson, "February 4," Once Around the Sun (1951)

———————

741 Donald Trump 'Obsessed With His Own Self-Image' Says Visiting Senior Republican

— *ABC, 8/6/17*

People can die of mere imagination.

— Chaucer, "The Miller's Tale," The Canterbury Tales (1387)

———————

742 Trump Complains About Polls Showing He's the Least Popular President Ever

— *Newsweek, 8/7/17*

Suspicion is a thing very few people can entertain without letting the hypothesis turn, in their minds, into fact.

— David Cort, "Social Astonishments" (1963)

---

743 Hounded on All Sides a Cornered President Snarls

— Politico, 8/19/17

A Wounded Deer – leaps highest.

— Emily Dickinson, Poem (1860)

---

744 Donald and Melania Trump to Skip Kennedy Center Honors

— New York Times, 8/19/17

There is no character howsoever good and fine, but it can be destroyed by ridicule, howsoever poor and witless.

— Mark Twain, "Pudd'nhead Wilson" (1894)

---

745 As Hurricane Harvey's Aftermath Slams Texas, Trump Tweets a Storm of Self-Congratulations and Grievances

— Huffington Post, 8/2717

O man! Thou feeble tenant of an hour, / Debased by slavery, or corrupt by power, / Who knows thee well must quit thee with disgust, / Degraded mass of animated dust! / Thy love is lust, thy friendship all a cheat, / Thy smiles hypocrisy, thy word deceit! / By nature vile, ennobled but by name, / Each kindred brute might bid thee blush for shame.

— Byron, "On The Monument Of A Newfoundland Dog" (1808)

---

746 Matt Damon: Directors Had to Write Trump a Part to Shoot Movies in His Buildings

— The Hill, 9/1/17

He wanted to be the bride at every wedding and the corpse at every funeral.

— *Alice Roosevelt Longworth, Quoted In NY Times Book Review (Nov., 1993)*

———————

747 Trump Uses Meeting With Hurricane Victims to Praise Himself, Diss Reporters

— *Shareblue Media, 9/3/17*

Whenever Nature leaves a hole in a person's mind, she generally plasters it over with a thick coat of self-conceit.

— *Longfellow, "The Blank-Book Of A Country Schoolmaster" (1857)*

———————

748 Trump Anger at Gary Cohn [Economic Advisor] Raises Doubts About White House Tenure

— *The Guardian, 9/7/17*

Crime and punishment grow out of one stem.

— *Emerson, "Compensation," Essays: First Series (1841)*

———————

749 Trump Demands ESPN Apologize for Untruth

— *Politico, 9/15/17*

Glory consists of two parts: The one in setting too great a value upon ourselves, and the other in setting too little a value upon others.

— *Montaigne, "Of Presumption," Essays (1580)*

———————

750 Trump and The Fox & Friends Show. Think Ego, Not News

— *The Guardian, 9/17/17*

When comedy fails, seriousness begins to leak back in.

— *Susan Sontag, "Going To the Theatre, Etc.," Against Interpretation (1966)*

———————

751 Trump Tweets He Was 'Saddened' by 'Bad' Emmy Ratings
— *New York Times, 9/19/17*

Judge not, that ye be not judged.
— *Bible, Mathew 7:1*

---

752 Poll: Donald Trump Has Embarrassed America and Really Needs to Stop Tweeting Now
— *Huffington Post, 9/28/17*

The big drum only sounds well from afar.
— *Persian Proverb*

---

753 Trump Lashes Out at Puerto Rico Mayor Who Criticized Storm Response
— *New York Times, 9/30/17*

The best defense is a good offense.
— *George Washington, Adage From Congress Speech (Jan., 1790)*

---

754 Trump Takes on All Comers Believing Himself the Victor
— *New York Times, 10/1/17*

In every sort of danger there are various ways of winning through, if one is ready to do and say anything whatever.
— *Socrates, "On Plato's Apology" (4th C. BCE)*

---

755 Trump Slams Late Night Comedians for 'Unfunny' Anti-Trump Jokes
— *The Hill, 10/7/17*

A wit would often be embarrassed without the company of fools.
— *La Rochefoucauld, "Maxims" (1665)*

---

756 Trump Offers to 'Compare IQ Tests' With Tillerson After 'Moron' Report

— *The Hill, 10/10/17*

Conceit is vanity driven from all other shifts, and forced to appeal to itself for admiration.

— *William Hazlitt, "Characteristics" (1823)*

---

757 Trump Apparently Pressed Forbes for a Higher Wealth Ranking Every Year for Decades

— *The Week, 10/11/17*

Those who apply themselves too much to little things usually become incapable of great ones.

— *La Rochefaucauld, "Maxims" (1665)*

---

758 Trump [in Tweet] Accuses New York Times Article of Ignoring Accomplishments

— *News Source, 10/15/15*

I wonder that you will still be talking: nobody marks you.

— *Shakespeare, "Much Ado About Nothing" (1598)*

---

759 Donald Trump Tries a New Tactic to Attack Congresswoman ['She's Killing Democratic Party'] Who Exposed His Lies

— *Huffington Post, 10/21/17*

Why appear you with this ridiculous boldness?

— *Shakespeare, "Twelfth Night" (1601- 1602)*

---

760 Donald Trump: Bob Corker 'Couldn't Get Elected Dog Catcher' in Tennessee

— *News Source, 10/24/17*

No man can tell another his faults so as to benefit him, unless he loves him.
— Henry Ward Beecher, "Proverbs From Plymouth Pulpit" (1887)

---

761 Trump Makes Spectacle Even of His Pick for Fed
— New York Times, 10/27/17

A dramatist is one who from his earliest years has found that sheer gazing at the shocks and counter-shocks among people is quite sufficiently engrossing without having to encase it in comment.
— Thornton Wilder, Interview, "Writer's At Work: First Series" (1958)

---

762 President Trump Blasts Michael Moore's Broadway Show
— News Source, 10/29/17

The Stones that Critics hurl with Harsh Intent / A Man may use to build his Monument.
— Arthur Guiterman, "A Poet's Proverbs" (1924)

---

763 Trump: I'm the Only One That Matters
— CNN, 11/3/17

He is very proud, revengeful, ambitious, with more offenses at his beck than he has thoughts to put them in, imagination to give them shape, or time to act them in.
— Shakespeare, "Hamlet" (1601)

---

764 George H. W. Bush Calls Trump a 'Blowhard' in New Book: 'I Don't Like Him'
— News Source, 11/4/17

Nowadays most men lead lives of noisy desperation.
— James Thurber, "Further Fables For Our Time" (1956)

---

765 Trump Trades 'Short and Fat' Barb With N Korea's Kim
— *BBC, 11/12/17*

Boys will be boys and do childish things.
— *The American Heritage Idioms Dictionary (1995)*

———————

766 Donald Trump Says His Approval Rating Could Be in the 50s Despite 'Fake News Claiming They're in the 30s'
— *Independent. 11/14/17*

I talk of dreams; which are the children of an idle brain, begot of nothing but vain fantasy.
— *Shakespeare, "Romeo And Juliet" (1591 - 1595)*

———————

767 Trump's Tweets Are Hurting Him With the Voters He Needs Most
— *Politico, 11/19/17*

More of your conversation would infect my brain.
— *Shakespeare, "Coriolanus" (1605 - 1608)*

———————

768 Trump Tweets He Should've Left UCLA Players in Chinese Jail
— *News Source, 11/19/17*

Don't mistake my kindness for weakness. I'll choke you with the same hand I fed you with.
— *Someecards, Pinterest.com (Est. 2010)*

———————

769 Donald Trump's Childish 'IT WAS ME' Plea for Credit Sets Twitter on Fire
— *Huffington Post, 11/22/17*

Listen to a man's words and look at the pupil of his eye. How can a man conceal his character?
— *Mencius, "Works" (4th - 3rd C. BCE)*

770 Trump Visits Coast Guard Station in Florida, Touts Own Accomplishments in Thanksgiving Tweets

— *News Source, 11/23/17*

To say that a man is vain means merely that he is pleased with the effect he produces on other people. A conceited man is satisfied with the effect he produces on himself.

— *Max Beerbohm, "Quia Imperfectum," And Even Now (1920)*

771 For Trump, A Moment of Defeat [in Alabama] but Maybe Not Recalibration

— *New York Times, 12/13/17*

There are some men who turn a deaf ear to reason and good advice, and willfully go wrong for fear of being controlled.

— *La Bruyere, "Characters" (1688)*

772 'I'm Very Spoiled.' Marines Forced to Sit Through 12-Minute Trump Brag-a-Thon.

— *Shareblue Media, 12/15/17*

You are a cock and capon too, and you crow, cock, with your comb on.

— *Shakespeare, "Cymbeline" (1611)*

773 Tweeters Ridicule Mike Pence's Fawning Praise of Donald Trump at Cabinet Meeting

— *Huffington Post, 12/20/17*

No, I don't "understand" nor do I "get it." The only thing I get is nauseous when I sit and think about it.

— *Image Quote, Pinterest (Launched 2010)*

774 Trump Replaces 'E Pluribus Unum' With 'Make America Great Again' on Presidential [Challenge] Coin

— *Business Insider, 12/22/17*

You snapper up of unconsidered trifles.

— *Shakespeare, "The Winter's Tale" (1609 - 1611)*

———————

775 Trump Attacks 'Fake Polls and Fake News' as Reports Say He Has Worst Approval Rating in History

— *Independent, 12/24/17*

He seeks their hate with greater devotion than they can render it to him.

— *Shakespeare, "Coriolanus" (1605 - 1608)*

———————

776 Obama Beats Trump Again as Most Admired American Man in Poll

— *The Guardian, 12/27/17*

I hate to cry and I hate to sound like sour grapes, but no one ever listens to me. No one ever hears what I have to say.

— *Mike Tyson, Professional Boxer, articles.latimes.com (1985 - 2005)*

———————

777 'What a Year It's Been': Trump Lauds Major Feats of 2017 in End-of-Year Video

— *The Guardian, 12/31/17*

What does an ant, with an erection, lying on its back on a leaf floating down the river, cry out in alarm? "Open the drawbridge!"

— *Michael J. Weinstock, "Aphorisms" (1975)*

———————

778 Trump Speaks at Fourth-Grade Level, Lowest of Last 15 U.S. Presidents, New [Speech Pattern] Analysis Finds

— *Newsweek, 1/8/18*

If I wanted to kill myself, I would climb your ego and jump to your IQ.
— Hand-Picked Funny Picture, Loldamn.com (Oct., 17, 2017)

---

779 Trump Again Blasts Libel Laws, Calling Them 'A Sham'
— NPR, 1/10/18

There are few nudities so objectionable as the naked truth.
— Agnes Repplier, "The Gaiety Of Life," Compromises (1904)

---

780 Colbert: They're Not S---hole Countries Because Trump Isn't Their President
— The Hill, 1/12/18

There's neither honesty, manhood, nor good fellowship in thee.
— Shakespeare, "Henry IV, Part 1" (1597)

---

781 Donald Trump is Bad in Bed, Porn Star Stormy Daniels Claims, but They Had an Affair for 'Nearly a Year' Anyway: Report
— Newsweek, 1/17/18

The spirit is willing, but the flesh is weak.
— Bible, Matthew 26:41

CHAPTER 12

OUAGADOUGOU COLLEGE OF THE BIBLICAL SCIENCES

TOPICS:
HONORABLE AND LAW ABIDING

Ouagadougou College of the Biblical Sciences

782 In a Swirl of 'Untruths' and 'Falsehoods,' Calling a Lie a Lie

— *New York Times, 1/25/17*

If a man will kick a fact out the window, when he comes back he finds it again in the chimney corner.

— *Emerson, "Journals" (1842)*

---

783 Trump's Dual Roles Collide With [Hotel] Openings in Dubai and Vancouver

— *New York Times, 2/19/17*

Landlords, like all other men, love to reap where they never sowed.

— *Karl Marx, "First Manuscript" (1884)*

---

784 Budget Deal Includes Money for Trump's Mar-a-Lago Visits

— *Tampa Bay Times, 3/5/17*

For greed, all nature is too little.

— *Seneca, "Hercules Oetaeous" (1st C. CE)*

---

785 This Level of Corruption Is Unprecedented in the Modern History of the Presidency

— *Reddit, 3/12/17*

A thief passes for a gentleman when stealing has made him rich.

— *Thomas Fuller, M.D. "Gnomologia" (1732)*

---

786 Trump Had to Pay Millions Due to Law He Wants to Scrap

— *The Guardian, 3/15/17*

I know sage, wormwood, and hyssop, but I can't smell character unless it stinks.
— Edward Dahlberg, "On Human Nature," Reasons Of The Heart (1965)

_____

787 Former Trump University Student Refuses Settlement Because She Wants to Hold President 'Accountable for This Fraud'
— Reddit, 3/30/17

Whatsoever a man soweth, that shall he also reap.
— Bible, Exodus 21:23-25

_____

788 Robert Reich: Trump Is Fleecing America, and the Department of Justice Is Letting It Happen
— Reddit, 4/13/17

Man is the only animal that can remain on friendly terms with the victims he intends to eat until he eats them.
— Samuel Butler, "Mind And Matter," Notebooks (1912)

_____

789 Bring on the Wall: For Mexican Drug Smugglers, the Greater the Challenge, the Greater the Profits
— New York Times, 5/7/17

Crime is a logical extension of the sort of behavior that is often considered perfectly respectable in legitimate business.
— Robert Rice, "The Business Of Crime" (1956)

_____

790 Financial-Crimes Monitor to Share Records in Trump-Russia Probe
— Wall Street Journal, 5/13/17 (Misconstrued)

Corruption is like a ball of snow; whence once set a-rolling it must increase.
— Charles Caleb Colton, "Lacon" (1825)

791 The Trump Organization Says 'It's Not Practical' to Comply With the Emoluments Clause
— *The Atlantic, 5/24/17*

The faults of the burglar are the qualities of the financier.
— *George Bernard Shaw, "Preface, Major Barbara" (1905)*

792 Concerns Over Trump Still Allowing His Company to Profit From Foreign Officials
— *The Guardian, 5/24/17*

The smell of profit is clean / And sweet, whatever the source.
— *Juvenal, "Satires" (C. 100 CE)*

793 On JFK's 100th Birthday, Trump Repudiates His Legacy
— *Washington Post, 5/24/17*

He that cannot possibly mend his own case will do what he can to impair another's.
— *Francis Bacon, "Of Envy," Essays (1625)*

794 Comey Told Sessions Don't Leave Me Alone With Trump
— *New York Times, 6/6/17*

The thing that used to worry him the most was the fact that people always used to ask him what he was looking so worried about.
— *Douglas Adams, "The Hitchhiker's Guide To The Galaxy" (1979)*

795 Former Spy Chief Says Watergate 'Pales' in Comparison to Trump's Scandals
— *BuzzFeed News, 6/6/17*

Greatest scandal waits on greatest state.
— Shakespeare, "The Rape of Lucrece" (1594)

---

796 Ex-U.S. Attorney Bahara Tells of 'Unusual Calls' He Received From Trump
— Reuters, 6/11/17

He divides conversation into two categories: when you speak, and when you listen to yourself speak.
— John Fowles, "Daniel Martin" (1977)

---

797 Pelosi Predicts Trump Will 'Self-Impeach'
— Politico, 6/13/17

Troubles hurt the most, / when they prove self-inflicted.
— Sophocles, "Oedipus The King" (430 BCE)

---

798 A Legal 'Dream Team' Looking at Trump
— BBC News, 6/13/17

A sudden, bold, and unexpected question doth many times surprise a man and lay him open.
— Francis Bacon, "Of Cunning," Essays (1625)

---

799 Trump Property Sold to Secretive Buyers
— USA Today, 6/14/17

Every man wishes to be wise, and they who cannot be wise are almost always cunning.
— Samuel Johnson, "The Idler" (1758)

---

800 Democrats in Congress Sue Trump Over Foreign Business Dealings
— New York Times, 6/14/17

I do suspect thee very grievously.

— *Shakespeare, "King John" (1594 – 1596)*

---

801 China Approves 9 Trump Trademarks Previously Rejected

— *ABC, 6/14/17*

How I like to be liked, and what I do to be liked!

— *Charles Lamb, Letter To Dorothy Wordsworth (1821)*

---

802 The Head of Trump Voter Integrity Probe Just Got Sanctioned for a Lack of Integrity

— *Huffington Post, 6/23/17*

The truth is, hardly any of us have ethical energy enough for more than one really inflexible point of view.

— *George Bernard Shaw, "The Doctor's Dilemma" (1913)*

---

803 Resigning Ethics Director Says Trump Businesses Appear to Profit From Presidency

— *The Hill, 7/6/17*

A guilty conscience needs no accuser.

— *English Proverb*

---

804 Trump Team Met With Lawyer Linked to Kremlin During Campaign

— *New York Times, 7/8/17*

For a wrongdoer to be undetected is difficult; and for him to have confidence his concealment will continue is impossible.

— *Epicurus, "Vatican Sayings" (3rd C. BCE)*

---

805 Howard Dean: 'Criminal Enterprise' Running the Country Now

— *The Hill, 7/10/17*

Most men only commit great crimes because of their scruples about petty ones.

— Cardinal De Retz, "Memoires" (1718)

———————

806 Donald Trump's Deep Connections to Dirty Russian Money: The Trail Leads Back More Than 30 Years

— Salon, 7/14/17

No man is worthy of unlimited reliance - his treason, at best, only waits for sufficient temptation.

— H. L. Mencken, "The Skeptic," The Smart Set (1919)

———————

807 Trump 2020 Campaign Donors Paying for Family's Lawyers

— MSNBC, 7/17/17

Old burglars never die, they just steal away.

— Glen Gilbreath, Chicago Sun-Times (Apr. 26, 1958)

———————

808 Trump Especially Upset After Hearing Mueller Would Access Tax Returns: Report

— The Hill, 7/21/17

Man can only endure a certain degree of unhappiness; what is beyond that either annihilates him or passes by and leaves him apathetic.

— Goethe, "Elective Affinities" (1809)

———————

809 White House as Crime Scene: How Robert Mueller Is Closing In on Trump

— The Guardian, 8/5/17

Honor is like a steep island without a shore: One cannot return once one is outside.

— Nicolas Boileau, "Satires" (1666)

810 Trump Eases Post-Crisis Wall Street Rules
— *Wall Street Journal, 8/14/17 (Misconstrued)*

There are some things the arrogant mind does not see; it is blinded by its vision of what it desires.
— *Wendell Berry, "People, Land And Community," Standing By Words (1983)*

811 Secrecy and Suspicion Surround Trump's Deregulation Teams
— *New York Times, 8/17/17*

At no time are people so sedulously careful to keep their trifling appointments, attend to their ordinary occupations, and thus put a commonplace aspect on life, as when conscious of some secret that if suspected would make them look monstrous in the general eye.
— *Nathaniel Hawthorne, "The Marble Fawn" (1860)*

812 Bahara Accuses Trump Pardon [of Former Arizona Sheriff] of Violating DOJ Guidelines
— *The Hill, 8/26/17*

(It) is in fact far easier to act under conditions of tyranny than it is to think.
— *Hannah Arendt, "The Human Condition" (1958)*

813 Trump Organization Executive Asked Putin Aide for Help [During 2016 Campaign] On Deal
— *Washington Post, 8/28/17*

The bird thinks it is an act of kindness to give the fish a lift in the air.
— *Rabindranath Tagore, "Stray Birds" (1916)*

814 How to Get Rich In Trump's Washington

— *New York Times, 8/30/17*

It is hard to fight against impulsive desire; whatever it wants it will buy at the cost of the soul.

— *Heraclitus, "Fragments" (5th C. BCE)*

———————

815 Report: Mueller Partners With New York Attorney General to Investigate Manafort [Trump's Former Campaign Manager]

— *Huffington Post, 8/30/17*

Who saves his country violates no law.

— *Napoleon I, "Maxims" (1804)*

———————

816 Trump Lawyers Argue to End Obstruction Probe

— *Wall Street Journal, 9/1/17 (Misconstrued)*

Those who in quarrels interpose, / Must often wipe a bloody nose.

— *John Gay, "The Mastiffs," Fables (1727)*

———————

817 Massachusetts Moves to Require Presidential Candidates to Release Tax Returns

— *The Hill, 9/6/17*

Stolen waters are sweet, and bread eaten in secret is pleasant.

— *Bible, Proverbs 9:17*

———————

818 Trump Hires Chinese Government-Owned Firm Despite Promise: Report

— *The Hill, 9/11/17*

Power tends to corrupt and absolute power corrupts absolutely.

— *Lord Acton, Letter To Mandell Creighton (April, 1887)*

———————

819 Trump Lawyer Will Now Have to Testify in Public After Defying the Senate Intel Committee

— *Business Insider, 9/19/17*

This is servitude, / To serve the unwise.

— *Milton, "Paradise Lost" (1667)*

---

820 Mueller Seeks White House Documents Related to Trump's Actions as President

— *New York Times, 9/20/17*

Many strokes overthrow the tallest oaks.

— *John Lyly, "Euphues: The Anatomy Of Wit" (1579)*

---

821 Trump Administration: The Most Corrupt and Unethical in American History

— *Newsweek, 9/23/17*

Between two evils, I always pick the one I never tried before.

— *Mae West, In "Klondike Annie" (1936)*

---

822 Trump Tax Plan Benefits Wealthy, Including Trump

— *New York Times, 9/27/17*

We may see the small value God has for riches by the people he gives them to.

— *Alexander Pope, "Thoughts On Various Subjects" (1727)*

---

823 The $2.8 Billion Winners of Trump's Proposed [Estate] Tax Cuts Are His Kids

— *MarketWatch, 9/28/17*

Nothing in the world is so incontinent as a man's accursed appetite.

— *Homer, "Odyssey" (9th C. BCE)*

---

824 Trump's Tax Plan Is Very Good for Trump: $757 Million Over 10 Years

— *Huffington Post, 9/29/17*

It is not greedy to enjoy a good dinner, any more than it is greedy to enjoy a good concert. But I do think there is something greedy about trying to enjoy the dinner and the concert at the same time.

— *G. K. Chesterton, "On Pleasure-Seeking," Generally Speaking (1928)*

---

825 Trump Scandals, a List

— *New York Times, 10/5/17*

No such thing as a man willing to be honest - that would be like a blind man willing to see.

— *F. Scott Fitzgerald, "The Note-Books," The Crack-Up (1945)*

---

826 Trump Campaign Subpoenaed Over Sexual Assault Allegations

— *CNN, 10/15/17*

If venereal delight and the power of propagating the species were permitted only to the virtuous, it would make the world very good.

— *James Boswell, "London Journal" (Mar., 1763)*

---

827 The Iran Business Ties Trump Didn't Disclose

— *New Yorker, 10/20/17*

Though authority be a stubborn bear, yet he is oft lead by the nose with gold.

— *Shakespeare, "The Winter's Tale" (1609 - 1611)*

---

828 Wall Street Is on the Verge of Its First Major Win in Trump's Washington

— *Washington Post, 10/24/17*

Dry happiness is like dry bread. We eat, but we do not dine. I wish for the superfluous, for the useless, for the extravagant, for the too much, for that which is not good for anything.
— Victor Hugo, "Jean Valjean," Les Miserables (1862)

_____

829 Trump Tries to Shift Focus as First Charges Reportedly Loom in Russia Case
— New York Times, 10/29/17

Imagination is the mad boarder.
— Nicolas Malebranche, Preface To "Recherche De La Verite" (1674)

_____

830 Democrats Warn Trump Not to Fire Mueller
— Wall Street Journal, 10/30/17 (Misconstrued)

A word to the wise is enough.
— Benjamin Franklin, "The Way To Wealth," Essay (1758)

_____

831 Dershowitz: Mueller Is Very 'Zealous' - Won't Be Happy Until He Gets POTUS Or People Close to Him
— News Source, 10/31/17

How can justice fall victim, ever, to what is right?
— Philip K. Dick, "A Scanner Darkly" (1977)

_____

832 Mueller Drains the Swamp
— Wall Street Journal, 11/1/17 (Misconstrued)

In times of stress and danger such as come about as the result of an epidemic, many tragic and cruel phases of human nature are brought out, as well as many brave and unselfish ones.
— William Crawford Gorgas, "Sanitation In Panama" (2015)

_____

833 Warren to Trump: 'I Understand Your Desperation to Change the Subject'

— *Politico, 11/3/17*

In despair there are the most intense enjoyments, especially when one is very acutely conscious of the hopelessness of one's position.

— *Dostoyevsky, "Notes From The Underground" (1864)*

———

834 Trump Coal Backer Wins Big Under [Energy Secretary] Perry's Power Plan

— *Politico, 11/6/17*

Most vices may be committed very genteelly: a man may debauch his friend's wife genteelly; he may cheat at cards genteelly.

— *Samuel Johnson, Boswell's "Life Of Samuel Johnson" (April, 1775)*

———

835 Billionaire [Supporter] Used Tax Haven to Build War Chest for Pro-Trump Populists: Report

— *Newsweek, 11/9/17*

Fortunate persons hardly ever amend their ways: they always imagine they are in the right when fortune upholds their bad conduct.

— *La Rochefaucauld, "Maxims" (1665)*

———

836 Trump Administration to Bankers: You're Not the Villain Anymore

— *Wall Street Journal, 11/12/17 (Misconstrued)*

Hear now this, O foolish people, and without understanding; which have eyes and see not; which have ears and hear not.

— *Bible, Jeremiah 5:21*

———

837 Wall Street Fines Fall During First Year of Trump Administration, Research Shows
— *Wall Street Journal, 11/14/17 (Misconstrued)*

Never wrestle with pigs. You get both dirty and the pig likes it.
— *George Bernard Shaw, Playwright, Critic And Polemicist (1856 - 1950)*

———————

838 Trump Made Millions of Dollars From Drug Money in Panama: Report
— *Newsweek, 11/17/17*

Avarice is a fine, absorbin', passion an' manny an ol' fellow is as happy with his arm around his bank account as he was sleigh ridin' with his first girl.
— *Finley Peter Dunne, ""Mr. Dooley On Making A Will" (1919)*

———————

839 A Split From Trump Indicates That Flynn Is Moving to Cooperate With Mueller
— *New York Times, 11/23/17*

Good night, good night! Parting is such sweet sorrow.
— *Shakespeare, "Romeo And Juliet" (1591- 1595)*

———————

840 McCain: Trump Doesn't Have Any 'Principles and Beliefs'
— *The Hill, 11/27/17*

A mile wide and an inch deep.
— *Urban Dictionary, By Octopod (April, 2004)*

———————

841 Mueller Has Subpoenaed Deutsche Bank for Information on Trump and His Family
— *Business Insider, 12/5/17*

Where God hath a temple, the Devil will have a chapel.
— *Robert Burton, "The Anatomy Of Melancholy" (1621)*

842 Trump's Richest Friends Are Asking for Changes to the GOP Tax Plan, and He's Listening
— *Washington Post, 12/7/17*

Avarice is a cursed vice: offer a man enough gold, and he will part with his own small hoard of food, however great his hunger.
— *Lucan, "On The Civil War" (1st. C. CE)*

843 Trump Administration Is the Most Corrupt Government Institution in the United States, Americans Believe
— *Newsweek, 12/12/17*

I generally avoid temptation unless I can't resist it.
— *Mae West, in "My Little Chickadee" (1940)*

844 Welcome to the Trump Family Swamp [Nepotistic Profit Center]
— *Washington Post, 12/18/17*

Public money is like holy water; everyone helps himself to it.
— *Italian Proverb*

845 Report: Trump DC Hotel Employee Wrote in Email That Trump 'Is Definitely Still Involved' in Trump Org.
— *The Hill, 12/28/17*

There are no .400 hitters in Washington.
— *George F. Will, "Men At Work: The Craft Of Baseball" (1990)*

846 After Becoming President, Trump Has Sold Millions in Real Estate in Secret Deals
— *Newsweek, 1/10/18*

The only way to get rid of a temptation is to yield to it. Resist it, and your soul grows sick with longing for the things it has forbidden to itself.

— Oscar Wilde, "The Picture Of Dorian Gray" (1891)

CHAPTER 13

FROBISHER INSTITUTE OF ABANDONED LANGUAGES AND INFORMAL PATOIS

TOPICS:
RESPONSIBILITY AND OWNERSHIP

Frobisher Institute of English Languages and Informal Patois

847 White House Blames 'Professional Protesters' for Rowdy GOP Town Halls

— *Politico, 1/22/17*

I respect only those that resist me, but I cannot tolerate them.

— *Charles De Gaulle, Quoted In The New York Times Magazine (1968)*

---

848 As Trump Thunders, G.O.P. Lawmakers Duck and Cover

— *New York Times, 1/26/17*

I've always felt, as a writer, that radicals are fascinating because they're relations; they have a place in the American family. They're the relatives everyone wishes would go away. They're the embarrassments to decorum and good taste.

— *E. L. Doctorow, Interview (1993)*

---

849 Trump Fires Acting Attorney General Who Defied Him

— *New York Times, 1/30/17*

Abuse a man unjustly, and you will make friends for him.

— *Edgar Watson Howe, "Country Town Sayings" (1911)*

---

850 Trump's Approval Ratings Are Down. How Much Does It Mean?

— *New York Times, 2/3/127*

Every hero becomes a bore at last.

— *Emerson, "Uses Of Great Men," Representative Men (1850)*

---

851 In Trump's Volleys, Echoes of a Host's Conspiracy Theories
— *New York Times, 2/20/17*

Our natural egoism leads us to judge other people by their relations to ourselves. We want them to be certain things to us, and for us that is what they are; because the rest of them is no good to us, we ignore it.
— *W. Somerset Maugham, "The Summing Up" (1938)*

---

852 'I Think He's Behind It': Trump Suggests Obama Is Organizing Protests Against Him
— *New York Times, 2/28/17*

In jealousy, there is more of self-love than love.
— *La Rouchefoucauld, "Maxims" (1665)*

---

853 Trump: It's 'Pathetic' Dems Are Holding Up Cabinet Picks
— *Politico, 3/3/17*

He spoke with a certain what-is-it in his voice, and I could see that, if not actually disgruntled, he was far from being gruntled.
— *P. G. Wodehouse, "The Code Of The Woosters" (1938)*

---

854 Trump Accuses Obama of Wiretapping Trump Tower
— *Reddit, 3/4/17*

Some men have a necessity to be mean, as if they were exercising a faculty which they had to practically neglect since early childhood.
— *F. Scott Fitzgerald, "The Crack-Up" (1945)*

---

855 The President Accused Obama of 'McCarthyism.' But Trump's Mentor Helped Enforce It
— *Washington Post, 3/5/17*

If a man could say nothing against a character but what he can prove, history could not be written.

— Samuel Johnson, Quoted In Boswell's "Life Of Samuel Johnson" (1776)

---

856 Trump's Obamacare Fallback: Blame the Democrats

— Politico, 3/10/17

There is no greater hindrance to the progress of thought than an attitude of irritated party-spirit.

— Alfred North Whitehead, "Adventures In Ideas" (1933)

---

857 Justice Dept. Tells Remaining Obama Administration U.S. Attorneys to Resign

— Washington Post, 3/11/17

Many punishments sometimes, and in some cases, as much discredit a prince as many funerals a physician.

— Ben Johnson, "Of Statecraft," Timber (1640)

---

858 Trump Blames Everyone But Himself for Failure of GOP Reform

— The Guardian, 3/27/17

Ah, snug lie those that slumber / Beneath Conviction's roof. / Their floor are sturdy lumber, / Their windows weatherproof. / But I sleep cold forever / And cold sleep all my kind, / For I was born to shiver / In the draft from an open mind.

— Phyllis McGinley, "Lament For A Wavering Viewpoint" (1940)

---

859 Blame Game Intensifies as Trump Agenda Stalls

— Politico, 3/27/17

Satire is a sort of glass, wherein beholders do generally discover everybody's face but their own.
— Jonathan Swift, Preface To "The Battle of the Books" (1704)

_____

860 Personal Responsibility: A Concise History of Trump's Buck Passing
— Washington Post, 4/6/17

Responsibility, n. A detachable burden easily shifted to the shoulders of God, Fate, Fortune, Luck or one's neighbor. In the days of astrology, it was customary to unload it on a star.
— Ambrose Bierce, "The Devil's Dictionary" (1881-1911)

_____

861 Trump Attacks His Own FBI Director in Effort to Hit Back at Clinton
— New York Magazine, 5/3/17

A man that studieth revenge keeps his own wounds green, which otherwise would heal and do well.
— Francis Bacon, "Of Revenge," Essays (1625)

_____

862 Trump: No Politician 'Has Been Treated Worse or More Unfairly'
— Politico, 5/18/17

To sense when a teenager needs understanding, and when misunderstanding, is a difficult and delicate task. The sad truth is that no matter how wise we are, we cannot be right for any length of time in our teenager's eyes.
— Haim G. Ginotte, "Between Parent & Teenager" (1969)

_____

863 The Unbearable Weakness of President Trump in the Face of Terrorism
— Huffington Post, 6/4/17

The weak can be terrible / because they try furiously to appear strong.
— *Rabindranath Tagore, "Fireflies" (1928)*

---

864 Trump Grows Discontented With Attorney General Jeff Sessions
— *New York Times, 6/5/17*

To have a grievance is to have a purpose in life.
— *Eric Hoffer, "The Passionate State of Mind" (1954)*

---

865 Gulf Crisis: Trump Escalates Row by Accusing Qatar of Sponsoring Terrorism
— *The Guardian, 6/9/17*

Exaggeration is a prodigality of the judgement which shows the narrowness of one's knowledge or one's taste.
— *Baltasar Gracian, "The Art Of Worldly Wisdom" (1647)*

---

866 Trump Loses Patience With His White House Counsel
— *Politico, 6/23/17*

Only those sadnesses are dangerous and bad which one carries about among people in order to drown them out.
— *Rainer Maria Rilke, "Letters To A Young Poet" (1904)*

---

867 Trump Blames the Biggest Mistake of His Presidency on Obama
— *Vanity Fair, 6/23/17*

I have never found, in a long experience of politics, that criticism is ever inhibited by ignorance.
— *Harold MacMillan, Wall Street Journal (Aug., 1963)*

---

868 Pro-Trump Group Launches New Attack Ad Against Special Counsel Robert Mueller

— *Los Angeles Times, 6/24/17*

Evil communications corrupt good manners.

— *Bible, I Corinthians 15:33*

---

869 Hey Republicans, Nobody Is Buying Your Fake Outrage Over Trump's Sexist Tweets. You Endorsed This

— *Huffington Post, 6/30/17*

The conservatives nearly always tolerate the demagogue while he is destroying liberals.

— *Harry Golden, "Only In America" (1958)*

---

870 Trump: Basically, It's Obama's Fault That Russian Lawyer Took Advantage of 'Young Man' Donald Trump, Jr.

— *Washington Post, 7/13/17*

Everyone in a crowd has the power to throw dirt: nine out of ten have the inclination.

— *WIlliam Hazlitt, "On Reading New Books," Sketches And Essays (1839)*

---

871 Governors Go Around Trump on Global Diplomacy

— *New York Times, 7/15/17*

A prudent man does not make the goat his gardener.

— *Hungarian Proverb*

---

872 Trump Lawyer Blames Secret Service for Not Preemptively Stopping Jr.'s [Russian] Meeting

— *TPM Livewire, 7/16/17*

In the world of imagination, anything goes that is imaginatively possible, but nothing really happens.

— Northrop Frye, "The Educated Imagination" (1964)

---

873 Donald Trump Signs Off on Obama's Iran Deal, Which He Promised to Scrap

— *Salon, 7/18/17*

It is one thing to show a man he is in error, and another to put him in possession of the truth.

— John Locke, "An Essay Concerning Human Understanding" (1690)

---

874 Trump Suggests States Resisting Voter-Records Request Have Something to Hide

— *Wall Street Journal, 7/19/17 (Misconstrued)*

The most distrustful are often the greatest dupes.

— Cardinal De Retz, "Memoires" (1718)

---

875 Trump Goes Off-Script and Fumes About Sessions and Russia Probe

— *Politico, 7/20/17*

There is something so showy about desperation; it takes hard wits to see it's a grandiose form of funk.

— Elizabeth Bowen, "The Death Of The Heart" (1938)

---

876 Senators Move to Block Trump From Ousting Sessions as Attorney General

— *Wall Street Journal, 7/28/17 (Misconstrued)*

The complaints I [Trump] have heard of you [Sessions] I do not believe; 'tis my slowness that I do not; for I know you lack not folly to commit them and have ability enough to make such knaveries yours.
— *Shakespeare, "All's Well That Ends Well" (1604 – 1605)*

―――――――

877 De Blasio Fundraises Off of Trump's 'Pathetic Mayor' Remarks
— *Politico, 7/28/17*

Oratory is just like prostitution, you must have little tricks.
— *Vittorio Emanuele Orlando, Time (Dec., 1952)*

―――――――

878 Trump Suggests Russia Probe Investigate Clinton Amid Reports of Grand Jury
— *Huffington Post, 8/3/17*

There is a prodigious selfishness in dreams: they live perfectly deaf and invulnerable amid the cries of the real world.
— *George Santayana, "Life Of Reason: Reason In Common Sense" (1905)*

―――――――

879 Trump Advisor Suggests Minnesota Mosque Attack Could Have Been Faked 'By The Left'
— *Huffington Post, 8/8/17*

A man who doesn't trust himself can never really trust anyone else.
— *Cardinal De Retz, "Memoires" (1718)*

―――――――

880 Trump's Jabs at Lawmakers Fire Up GOP Senators
— *Wall Street Journal, 8/18/17 (Misconstrued)*

Pay attention to your enemies, for they are the first to discover your mistakes.
— *Laertius "Lives And Opinions Of Eminent Philosophers" (3rd C. C.E.)*

―――――――

881   At [Phoenix] Rally, Trump Blames the Media for Country's Deepening Divisions
— *New York Times, 8/23/17*

Our history is every human history; a black and gory business with more scoundrels than wise men at the lead, and more louts than both put together to cheer and follow.
— *Phillip Wylie, "Generation of Vipers" (1942)*

---

882   Trump Blames GOP Leaders for Debt Ceiling 'Mess'
— *The Hill, 8/24/17*

It is often pleasant to stone a martyr, no matter how much we may admire him.
— *John Barth, "The Floating Opera" (1956)*

---

883   Trump Humiliated Jeff Sessions After Mueller Appointment
— *New York Times, 9/14/17*

Whoever touches pitch will be defiled.
— *"Apocrypha," Ecclesiasticus 13:1*

---

884   'Burned' [By the Republican Leadership] Trump Finds Comfort With Democrats
— *Politico, 9/15/17*

Nothing on earth consumes a man more quickly than the passion of resentment.
— *Nietzsche, "Ecce Homo" (1888)*

---

885   Trump's Top Supporters Are in a Full-Blown Panic. They're Right to Be Afraid
— *Washington Post, 9/15/17*

Tenterhooks are the upholstery of the anxious seat.
— *Robert Sherwood, News Reports (Nov., 1955)*

---

886 Dear Trump Voter: WTF Is Wrong With You?
— *Huffington Post, 9/26/17*

People on the whole are very simple-minded, in whatever country one finds them. They are so simple as to take literally, more often than not, the things their leaders tell them.
— *Pearl S. Buck, "What America Means To Me" (1943)*

---

887 Corker Mocks Trump in Escalating Twitter Feud
— *Politico, 10/8/17*

Though familiarity may not breed contempt, it takes the edge off admiration.
— *William Hazlitt, "Characteristics" (1823)*

---

888 Trump Vents to Wealthy Donors About Failure to Repeal Obamacare
— *Politico, 10/8/17*

A critic is a man who knows the way but can't drive the car.
— *Kenneth Tynan, The New York Times Magazine (Jan., 1966)*

---

889 A 'Pressure Cooker': Trump's Frustration and Fury Rupture Alliances, Threaten Agenda
— *Washington Post, 10/9/17*

The man who acts the least, upbraids the most.
— *Homer, "Iliad" (9th C. BCE)*

---

890 Trump Blames Republicans in Congress for His Woes. Does He Have a Point?

— *Washington Post, 10/10/17*

A confederacy of dunces doesn't need to "develop" - but it does.

— *John Kennedy Toole, "A Confederacy Of Dunces," Guardian (June, 2017)*

891 Trump Says the U.S. Is the Highest Taxed Country in the World. No, It's Not

— *CNN, 10/12/17*

I'm inclined to think we are all ghosts - every one of us. It's not just what we inherit from our mothers and fathers that haunts us. It's all kinds of old defunct theories, all sorts of old defunct beliefs, and things like that.

— *Henrik Ibsen, "Ghosts" (1881)*

892 Trump's Frustration With Congress Reaches a Breaking Point

— *Politico, 10/13/17*

Do as I say, not as I do.

— *John Seldon, "Table Talk" (1654)*

893 Trump Slams 'Unhinged' Billionaire Steyer [in Tweet] After Impeachment Ad

— *News Source, 10/27/17*

Manners require time, as nothing is more vulgar than haste.

— *Emerson, "Behavior," The Conduct Of Life (1860)*

894 Edward Klein: New Book Reveals FBI Report on Deep State's 'All Out War' to Destroy Trump

— *News Source, 10/29/17*

It is more blessed to give than to receive.
— Bible, Acts 20:35

___

895 Trump: I'm Disappointed in the DOJ for Not Looking Into Dems
— News Source, 11/3/17

Persistence in one opinion has never been considered a merit in political leaders.
— Cicero, "Ad Familiares" (1st C. BCE)

___

896 'Very Frustrated'Trump Becomes Top Critic of Law Enforcement
— New York Times, 11/3/17

Rash and incessant scolding runs into custom and renders itself despised.
— Montaigne, "Of Anger," Essays (1580 - 1588)

___

897 Trump Voters Disappointed by His Presidency Threaten GOP
— Los Angeles Times, 11/8/17

They that sow the wind, shall reap the whirlwind.
— Hebrew Bible. Hosea 8:7

___

898 Trump Blames Gillespie for Election Loss: Did Not Embrace Me
— News Source, 11/8/17

A scapegoat is not necessarily a goat at all, of course. A scapegoat is one who is to be blamed for the wrongdoing of others.
— William Holman Hunt, "The Scapegoat" (1854)

___

899 Donald Trump: I Blame Previous Presidents for Massive Trade Deficit, Not China

— *News Source, 11/9/17*

Children are natural mythologists: they beg to be told tales, and love not only to invent but to enact falsehoods.

— *George Santayana, "Dialogues In Limbo" (1925)*

————

900 Donald Trump Mocks 'Sen. Jeff Flakey' on Twitter

— *News Source, 11/20/17*

You shall judge of a man by his foes as well as by his friends.

— *Joseph Conrad, "Lord Jim" (1900)*

————

901 The Hill: Trump and McConnell at Odds Over Roy Moore

— *News Source, 11/22/17*

Your worst enemy / Becomes your best friend, once he's underground.

— *Euripides, "Herakleidia" (429 BCE)*

————

902 Trump: 'I Would Absolutely Blame the Democrats' If There Was a Government Shutdown

— *Washington Post, 11/28/17*

The fault, dear Brutus, is not in our stars, but in ourselves, that we are underlings.

— *Shakespeare, "Julius Caesar" (1599 -1600)*

————

903 Tillerson Faces 'Death Blow' After Repeated Clashes With Trump

— *Bloomberg, 12/1/17*

You can be a king or a street sweeper, but everybody dances with the Grim Reaper.

— *Robert Alton Harris, Criminal And Murderer At His Execution (1992)*

———————

904 Trump Says Democrats Will Pay After Acquittal of Immigrant in Murder Case

— *Los Angeles Times, 12/1/17*

There is no idea, no fact, which could not be vulgarized and presented in a ludicrous light.

— *Dostoyevsky, "Mr.-bov And The Question Of Art' "1895)*

———————

905 In Florida, Trump Attacks Credibility of Roy Moore Accuser as He Rallies Support for Alabama Senate Hopeful

— *Los Angeles Times, 12/8/17*

Woman was God's second mistake.

— *Nietzsche, "The Antichrist" (1888)*

———————

906 Report: Trump Furious [U. N. Ambassador] Haley Said his [Sexual Assault] Accusers Should be Heard

— *Axios, 12/11/17*

Of all plagues, good Heaven, thy wrath can send, / Save, save, Oh, save me from the candid friend!

— *George Canning, "New Morality" (1798)*

———————

907 Trump Blames Democrats for 'Fabricated Stories' of Sexual Misconduct

— *The Guardian, 12/12/17*

It's always the ones with dirty hands pointing the fingers.

— *Sonya Teclai, Singer/Song Writer And Poet, Facebook Meme*

———————

908 Steve Bannon's Political Science Experiment [in Alabama] Blew Up in Trump's Face

— *CNN, 12/13/17*

Whatever folly men commit, be their shortcomings or their vices what they may, let us exercise forbearance; remember that when these faults appear in others it is our vices and follies that we behold.

— *Schopenhauer, "Parega And Paralipomena" (1851)*

———————

909 Trump 'Dossier' Firm: Republicans Leaked [Its] Bank Records in Retaliation [for Linking Trump Campaign to Russia]

— *Reuters, 12/13/17*

Why is it that when political ammunition runs low, inevitably the rusty artillery of abuse is always wheeled into action?

— *Adlai Stevenson, Speech, New York City (Sept., 1952)*

———————

910 Plot to Stop Mueller Enters a New and Dangerous Phase

— *MSNBC, 12/15/17*

Wherever law ends, tyranny begins.

— *John Locke, "Two Treatises On Government" (1690)*

———————

911 'Trump, Trump, Trump!' How [Calling Out] a President's Name Became a Racial Sneer

— *New York Times, 12/16/17*

Logical consequences are the scarecrows of fools and the beacons of wise men.

— *Thomas Henry Huxley, "Animal Automatism" 1874)*

———————

912 Trump Threatens to Cut Aid to Countries Over UN Jerusalem Vote

— The Guardian, 12/21/17

Political language - and with variations this is true of all political parties, from Conservatives to Anarchists - is designed to make lies sound truthful and murder respectable, and to give an appearance of solidity to pure wind.

— George Orwell, "Politics/The English Language," Shooting An Elephant (1950)

———————

913 United Nations Rebukes U.S. Over Jerusalem in 128-to-9 Vote

— New York Times, 12/21/17

This is sweet: to see your foe / perish and pay to justice all he owes.

— Euripides, ""Heracles" (422 BCE)

———————

914 Trump Takes Aim at Top FBI Officials

— CNN, 12/24/17

Suspicion always haunts the guilty mind, the thief doth fear each bush an officer.

— Shakespeare, "Henry VI, Part 3" (1591)

———————

915 Thanks to President Donald Trump, Our World Is a Less Safe Place for Everybody

— The Sydney Morning Herald, 12/25/17

They're ain't no fans nor no rest and brother, they're ain't no Cokes in hell.

— Wilma Dykeman, Anonymous Quote In "The French Broad" (1955)

———————

916 Trump Partly Blames Sessions for Alabama Senate Loss: Report

— The Hill, 12/26/17

For God's sake, take away this captive scold.
— *Shakespeare, "Henry VI, Part 3" (1591)*

---

917 With Trump, It's Always Someone Else's Fault
— *Chicago Sun Times, 12/27/17*

There is an old and very wise Native American saying: Every time you point your finger in scorn - there are three remaining fingers pointing right back at you.
— *Alyson Noel, "Fated" (2012)*

---

918 The White House Loves to Rewrite Resumes of Ex-Trump Aides Who Cause Trouble for Him
— *Huffington Post, 1/3/18*

History is largely concerned with arranging good entrances for people; and later exits not always quite so good.
— *Heywood Broun, ""Pieces Of Hate, And Other Enthusiasms" (1922)*

---

919 Trump's Outburst Against Bannon Removes Any Shred of Presidential Decorum
— *The Guardian, 1/3/18*

Bullying creates character like nuclear waste creates superheroes. It's a rare occurrence and often does much more damage than endowment.
— *Zack W. Van, "Inanimate Heroes" (2011)*

---

920 Trump Unloads on Russia Investigation, Libel Laws, and Explosive New Tell-All Book During Press Conference
— *Business Insider, 1/6/18*

The world will never be long without some good reason to hate the unhappy; their real faults are immediately detected; and if those are not sufficient to sink them into infamy, an additional weight of calumny will be superadded.

— Samuel Johnson, "The Adventurer" (1753)

––––––––––

921 Majority of Americans See Trump's First Year as a Failure

— NPR, 1/18/18

You know it's cold outside when you go outside and it's cold.

— Bill Murray, Twitter (May, 2013)

CHAPTER 14

THE UNIVERSITY OF BARROW AT USHUAIA

TOPICS:
FAITHFULNESS AND
STEADFASTNESS

The University of Barrow at Ushuaia

922 Losing Hope in U.S., Migrants Make Icy Crossing to Canada
— *New York Times, 2/11/17*

The mass of men lead lives of quiet desperation. What is called resignation is confirmed desperation. From the desperate city you go into the desperate country, and have to console yourself with the bravery of minks and muskrats.
— *Thoreau, "Economy," Walden (1854)*

923 Trump Will Likely Sell Out His Working-Class Base
— *Washington Post, 2/23/17*

The trouble with the profit system has always been that it is highly unprofitable to most people
— *E. B. White, "Control, One Man's Meat" (1944)*

924 Trump's Promise to Bring Back Coal Jobs Is Worse Than a Con
— *Washington Post, 3/5/17*

You can fool too many of the people too much of the time.
— *James Thurber, "The Owl Who Was God," The Thurber Carnival (1945)*

925 Former Obama Official: Trump Has Turned Our Traditional Openness Into Weakness.
— *Washington Post, 3/14/17*

Primitive, simplistic anti-communism [Muslimism?] is all too often used as a common denominator for diverse efforts to perpetuate one's own power in a democratic system, convert opinions into dogma, and kill off all opposition, even silent.
— *Eugene Kogen, "The Path To Dictatorship" (1966)*

926 Trump Is Leading Coal Miner's Out of a Ditch – And Into the Abyss
— *The Guardian, 3/30/17*

No man [coal miner] will be found in whose mind airy notions do not sometimes tyrannize, and force him to hope or fear beyond the limits of sober probability.
— *Samuel Johnson, "Rasselas" (1759)*

———————

927 Poll: Trump More Unpopular Than Obama Ever Was
— *Reddit, 4/5/17*

By their fruits ye shall know them.
— *Bible, Matthew 7:20*

———————

928 President Trump Just Cost Americans Saving for Their Retirement $3.7 Billion
— *Huffington Post, 4/10/17*

What renders us so bitter against those who trick us is that they believe themselves to be more clever than we are.
— *La Rochefoucald, "Maxims" (1665)*

———————

929 Trump's Tax Cuts May Be More Damaging Than Reagan's
— *New York Times, 5/1/17*

It is the part of a good shepherd to shear his flock, not flay it.
— *Tiberius, Quoted In Suetonius "Lives Of The Caesars Tiberius" (2nd C. CE)*

———————

930 Who Gets Hurt - And When - If Trumpcare Becomes Law
— *Washington Post, 5/7/17*

He that plants thorns must never expect to gather roses.
— *Vishnu Sharma, "The Fables Of Bidpal," Panchatantra (300 BCE)*

———————

931 Trump Has a Long History of Secretly Recording Calls, According to Former Associates
— *Washington Post, 5/13/17*

We are never so easily deceived as when we imagine we are deceiving others.
— *La Rochefoucauld, "Maxims" (1665)*

---

932 Trump Plans Likely to Aggravate U. S. Inequality: Nobel Winner Deaton
— *Huffington Post, 5/15/17*

Whatever may be the general endeavor of a community to render its members equal and alike, the personal pride of individuals will always seek to rise above the line, and to form somewhere an inequality to their own advantage.
— *Alexis De Tocqueville, "Democracy In America" (1835)*

---

933 I Was in the CIA. We Wouldn't Trust a Country Whose Leader Did What Trump Did [Sharing Classified Information With Russian Diplomat]
— *Washington Post, 5/20/17*

We have to distrust each other. It is our only defense against betrayal.
— *Tennessee Williams, "Camino Real" (1953)*

---

934 Trump's Budget Hits His Own Supporters Hardest
— *Politico, 5/22/17*

A false friend and a shadow attend only while the sun shines.
— *Benjamin Franklin, "Poor Richard's Almanack" (1732-57)*

---

935 The Pentagon Can't Believe Trump Told Another President [of the Philippines] About Nuclear Subs Near North Korea
— *BuzzFeedNews, 5/25/17*

There is no crime in the cynical American calendar more humiliating than to be a sucker.
— *Max Lerner, "Actions And Passions" (1949)*

————————

936 Thanks to Trump, Germany Says It Can't Rely on the United States. What Does That Mean?
— *Washington Post, 5/28/17*

It is as foolish to make experiments on the constancy of a friend, as upon the chastity of a wife.
— *Samuel Johnson, Quoted In Boswell's "Life of Samuel Johnson" (1779)*

————————

937 White House Hands Say Over Afghan Troop Levels to Military
— *Wall Street Journal, 6/14/17 (Misconstrued)*

If you leap into a well, Providence is not bound to fetch you out.
— *Thomas Fuller, M.D. "Gnomologia" (1732)*

————————

938 Trump Administration Sides with Employers Over Workers on Arbitration Agreements
— *Huffington Post, 6/16/17*

Blow, blow, blow thou winter wind, thou are not so unkind as man's ingratitude.
— *Shakespeare, "As You Like It" (1599)*

————————

939 Deputy AG Is Latest Target of Trump Twitter Ire
— *Washington Post, 6/17/17*

He declares himself guilty who justifies himself before accusation.
— *Thomas Fuller, M.D. "Gnomologia" (1732)*

---

940 Trump Just Sold Us All Out on Drug Pricing
— *Business Insider, 6/21/17*

There's no more faith in thee than in a stewed prune.
— *Shakespeare, "Henry IV, Part 1" (1591)*

---

941 Trumpcare Isn't About Health. It's a Tax Cut for the 1%
— *The Guardian, 6/27/17*

There is a mistaken idea, ancient but still with us, that an overdose of anything from fornication to hot chocolate will teach restraint by the very results of its abuse.
— *M. K. Fisher, In "The Art Of The Personal Essay" (1994)*

---

942 Trump's 'No One Will Lose Coverage' Is Turning Out to Be the Worst Campaign Promise Since 'Read My Lips'
— *New Republic, 6/27/17*

A promise is binding in the inverse ratio of the numbers to whom it is made.
— *Thomas De Quincy, "Confessions Of An English Opium-Eater" (1821-56)*

---

943 Don't Sugarcoat This. Trump Just Called for 32 Million People to Lose Health Coverage
— *Washington Post, 6/30/17*

Cruelty ever proceeds from a vile mind, and often from a cowardly heart.
— *Lodovico Ariosto, "Orlando Furiouso" (1516)*

---

944 Clinton Running Mate: Russian Probe Moving Into 'Potentially Treason'

— *The Hill, 7/11/17*

There are certain truths so true that they are practically unbelievable.

— *Gore Vidal, "The Second American Revolution And Other Essays" (1982)*

_____

945 Trump Threatens Insurer Payments to Push Congress on Health-Care Repeal

— *Wall Street Journal, 7/31/17 (Misconstrued)*

A tart temper never mellows with age, and a sharp tongue is the only edged tool that grows keener with constant use.

— *Washington Irving, "The Sketch Book of Geoffrey Crayon, Gent." (1819)*

_____

946 Studies Show That School Vouchers Lead to Lower Math and Reading Scores. Why Has the Trump Administration Embraced Them?

— *Scientific American, 8/1/17*

It is error alone which needs the support of government. Truth can stand by itself.

— *Thomas Jefferson, "Notes On The State Of Virginia" (1784)*

_____

947 Trump Admits He Punked His Supporters on Mexico Paying for the Wall

— *Washington Post, 8/3/17*

If human beings don't keep exercising their lips, he thought, their mouths probably seize up. After a few months' consideration and observation he abandoned this theory in favor of a new one. If they don't keep on exercising their lips, he thought, their brains start working.

— Douglas Adams, "The Hitchhikers Guide To The Galaxy" (1979)

---

948 Trump's Stalled Trade Agenda Leaves Industries in the Lurch

— New York Times, 8/7/17

American Society has tried so hard and so ably to defend the practice and theory of production for profit and not primarily for use that now it has succeeded in making its jobs and products profitable and useless.

— Paul Goodman, "Growing Up Absurd" (1960)

---

949 New Chief Of Staff John Kelly Said to Be Frustrated, Dismayed at Trump's Lack Of Discipline

— Chicago Tribune, 8/16/17

How shall I be able to rule over others, that have not full power and command of myself?

— Rabelais, "Gargantua And Pantagruel" (1532)

---

950 Infrastructure Advisers Quit, Say Trump's Actions Threaten Homeland Security

— Huffington Post, 8/23/17

If one must do wrong, its best to do it / pursuing power – otherwise, let's have virtue.

— Euripides, "The Phoenician Women" (411 BCE)

---

951 Trump Setting Records for Low Presidential Approval
— *CNBC, 8/26/17*

A man with a host of friends who slaps on the back everybody he meets is regarded as the friend of nobody.
— *Aristotle, "Nicomachean Ethics" (4th C. BCE)*

---

952 Trump Is Shedding Supporters Like No Other President in Modern History
— *Los Angeles Times, 8/27/17*

To every thing there is a season, and a time to every purpose under the heaven.
— *Bible, Ecclesiastes 3:1*

---

953 [Trump] Infrastructure Plan Shifts Burden To States, Cities
— *Wall Street Journal, 9/2/17 (Misconstrued)*

The great majority of men are bundles of beginnings.
— *Emerson, "Journals" (1828)*

---

954 Meet the Swamp: Donald Trump Punts September Agenda to December After Meeting With Congress
— *News Source, 9/6/17*

Defeat is a school in which truth always grows strong.
— *Henry Ward Beecher, "Proverbs From Plymouth Pulpit" (1887)*

---

955 'Trump Betrays Everyone': The President Has a Long Record as An Unpredictable Ally
— *Washington Post, 9/9/17*

The life of children, as much as that of intemperate men, is wholly governed by their desires.
— *Aristotle, "Nicomachean Ethics" (4th C. BCE)*

956 Trump Voters Throw MAGA [Make America Great Again] Hats Into Twitter Bonfire [in Protest]

— *News Source, 9/14/17*

They fall for the latest isms gullibly as pups for rubber bones.

— *Dylan Thomas, "Quite Early One Morning" (1954)*

957 Donald Trump Deletes Tweets Supporting Luther Strange [Alabama Senator]

— *News Source, 9/26/17*

Damn with faint praise, assent with civil leer, And without sneering teach the rest to sneer.

— *Alexander Pope, "Epistle To Doctor Arbuthnot" (1735)*

958 Report: Trump 'Deeply Worried' His Cave on DACA Amnesty 'Endangers' Standing With Base

— *News Source, 9/27/17*

My apprehensions come in crowds; / I dread the rustling of the grass; / The very shadows of the clouds / Have power to shake me as they pass; / I question things and do not find / One that will answer to my mind; / And all the world appears unkind.

— *William Wordsworth, "The Affliction Of Margaret " (1804)*

959 Trump Adviser 'Can't Guarantee' Taxes Won't Go Up for the Middle Class

— *ABC News, 9/28/17*

We promise much to avoid giving little.

— *Vauvenargues, "Reflections And Maxims" (1746)*

960 Stephen King on Trump's Tax Plan: Trump 'Couldn't Give a S—' About Working Class

— *The Hill, 9/28/17*

Just as war is waged with the blood of others, fortunes are made with other people's money.

— *Andre Suares, "Voici L'Homme" (1906)*

---

961 Trump's Upbeat Puerto Rico Rhetoric Clashes With Reality on the Ground

— *Politico, 9/29/17*

Optimism is the content of small men in high places.

— *F. Scott Fitzgerald, "Note-Books," The Crack-Up (1945)*

---

962 Trump Contradicts Tillerson on North Korea, the Latest in a Series of Put-Downs

— *Washington Post, 10/1/17*

It is one of the blessings of old friends that you can afford to be stupid with them.

— *Emerson, "Journals" (1836)*

---

963 An Unfit President Fails Puerto Rico

— *New York Times, 10/3/17*

There is not a fiercer hell than the failure in a great object.

— *Keats, Preface, "Endymion" (1818)*

---

964 Trump Puerto Rico Debt Wipe Out - Crushes Wall Street

— *News Source, 10/4/17*

The lie of a pipe dream is what gives life to the whole misbegotten mad lot of us, drunk or sober.

— *Eugene O'Neill, "The Iceman Cometh" (1946)*

---

965 Trump Administration Releases Hard-Line Immigration Principles, Threatening Deal on 'Dreamers'
— *Washington Post, 10/8/17*

Politics, n. A strife of interests masquerading as a contest of principles.
— *Ambrose Bierce, "The Devil's Dictionary" (1881-1911)*

---

966 Trump vs. Clinton: The Feud Continues Even After the Election
— *News Source. 10/16/17*

Get thee to a nunnery.
— *Shakespeare, "Hamlet" (1601)*

---

967 Trump to Shrink Two Utah National Monuments, Senator Says
— *News Source, 10/27/17*

Would the fountain of your mind were clear again, that I might water an ass at it.
— *Shakespeare, "Troilus And Cressida" (1602)*

---

968 White House Distances Itself From Manafort, Papadopoulos Charges
— *News Source, 10/30/17*

Friendship: A ship big enough for two in fair weather; but only one in foul.
— *Ambrose Bierce, "The Devil's Dictionary" (1881-1911)*

---

969 Keith Olbermann Argues Claim That Trump Did More Damage to the US Than Bin Laden
— *News Source, 11/3/17*

If experience teaches us anything at all, it teaches us this: that a good politician, under democracy, is quite as unthinkable as an honest burglar.

— H. L. Mencken, "Prejudices: Fourth Series" (1924)

---

970 Farmers Move to Defy Trump on NAFTA

— Politico, 11/9/17

A doubtful friend is worse than a certain enemy. Let a man be one thing or the other, and we then know how to meet them.

— Aesop, "The Hound And The Hare," Fables (6th C. BCE)

---

971 Most Americans Blame Donald Trump for Obamacare Problems, Poll Finds

— Independent, 11/18/17

Be thou [voters], in rebuking evil, / Conscious of thine own.

— John Greenleaf Whittier, "What The Voice Said" (1847)

---

972 Robinson: Congress Should Investigate Trump's Alleged Sexual Misconduct

— Post-Tribune, 11/22/17

In this counthry a man is presoomed to be guilty ontil he's proved guilty an' afther that he's presoomed to be innocent.

— Finley Peter Dunne, "Mr. Dooley On Making A Will" (1919)

---

973 Donald Trump: A 'Populist' Who Wages Class War on Behalf of the Rich

— Salon, 11/25/17

Oh, it is vile for a man, if he be noble, / And when he has won to the heights of power, / To put on new manners for old and change / His countenance.
— *Euripides, "Iphigenia In Aulis" (405 BCE)*

_____

974 Carly Fiorina on Roy Moore: 'Donald Trump Cares About a Vote in the Senate - No More, No Less'
— *News Source, 11/26/17*

If there are obstacles, the shortest line between two points may be the crooked line.
— *Bertold Brecht, "Galileo" (1938)*

_____

975 Embracing the Far Right, Trump Stains a History of Democratic Ideals
— *BBC, 12/1/17*

If Despotism failed only for want of a capable benevolent despot, what chance has Democracy, which requires a whole population of capable voters.
— *George Bernard Shaw, "Epistle Dedicatory," Man And Superman (1903)*

_____

976 Polls Show Trump's Support Dwindling Among White Evangelicals
— *Huffington Post. 12/7/17*

A good salad may be the prologue to a bad supper.
— *Thomas Fuller, M. D., "Gnomologia" (1732)*

_____

977 With Omarosa's Exit, Trump Now Appears to Have No Black Senior Advisers
— *Washington Post. 12/15/17*

[He threw] the baby out with the bathwater.
— *Thomas Murner, "Narrenbeschworung" (1512)*

---

978 Billionaire Michael Bloomberg: 'The [GOP] Tax Bill is An Economically Indefensible Blunder'
— *Money, 12/15/17*

I believe that much of the maladjustment in our societies is caused, not by malevolence and corruption, but simply by ignorance.
— *Gilbert Highet, "The Art Of Teaching" (1950)*

---

979 Donald J. Trump: The 'Least Popular First-Year President on Record'
— *Common Dreams, 12/17/17*

The horror! The horror!
— *Joseph Conrad, "Heart Of Darkness" (1899)*

---

980 The Real Reason Trump Allies Are Attacking Mueller [Provide Cover for Future Pardons]
— *Politico, 12/19/17*

Do not believe his vows; for they are brokers breathing like sanctified and pious bawds, the better to beguile.
— *Shakespeare, "Hamlet" (1601)*

---

981 After Tax Cuts, Republicans May Suddenly Find Trump Is More Trouble Than He's Worth
— *USA Today, 12/20/17*

Some people are like clouds. When they go away, it's a beautiful day.
— *Bill Murray, Actor And Comedian, Tweet (June, 2015)*

---

982 Dave Chappelle to Trump Voters in Netflix Special: 'You are poor. He's fighting for me [a Rich Guy]."
— *USA Today, 12/20/17*

When you've been had, your only recourse is REVENGE!
— *Peter Moore, British Business Executive, Pinterest (b. 1955)*

---

983 5.3 Million Puerto Ricans Will Take Revenge on Trump, Governor Says
— *Newsweek, 12/20/17*

God gives each is due at the time allotted.
— *Euripides, "Electra" (413 BCE)*

---

984 Palestinian Christian Leaders Denounce Trump's Decision [Recognizing Jerusalem as Israeli Capital]
— *Aljazeera, 12/24/17*

For those who like to stir the pot...you should know what you're cooking before you get burned!!!
— *Image Quote, Pinterest (Founded 2010)*

---

985 Trump's First Year Was Even Worse Than Feared
— *Washington Post, 12/25/17*

Every calamity is a spur and valuable hint.
— *Emerson, "Fate, The Conduct Of Life" (1860)*

---

986 2017 Marked a Year of Tearing Down Consumer Protections 'Brick by Brick'
— *Los Angeles Times, 12/31/17*

Little pig, little pig, let me come in. / Not by the hair on my chinny chin chin. / Then I'll huff, and I'll puff, and I'll blow your house down.
— *Joseph Jacobs, "The Three Little Pigs," English Fairy Tale (1890)*

987 Late Night Hosts on Trump and Bannon: 'The Rats Are Eating Their Young'

— *The Guardian, 1/4/18*

I could give a shit.

— *Popular Phrase, Urban Dictionary (Mar., 2007)*

988 Trump Has Declared War on California: State Defiant as White House Takes Aim

— *The Guardian, 1/5/18*

Oh, I'm sorry. Did my back hurt your knife?

— *Visual Bookmark (Pin), Tumblr.com (Founded 2007)*

989 Trump: Bannon 'Cried When He Got Fired,' 'Total Loser' Wolff's Book Is 'Really Boring and Untruthful'

— *The Washington Free Beacon, 1/5/18*

He was a frantic fool, hiding his bitter jests in blunt behavior.

— *Shakespeare, The Taming Of The Shrew" (1590 - 1592)*

990 'Learn His Name First': The Politicizing [by Trump] of Military Widows Is Touching a Nerve

— *The Washington Post, 1/7/18*

How low can you go?

— *American Proverb*

991 'He Made Promises That He Didn't Keep': Laid Off Factory Workers Feel Betrayed by Trump

— *Politico, 1/18/18*

Promises and pie-crust are made to be broken.

— Jonathan Swift, "Polite Conversation" (1738)

---

992 As Shutdown Looms, Trump Undercuts Chief of Staff and GOP on Key Issues

— Huffington Post, 1/18/18

There is no peace, saith the Lord, unto the wicked.

— Bible, Isaiah 48:22

CHAPTER 15

THE ACADEMY OF OUR LADY OF PERPETUAL GUILT

TOPICS:
PARTY LOYALTY
AND PARTY IDEOLOGY

The Academy of Our Lady of Perpetual Guilt

993 GOP to Bury House Resolution on Trump Conflict
— *Politico, 1/23/17*

Party loyalty lowers the greatest men to the petty level of the masses.
— *La Bruyere, "Characters" (1688)*

---

994 A Trump News Conference Filters Out the Tough Questions
— *New York Times, 2/13/17*

The only thing we have to fear is fear itself - nameless, unreasoning, unjustified terror which paralyzes needed efforts to convert retreat into advance.
— *Franklin D. Roosevelt, First Inaugural Address (Mar., 1933)*

---

995 Trump GOP Enablers Take a Page From the Fascist-Era Vatican
— *Washington Post, 2/28/17*

Party is the madness of many for the gain of a few.
— *Jonathan Swift, "Thoughts On Various Subjects" (1711)*

---

996 Every Single False Republican Criticism of Obamacare Applies Perfectly to Trumpcare
— *Reddit, 3/15/17*

You will always find some Eskimos ready to instruct the Congolese on how to cope with heat waves.
— *Stanislaw Lee, "Unkempt Thoughts" (1962)*

---

997 The Right Has Its Own Narrative About Trump's Crises
— *New York Times, 5/18/17*

Imagination, n. A warehouse of facts, with poet and liar in joint ownership.
— *Ambrose Bierce, "The Devil's Dictionary" (1881-1911)*

---

998 Trump's Scandals Stoke Fear for 2018 Midterms Among Republicans Nationwide
— *Washington Post, 5/19/17*

Grief has limits, whereas apprehension has none. For we grieve only for what we know has happened, but we fear all that possibly may happen.
— *Pliny The Younger, "Letters" (1st C. 97-110)*

---

999 The GOP-Trump Bargain May Be Unraveling
— *Wall Street Journal, 5/22/17 (Misconstrued)*

...and it becomes a falling out among thieves, and we are equal.
— *Richard Harding Davis, "The King's Jackal" (1898)*

1000 Brennan's Explosive Testimony Just Made It Harder for the GOP to Protect Trump
— *Washington Post, 5/23/17*

None of us can stand other people having the same faults as ourselves.
— *Oscar Wilde, "The Picture Of Dorian Gray" (1891)*

1001 GOP Leaders Play It Safe as Trump Scandals Grow
— *Politico, 5/25/17*

Our thought has been "Let every man look out for himself, let every generation look out for itself," while we reared giant machinery which made it impossible that any but those who stood at the levers of control should have a chance to look out for themselves.

— *Woodrow Wilson, First Inaugural Address (1913)*

1002 Boehner: Trump Has Been a Complete Disaster

— *Politico, 5/26/17*

What a miserable thing life is: you're living in clover, only the clover isn't good enough.

— *Bertolt Brecht, "Jungle Of Cities" (1924)*

1003 The U.S. Has a Homegrown Terrorist Problem - and It's Coming From the Right

— *Washington Post, 5/26/17*

You want to hate somebody if you can, just to keep your powers of discrimination bright, to save yourself from becoming a mere mush of good-nature.

— *Charles Dudley Warner, "Ninth Study," Backlog Studies (1873)*

1004 What's Less Popular Than Donald Trump? Pretty Much Everything Paul Ryan and Mitch McConnell Are Doing

— *New York Magazine, 5/29/17*

Politics, and the fate of mankind, are shaped by men without ideals and without greatness.

— *Albert Camus, "Notebooks 1935-1942" (1962)*

1005 GOP Attacked Obama as An 'Amateur,' But Trump Gets a Pass Because 'He's New to This'

— *Shareblue Media, 6/8/17*

The true hypocrite is the one who ceases to perceive his deception, the one who lies with sincerity.

— Andre Gide, "Journal Of The Counterfeiters," Second Notebook (1921)

———————

1006 What Will the GOP Do About Trump?

— USA Today, 6/13/17

That cowardice is incorrigible which the love of power cannot overcome.

— Charles Caleb Colton, "Lacon" (1825)

———————

1007 The GOP's Fantastically Anti-Democratic Quest to Kill Health Care in the Dark

— Washington Post, 6/14/17

The power of hiding ourselves from one another is mercifully given, for men are wild beasts, and would devour one another but for this protection.

— Henry Ward Beecher, "Proverbs From Plymouth Pulpit" (1887)

———————

1008 Beware of GOP Calls to 'Tamp Down' Criticism of Trump in Wake of Shooting

— Slate, 6/14/17

Policy sits above conscience.

— Shakespeare, "Timon of Athens" (1607)

———————

1009 House Republicans 'Can't Believe' Trump Called Their Health Bill 'Mean'

— Business Insider, 6/15/17

There is perhaps no phenomenon which contains so much destructive feeling as 'moral indignation,' which permits envy or hate to be acted out under the guise of virtue.

— Erich Fromm, "Man For Himself" (1947)

———

1010 Republicans Have Long Dreamed of Cutting Medicaid. Trumpcare Might Really Do It

— Washington Post, 6/16/17

There are far fewer ungrateful men than we believe, for there are far fewer generous men than we think.

— Saint-Evromond, "Sur Les Ingrats" (1705)

———

1011 'Trump Is Becoming Radioactive:' Why Republicans Won't Work for His Administration

— Washington Post, 6/17/17

Who will pity a snake charmer bitten by a serpent, or any who goes near wild beasts?

— "Apocrypha," Ecclesiasticus 12:13

———

1012 Sorry, Folks. The GOP's Devious Strategy for Ramming Trumpcare Through Is Working

— Washington Post, 6/20/17

It is more tolerable to be refused than deceived.

— Publilius Syrus, "Moral Sayings" (1st C. BCE)

———

1013 'Trump Is What Happens When a Political Party Abandons Ideas'

— Politico, 6/24/17

Our great democracies still tend to think that a stupid man is more likely to be honest than a clever man, and our politicians take advantage of this prejudice by pretending to be even more stupid than nature made them.

— *Bertrand Russell, "New Hopes For A Changing World" (1951)*

_____

1014 Hey Republicans, Nobody Is Buying Your Fake Outrage Over Trump's Sexist Tweets. You Endorsed This

— *Huffington Post, 6/30/17*

The conservatives nearly always tolerate the demagogue while he is destroying liberals.

— *Harry Golden, "Only In America" (1958)*

_____

1015 Republican Party Has 'Flat-Out' Lost Its Mind

— *Miami Herald, 7/5/17*

All political parties die at last of swallowing their own lies.

— *John Arbuthnot, Quoted In Richard Garnett's "Life of Emerson" (1887)*

_____

1016 A GOP Stunt Backfires, and Accidentally Reveals a Truth Republicans Want Hidden

— *Washington Post, 7/5/17*

The trouble with this country is that there are too many politicians who believe, with a conviction based on experience, that you can fool all of the people all of the time.

— *Franklin P. Adams, "Nods And Becks" (1944)*

_____

1017 GOP Health-Care Plan Is Reportedly the Most Unpopular Bill in Three Decades

— *TPM Livewire, 7/6/17*

Wickedness is always easier than virtue, for it takes the short cut to everything.
— Samuel Johnson, "Journal of A Tour To The Hebrides" (1773)

1018 Pew: Most Republicans View Higher Education as Bad for America
— The Daily Beast, 7/10/17

Those who think that all virtue is to be found in in their own party principles push matters to extremes; they do not consider that disproportion destroys a state.
— Aristotle, "Politics" (4th C. BCE)

1019 Republicans Block Effort to Remove Jared Kushner's Security Clearance
— Huffington Post, 7/13/17

Politics, in a sense, has always been a con game.
— Joe McGinniss, "The Selling Of The President 1968" (1969)

1020 If Republicans Love Their Country, When Will They Show It?
— New York Magazine, 7/14/17

The philosophical conservative is someone willing to pay the price of other people's suffering for his principles.
— L. Doctorow, "Jack London, Hemingway, And The Constitution" (1993)

1021 By a 2-to-1 Margin, Americans Prefer Obamacare to Republican Replacements
— Washington Post, 7/16/17

Politics is not the art of the possible. It consists of choosing between the disastrous and the unpalatable.
— John Kenneth Galbraith, "Ambassador's Journal" (1969)

1022 'Plan C' on Obamacare, Repeal Now and Replace Later, Has Collapsed
— *New York Times, 7/18/17*

O Human race? Born to ascend on wings, / Why do ye fall at such a little wind?
— *Dante, "Purgatorio," 12, The Divine Comedy (1308 - 1321)*

1023 Jeb Bush Calls Out GOP for Backing Trump Amid Russia Scandals
— *New York Post, 7/22/17*

Cowards never use their might, / But against such as will not fight.
— *Samuel Butler, "Hudibras" (1663)*

1024 Trump and Republicans Treat Their Voters Like Morons
— *Washington Post, 7/26/17*

One of the most fascinating aspects of politician watching is trying to determine to what extent any politician believes what he says.
— *Gore Vidal, "Reflections Upon A Sinking Ship" (1969)*

1025 Republicans Complain About White House Infighting
— *Politico, 7/28/17*

Great fleas have little fleas upon their backs to bite'em / And little fleas have lesser fleas and so on 'ad infinitum.'
— *Augustus De Morgan, "A Budget of Paradoxes" (1850)*

1026 House Republican Blames Trump for Healthcare Failure: He 'Never Laid Out a Plan'
— *The Hill, 7/29/17*

I don't care how unkind the things people say about me are / so long as they don't say them to my face.

— *Ogden Nash, "Versus From 1929 On" (1959)*

1027 Trump Deepens GOP Divide

— *Wall Street Journal, 7/31/17 (Misconstrued)*

After all, my erstwhile dear, / My no longer cherished, / Need we say it was no love, / Just because it perished?

— *Edna St. Vincent Millay, "The Harp-Weaver" (1923)*

1028 My Party Is in Denial About Donald Trump

— *Politico, 7/31/17*

A good scare is worth more to a man than good advice.

— *Edgar Watson Howe, "Country Town Sayings" (1911)*

1029 Republicans Ignore Trump's Obamacare Taunts

— *Politico, 7/31/17*

One of the misfortunes of our time is that in getting rid of false shame we have killed off so much real shame as well

— *Louis Kronenberger, "Company Manners" (1954)*

1030 Republicans Aren't Tired of Winning Under Trump. In Fact, More Think They're Losing

— *Washington Post, 8/5/17*

After a couple of days and after a hundred coffees and a thousand cigarettes and a million words and quite a few lunchtime beers we were able to agree that we didn't know nothing

— *James Herndon, "How To Survive In Your Native Land" (1971)*

1031 Report: GOP Insiders 'Privately Concede' Trump's Presidency Could End Early

— *Huffington Post, 8/8/17*

The drama is make-believe. It does not deal with truth but with effect.

— *W.Somerset Maugham, "The Summing Up" (1939)*

—————

1032 Trump: 'Can You Believe' McConnell Couldn't Repeal, Replace ObamaCare?

— *The Hill, 8/10/17*

There is so much good in the worst of us, / And so much bad in the best of us, / That it hardly behooves any of us / To talk about the rest of us.

— *Attributed To Edward Wallace Hoch (1849 - 1945)*

—————

1033 Republicans Must Impeach Trump to Save Country, Their Political Standing

— *Lexington Herald Leader, 8/18/17*

Popular men, / They must create strange monsters, and then quell them, / To make their arts seem something.

— *Ben Johnson, "Catiline His Conspiracy" (1611)*

—————

1034 Republicans Want To Stop Talking About White Supremacists So They Can Focus on Cutting Taxes for Rich People

— *Think Progress, 8/20/17*

There is no one so bound to his own face that he does not cherish the hope of presenting another to the world.

— *Antonio Machado, "Juan De Mairena" (1943)*

—————

1035 The New GOP Primary Litmus Test: Loyalty to Trump
— *Politico, 8/21/17*

Truth is a good dog; but beware of barking too close to the heels of an error lest you get your brains kicked out.
— *Samuel Taylor Coleridge, "Table Talk" (June, 1830)*

1036 Ryan Says 'There Are No Sides' to White Supremacy but Still Won't Call Out Trump
— *Huffington Post, 8/21/17*

Truth always lags last, limping along on the arm of Time.
— *Baltasar Gracian, "The Art Of Worldly Wisdom" (1647)*

1037 GOP on Eggshells as Trump Storms Into Phoenix
— *Politico, 8/22/17*

Whatsoe'er we perpetrate, / We do but row, we are steered by fate.
— *Samuel Butler, "Hudibras" (1663)*

1038 McConnell in Private, Doubts If Trump Can Save Presidency
— *New York Times, 8/22/17*

We should often feel ashamed of our best actions if the world could see all of the motives which produced them.
— *La Rochefoucauld, "Maxims" (1665)*

1039 Donald Trump Steps Up Feud With Mitch McConnell and Paul Ryan
— *Huffington Post, 8/24/17*

The laws of changeless justice bind / Oppressor and oppressed; / And, close as sin and suffering joined, / We march to Fate abreast.
— *John Greenleaf Whittier, "At Port Royal" (1862)*

1040 Bob Corker, Often An Ally of Trump, Is Latest Republican to Be Attacked by Him

— *New York Times, 8/25/17*

There are two modes of establishing our reputation; to be praised by honest men, and to be abused by rogues.
— *Charles Caleb Colton, "Lacon" (1825)*

———————

1041 Trump Divorces the GOP Congress

— *Wall Street Journal, 8/25/17 (Misconstrued)*

I have heard earnest American sociologists say that American children have a "right" to the divorce experience as an enriching element of an advanced civilization.
— *Anthony Burgess, "You've Had Your Time" (1990)*

———————

1042 Arpaio's Pardon Widens GOP Split

— *Wall Street Journal, 8/28/17 (Misconstrued)*

Quarrels would not last long if the fault was only on one side.
— *La Rochefoucauld, "Maxims" (1665)*

———————

1043 Republican Floats Measure to Kill Mueller Probe After 6 Months

— *Politico, 8/28/17*

There is a hundred things to single you out for promotion in party politics besides ability.
— *Will Rogers, "The Autobiography Of Will Rogers" (1949)*

———————

1044 Former Kushner Aide: Trump Told Jared Republicans Are Dumb

— *MSNBC, 8/31/17*

If he dropped a pun or a platitude into the conversation, it was just as if he had dropped a plate – there would be a moment of frozen silence, then the talk would go on as before.

— *Mary McCarthy, "The Company She Keeps" (1942)*

1045 Trump's Punt to Congress on DACA Threatens New GOP Rift

— *Politico, 9/4/17*

He who incites to strife is worse than he who takes part in it.

— *Aesop, "The Trumpeter Takes Prisoner," Fables (6th C. BCE)*

1046 GOP Leaders Prevent Votes to Ban Federal Spending at Trump Businesses

— *The Hill, 9/6/17*

There is no need of spurs when the horse is running away.

— *Publilius Syrus, "Moral Sayings" (1st C. BCE)*

1047 Trump Makes Deal on Debt, Irking GOP

— *Wall Street Journal, 9/7/17 (Misconstrued)*

Most people have seen worse things in private than they pretend to be shocked at in public.

— *Edgar Watson Howe, "Country Town Sayings" (1911)*

1048 Mercurial Trump Rattles Republican Party Ahead of Mid-Terms

— *New York Times, 9/8/17*

To take refuge with an inferior is to betray one's self.

— *Publilius Syrus, "Moral Sayings" (1st C. BCE)*

1049 Republicans in Congress Want to Roll Back Regulations on Credit Bureaus
— *NBC News, 9/11/17*

The Republicans believe the wagon train will not make it to the frontier unless some of our old, some of our young, and some of our weak are left behind by the side of the trail. We Democrats believe we can make it all the way with the whole family intact.
— *Mario Cuomo, Speech To The Democratic National Convention (1984)*

1050 Republicans Jumping Ship Amid Dissatisfaction With Trump Era
— *AP News, 9/12/17*

Achievement, n. The death of endeavor and the birth of disgust.
— *Ambrose Bierce, "The Devil's Dictionary" (1881)*

1051 GOP to Release Tax Overhaul as Trump Says Rich Won't Benefit
— *Wall Street Journal, 9/14/17 (Misconstrued)*

If some appalling disaster befalls, there's / Always a way for the rich.
— *Euripides, "Andromache" (426 BCE)*

1052 GOP Pushes Back on 'Dreamer's' Deal Sought by Trump, Democrats
— *New York Times, 9/15/17*

Politicians are the same all over. They promise to build a bridge even where there is no river.
— *Nikita Khrushchev, Comment To Reporters, Glen Cove, N.Y. (Oct., 1960)*

1053 Immigration's Sudden Emergence Scrambles Republican Agenda

— New York Times, 9/15/17

There are two infinities in this world: God up above, and down below, human baseness.

— Jules De Goncourt, Journal (Nov., 1862)

1054 Frustration With GOP Sent Trump to Cut Legislative Deals With Democrats

— Wall Street Journal, 9/16/17 (Misconstrued)

The desire for imaginary benefits often involves the loss of present blessings.

— Aesop, "The Kites and The Swans," Fables (6th C. BCE)

1055 As Usual, Republicans Won't Have Any Clue What Their New Obamacare Repeal Bill Does Before They Vote on It

— Slate, 9/18/17

An obstinacy's ne'er so stiff, / As when 'tis in a wrong belief.

— Samuel Butler, "Hudibras" (1663)

1056 GOP Will Spend Less Than 2 Minutes Debating a Bill to Decide Healthcare for 40 Million Kids

— Shareblue Media, 9/20/17

The man who regards his own life and that of his fellow-creatures as meaningless is not merely unfortunate but almost disqualified for life.

— Einstein, "The Meaning Of Life," The World As I See It (1934)

1057 The Tenuous Logic Behind Republicans' About Face on Debt

— Wall Street Journal, 9/28/17 (Misconstrued)

Pretending is a virtue. If you can't pretend, you can't be king.
— *Luigi Pirandello, "Liola" (1916)*

_____

1058 Republicans 'Death Tax Fixation' Tells You All You Need to Know About Their Concern for the Working Class
— *Los Angeles Times, 9/29/17*

Our political parties exist for no other reason than to win power; they are not ideological debating societies designed to present a particular political philosophy and to persuade voters to accept it.
— *Tom Wicker, "JFK And LBJ" (1968)*

_____

1059 The Only Thing the Republican Party Knows How to Do [Cut Taxes for the Rich]
— *Washington Post, 10/1/17*

God give you pardon from gratitude / and other mild forms of servitude.
— *Robert Creeley, "Song," For Love (1962)*

_____

1060 Republicans Were So Busy Trying to Repeal Obamacare, They Ran Out the [Health Care] Clock on 9 Million Kids
— *Esquire, 10/2/17*

If you trap the moment before it's ripe, / The tears of repentance you'll certainly wipe; / But if once you let the ripe moment go / You'll never wipe off the tears of woe.
— *William Blake, "The Marriage Ring" (1793)*

_____

1061 Republicans Won't Rule Out Tax Hikes for Some in the Middle Class
— *New York Times, 10/2/17*

In baiting a mouse-trap with cheese, always leave room for the mouse.
— *Saki, "The Infernal Parliament," The Square Egg (1924)*

1062 Republicans Trapped by Their [Tax Reform] Flimflam
— *New York Times, 10/3/17*

It is often easier to fight for principles than to live up to them.
— *Adlai Stevenson, Speech, New York City (Aug., 1952)*

1063 The Republican's Guide to Presidential Etiquette
— *New York Times, 10/8/17*

It is disgusting to pick your teeth; what is vulgar is to use a gold toothpick.
— *Louis Kronenberger, "The Cart And The Horse" (1908)*

1064 Other Republicans Nod (Silently) as Corker Blasts Trump
— *New York Times, 10/9/17*

The most mortifying infirmity in human nature, to feel in ourselves, or to contemplate in another, is, perhaps, cowardice.
— *Charles Lamb, "Stage Illusion," Last Essays Of Elia (1833)*

1065 Donald Trump, the President Without a Party
— *Wall Street Journal. 10/9/17 (Misconstrued)*

Nothing impresses the mind with a deeper feeling of loneliness than to tread the silent and deserted scene of former throng and pageant.
— *Washington Irving, "The Sketch Book Of Geoffrey Crayon, Gent. " (1819)*

1066 The Bizarre Situation Where Only Retiring Republicans Will Talk About Trump's Fitness for Office
— *Vox, 10/10/17*

He that will not sail till all dangers are over must never put to sea.

— *Thomas Fuller, M. D. "Gnomologia" (1732)*

1067 Republicans Split Over Trump's Move to End Health Subsidies

— *Wall Street Journal, 10/13/17 (Misconstrued)*

Like sheep being led to slaughter.

— *Bible, (Derived From) Isaiah 53:7*

1068 Trump, McConnell Set for Tense Talks at Monday Meeting

— *News Source, 10/15/17*

The Greater Fool Theory states that the price of an object is determined not by its intrinsic value, but rather by irrational beliefs and expectations of market participants.

— *Business Dictionary, "Greater Fool Theory" (2017)*

1069 Can Trump Forge a 'Workable Truce' Between the GOP's Wings?

— *News Source, 10/16/17*

A mighty pain to love it is, / And 'tis a pain that pain to miss; / But of all pains, the greatest pain / It is to love, but to love in vain.

— *Abraham Cowley, "Gold," From Anacreon (1656)*

1070 The G.O.P. Is No Party for Honest Men

— *New York Times, 10/16/17*

I am well acquainted with your manner of wrenching the true cause the false way.

— *Shakespeare, "Henry IV, Part 2" (1596 - 1599)*

1071 Republican's Desire to Retire Seen as Sign of Growing Frustration in Washington

— *The Hill, 10/19/17*

Get out while the getting's good.

— *McGraw-Hill's Dictionary Of American Slang/Colloquial Expressions (2006)*

1072 The Hill: GOP Senate Hopefuls Reluctant to Back McConnell as Leader

— *News Source, 10/22/17*

It is the peculiarity of the bore that he is the last person to find himself out.

— *Oliver Wendell Holmes, Sr., "Over The Teacups" (1891)*

1073 The GOP Tried Trump-Style Tax Cuts in Kansas. What a Mess [Revenues Plummeted]

— *NBC, 10/22/17*

Who can deny that all men are violent lovers of truth, when we see them so positive in their errors, which they will maintain out of their zeal to truth, although they contradict themselves every day of their lives.

— *Jonathan Swift, "Thoughts On Various Subjects" (1711)*

1074 The GOP's Big Lie [Trickle-Down Economics] About Tax Cuts

— *Huffington Post, 10/23/17*

I would have men of such constancy put to sea, that their business might be everything, and their intent everywhere, for that's it that always makes a good voyage of nothing.

— *Shakespeare, " Twelfth Night" (1601 - 1602)*

1075 Rift Widens Within GOP in Battle for Control of Party
— *Wall Street Journal, 10/24/17 (Misconstrued)*

To fight is a radical instinct; if men have nothing else to fight over they will fight over words, fancies, or women, or they will fight because they dislike each other's looks, or because they have met walking in the opposite directions.
— *George Santayana, "The Life Of Reason: Reason In Society" (1905)*

———————

1076 NY Times: As G.O.P. Bends Toward Trump, Critics Either Give In or Give Up
— *News Source, 10/27/17*

Cowards die many times before their deaths; / The valiant never taste of death but once.
— *Shakespeare, "Julius Caesar" (1599)*

———————

1077 Senate Republicans in No Rush to Shield Mueller From Trump
— *Politico, 10/31/17*

Expedients are for the hour, but principles are for the ages.
— *Henry Ward Beecher, "Proverbs From Plymouth Pulpit" (1887)*

———————

1078 Poll Shows Mitch McConnell, Senate Allies' Approval Ratings in Free Fall
— *News Source, 11/1/17*

For 'tis the sport to have the enginer hoist with his own petard, and't shall go hard.
— *Shakespeare, "Hamlet" (1601)*

———————

1079 House Republican: My Donors Told Me to Pass the Tax Bill 'Or Don't Ever Call Me Again'

— *Vox, 11/7/17*

Greed's worst point is its ingratitude.

— *Seneca, Letters To Lucilius (1st C. CE)*

———————

1080 GOP Tax Plan Would Slam California Housing Market

— *Wall Street Journal, 11/8/17 (Misconstrued)*

Revenge is a luscious fruit which you must leave to ripen.

— *Emile Gaboriau, "File 113," (1867)*

———————

1081 Republicans, Under Pressure From Election Losses, Struggle With Tax Reform

— *News Source, 11/10/17*

He that promises too much means nothing.

— *Thomas Fuller, M. D., "Gnomologia" (1732)*

———————

1082 McConnell to NYT: I 'Misspoke' on Tax Increase for Middle Class in Senate Tax Plan

— *CNN, 11/12/17*

Well said! That was laid on with a trowel.

— *Shakespeare, "As You Like It" (1599)*

———————

1083 The GOP Has Done the Impossible: Made Tax Cuts Unpopular

— *New York Magazine, 11/12/17*

It is far pleasanter to injure and afterwards beg forgiveness than to be injured and grant forgiveness. He who does the former gives evidence of power and afterwards of kindness of character.

— *Nietzsche, "Human, All Too Human" (1878)*

1084 Senate GOP Adds Health-Care Twist to Tax Overhaul Plan
— *Wall Street Journal, 11/15/17 (Misconstrued)*

O, give it up, old chap! Sleep it off!
— *James Joyce, "A Portrait Of The Artist As A Young Man" (1916)*

1085 GOP Senator Loses His Cool When Confronted About Tax Cuts for the Rich
— *Huffington Post, 11/17/18*

Don't confuse me with the facts. I've made up mind.
— *Roy S. Durstine, "Advertising And Selling" (1945)*

1086 Jeff Flake Caught on Live Mic Saying GOP is 'Toast' Under Leadershp of Moore, Trump
— *News Source, 11/18/17*

Hope springs eternal in the human breast: / Man never is, but always to be blest.
— *Alexander Pope, "An Essay On Man" (1733)*

1087 Texas 'Nightmare': Republicans Rage at Trump for 'Wholly Inadequate' Harvey Relief
— *Shareblue Media, 11/18/17*

It is awfully easy to be hard-boiled about everything in the daytime, but at night it is another thing.
— *Ernest Hemingway, "The Sun Also Rises" (1926)*

1088 GOP Plan Will Ultimately Raise Taxes on 50% of Americans, Nonpartisan Assessment Says
— *CNBC, 11/20/17*

In practice, such trifles as contradictions in principal are easily set aside; the faculty of ignoring them makes the practical man.

— Henry Adams, "The Education Of Henry Adams" (1907)

1089 [GOP] House Tax Bill Is Littered With Tax Loopholes for Wall Street's Wealthiest

— Bloomberg, 11/21/17

Familiarity breeds contentment.

— George Ade, "The Uplift That Moved Sideways," Hand-Made Fables (1920)

1090 Roy Moore Transforms GOP to 'Grand Old Pedophiles'

— Observer, 11/22/17

Some men wish evil and accomplish it / But most men, when they work in that machine, / Just let it happen somewhere in the wheels. / The fault is no decisive, villainous knife / But the dull saw that is the routine mind.

— Stephen Vincent Benet, ""John Brown's Body" (1928)

1091 Senate GOP Tax Bill Would Cost $1.4 Trillion, Hit Poor and Middle Class Harder Than Estimated, CBO [Congressional Budget Office] Says

— The Week, 11/27/17

Forgive us for pretending to care for the poor, when we do not like poor people and do not want them in our homes.

— United Presbyterian Church, "Litany For Holy Communion" (1968)

1092 [GOP] Senators Scramble to Advance Tax Bill That Increasingly Rewards Wealthy

— New York Times, 11/27/17

Shill: One who publicly promotes another's cause, especially in an extravagant or misleading way.

— *Slang, YourDictionary.com (2017)*

1093 Republicans Are Rejecting the Official [Congress' Joint Committee on Taxation] Analysis of Their Tax Bill's Cost

— *Vox, 12/1/17*

To find oneself jilted is a blow to one's pride. One must do one's best to forget it and if one doesn't succeed, at least one must pretend to.

— *Moliere, "Tartuffe" (1664)*

1094 Senate GOP Meeting This Morning

— *Reddit, 12/1/17*

Before we discuss raising taxes on the poor & middle class, adding $1 trillion to the deficit, taking health insurance away from 13 million, raising premiums by 10%, defending treason and swearing in a pedophile, let's begin with a prayer.

— *Ziegler Cartoon, "Political Humor," Reddit, [Submitted By Jefuchs] (2017)*

1095 'The Hypocrisy Is Astounding': This Tax Bill Shows the GOP's Debt Concerns Were Pure Fraud

— *Vox, 12/2/17*

Churchill:" Madam, would you sleep with me for five million pounds?" Socialite: "My goodness, Mr. Churchill…Well, I suppose… we would have to discuss terms, of course…" Churchill: "Would you sleep with me for five pounds?" Socialite: "Mr. Churchill, what kind of woman do you think I am?!" Churchill: "Madam, we've already established that. Now we are haggling about the price."

— *Winston Churchill, Joke, Wikiquote (2003)*

1096 U.S. Tax Reforms Expose a Republican Party Held Hostage by a Few Oligarchs
— *The Globe And Mail, 12/3/17*

Wealth is not without its advantages and the case to the contrary, although it has often been made, has never proved wildly persuasive.
— *John Kenneth Galbraith, "The Affluent Society" (1958)*

1097 Poll: Women Voters Favor Dems Over GOP by 20 Points
— *The Hill, 12/5/17*

Women and elephants never forget an injury.
— *Saki, "Reginald On Besetting Sins," Reginald (1904)*

1098 Trump Crony Admits Republican Tax Plan Is an Elaborate Middle Finger to Liberals
— *Vanity Fair, 12/5/17*

Revenge, the sweetest morsel to the mouth that ever was cooked in hell.
— *Walter Scott, Scottish Novelist, Playwright and Poet (1771 - 1832)*

1099 Senate Republicans Made a $289 Billion Mistake in the Handwritten Tax Bill They Passed at 2 A.M. Go Figure.
— *Slate, 12/6/17*

I do not mind lying, but I hate inaccuracy.
— *Samuel Butler, "Truth And Convenience," Note-Books (1912)*

1100 Republicans Turn to Industry For Advice on How to Reorganize Interior Department
— *Huffington Post, 12/7/17*

Everything I own is for sale except my wife and my hound dog, and they're for rent.
— Doc McGuire, Hunting Guide And Rotary Wing Instructor (1947 - 2013)

1101 Donald Trump Has Made Roy Moore the Face of the Republican Party
— The Nation, 12/8/17

There are mystically in our faces characters which carry in them the motto of our souls, wherein he that cannot read A, B, C may read our natures.
— Sir Thomas Browne, "Religio Medici" (1642)

1102 As Democrats Add Senate Seat, GOP Left to Bicker Over What Happened in Alabama
— Washington Post, 12/13/17

There is nothing like tasting the grit of fear for rediscovering that the umbilical cord [to Trump] is made of piano wire.
— Moss Hart, "Act One" (1959)

1103 Republicans Despise the Working Class
— New York Times, 12/14/17

Enmity is catching.
— Muriel Spark, "Momento Mori" (1959)

1104 Democrats See Plot to Fire Mueller in Escalating GOP Attacks
— Politico, 12/17/17

The rules I go by are: keep your villains bad, and keep the plot grounded and real. If you keep those stakes, the comedy will bounce off that and work.

— *Peter Segal, Film Director and Screenwriter, BrainyQuotes (1991+)*

1105 [GOP] Tax Bill Lets Trump and Republicans Feather Their Own Nest

— *New York Times, 12/18/17*

The avarice of the miser may be termed the grand sepulcher of all his other passions, as they successively decay.

— *Charles Caleb Colton, "Lacon" (1825)*

1106 White House Finally Admits Trump Will Benefit From Tax Bill

— *MSNBC, 12/21/17*

If you tell the truth you don't have to remember anything.

— *Mark Twain, "Notebook" (1935)*

1107 The [GOP] Tax Bill Should've Been Called The Inequality Exacerbation Act

— *The Hill, 12/22/17*

Experience demands that man is the only animal which devours his own kind, for I can apply no milder term to the general prey of the rich on the poor.

— *Thomas Jefferson To Edward Carrington (Jan., 1787)*

1108 GOP's New Hunt for 'Crooked Hillary': A Last Ditch Gamble to Save Trump?

— *Salon, 12/22/17*

While you're saving your face, you're losing your ass.

— *Lyndon B. Johnson, U.S. President (1963 - 1973)*

1109 Republicans Quietly Warn Trump: Don't Fire Mueller

— *Mother Jones, 12/23/17*

We did not tell him to cease and desist. It was a suggestion.

— *Ian Capstick, QuoteHD, Founder Of MediaStyle (2008)*

1110 Departing GOP Lawmakers Warn That Their Party Could Lose Majorities in 2018

— *Washington Post, 12/24/17*

My sympathy for you is rightfully thin.

— *Michael J. Weinstock, "Aphorisms" (1975)*

1111 'Never Trump' Will Be The Only [GOP] Faction Still Standing When He Is Gone

— *The Atlantic, 12/27/17*

Posterity is just.

— *Jean-Jacques Rousseau, "Grand Tour: Germany And Switzerland" (1928)*

1112 Republican Attacks on Mueller and F.B.I. Open New Rift in G.O.P.

— *New York Times, 12/30/17*

Magnanimity in politics is not seldom the truest wisdom; and a great empire and little minds go ill together.

— *Edmund Burke, "On Conciliation With The American Colonies" (Mar., 1775)*

1113 Iowa Starts to Sour on Trump and His Party

— *Washington Post, 1/1/18*

It is a flaw / In happiness, to see beyond our bourn, - / It forces us in summer skies to mourn, / It spoils the singing of the nightingale.
— *Keats, "Epistle To John Hamilton Reynolds" (1818)*

1114 Republicans Have 4 Convicted Criminals Running for Congress in 2018
— *Huffington Post, 1/10/18*

Every portrait that is painted with feeling is a portrait of the artist, not of the sitter.
— *Oscar Wilde, "The Picture Of Dorian Gray" (1868)*

1115 Few Republicans Acknowledged Trump's 'Shithole' Slur
— *Huffington Post, 1/12/18*

Sticks and stones are hard on bones. / Aimed with angry art, / Words can sting like anything. / But silence breaks the heart.
— *Phyllis McGinley, "The Love Letters Of Phyllis McGinley" (1954)*

1116 I'm a Republican. What on Earth Is Wrong With My Party?
— *Time, 1/14/18*

There are only two great currents in the history of mankind; the baseness which makes conservatives and the envy which makes revolutionaries.
— *Jules De Concourt, "Journal" (July, 1867)*

1117 Congressional Republicans Think Donald Trump's Sloth and Ignorance Is a Feature, Not a Bug. A Weak, Easy-To-Manipulate President Is What They Want
— *Vox, 1/16/18*

Custom adapts to expediency.
— *Tacitus, "Annals" (115 CE)*

1118 The Daily 202: Unexpected Defeat in Rural Wisconsin Special Election Sets Off Alarm Bells for Republicans

— *Washington Post, 1/17/18*

I suddenly remember something I've been told about fear. That amid a hail of machine gun fire you notice the existence of your skin.

— *Marguerite Duras, "The War: A Memoir" (1986)*

CHAPTER 16

THE UNIVERSITY OF THE COLLECTIVE UNCONSCIOUS AT LINZ

TOPICS:
HONESTY AND SINCERITY

The University of the Collective Unconscious at Linz

1119 White House Pushes 'Alternative Facts.' Here Are the Real Ones

— *New York Times, 1/22/17*

Man can certainly keep on lying (and does so), but he cannot make truth falsehood.

— *Karl Barth, Quoted In His Obituary, The New York Times (1968)*

1120 Trump Repeats Lie About Popular Vote in Meeting With Lawmakers

— *New York Times, 1/23/17*

You can't make the Duchess of Windsor into Rebecca of Sunnybrook Farm. The facts of life are very stubborn things.

— *Cleveland Armory, News Reports (1955)*

1121 Trump Won't Back Down From His Voting Fraud Lie. Here Are the Facts

— *New York Times, 1/24/17*

A fact is like a sack which won't stand up when it is empty. In order that it may stand up, one has to put into it the reason and sentiment which have caused it to exist.

— *Luigi Pirandello, "Six Characters In Search Of An Author" (1921)*

1122 Press Secretary Affirms That Trump Believes Lie of Millions of Illegal Voters

— *New York Times, 1/24/17*

There is no such flatterer as is a man's self.
— *Francis Bacon, "Of Friendship," Essays (1625)*

1123 Trump Falsely Claims That Obamacare Covers 'Very Few People'
— *Politico, 2/24/17*

What is a cynic? A man who knows the price of everything, and the value of nothing.
— *Oscar Wilde, "Lady Windermere's Fan" (1892)*

1124 Missing: Donald Trump's Infrastructure Plan
— *New York Times, 2/27/17*

Don't use that foreign word "ideals." We have that excellent native word "lies."
— *Henrik Ibsen, "The Wild Duck" (1884)*

1125 Trump Accuses Obama of Wiretapping Trump Tower
— *Reddit, 3/4/17*

Oh the nerves the nerves; the mysteries of this machine called man! Oh the little that unhinges it: poor creatures that we are!
— *Charles Dickens, "Third Quarter," The Crimes (1844)*

1126 Out of Control? Or Is Trump's Tweeting Designed to Distract?
— *The Guardian, 3/5/17*

The fraud delights my soul, and if he is big and clever and conceals his fraudulence for years, I am all the more impressed and entertained by his achievement.
— *William Saroyan, "The Actor In The Street" (1979)*

1127 19 Times Trump Called the Jobs Numbers 'Fake' Before They Made Him Look Good.

— *Reddit, 3/11/17*

Until the Donkey tried to clear / The Fence, he thought himself a Deer.

— *Arthur Guiterman, "A Poet's Proverbs" (1924)*

1128 Trump's 'Wiretap' Claims Are a Return to Old Birther Instincts

— *Huffington Post, 3/17/17*

Not on the stage alone, in the world also, a man's real character comes out best in his asides.

— *Alexander Smith, "William Dunbar," Dreamthorp (1863)*

1129 Keystone XL: The Final Leg and the Myth of Trump's Job Promises

— *The Guardian, 5/4/17*

The great enemy of the truth is very often not the lie - deliberate, contrived and dishonest - but the myth - persistent, persuasive and unrealistic.

— *John F. Kennedy, Commencement Address, Yale University ((1962)*

1130 This Bill Is Not the 'Insurance for Everybody' Trump Promised

— *Washington Post, 5/5/17*

Dishonesty is the raw material not of quacks only, but also in great part of dupes.

— *Thomas Carlyle, "Count Cagliostro" (1833)*

1131 Here's Even More Evidence Trump Is Lying About Massive Voter Fraud

— *Huffington Post, 5/7/17*

The history of our race, and each individual's experience, are sown thick with evidence that a truth is not hard to kill and that a lie told well is immortal.

— *Mark Twain, "Advice To Youth" (1923)*

1132 Why Trump Can't Do What He Said He'd Do

— *Washington Post, 5/8/17*

You must stir it and stump it, / And blow your own trumpet, / Or trust me you haven't a chance.

— *W. S. Gilbert, "Ruddigore" (1887)*

1133 All of Trump's Campaign Statements Just Vanished From His Website. So Let's Remember Them

— *Washington Post, 5/10/17*

Hypocrisy in anything whatever may deceive the cleverest and most penetrating man, but the least wide-awake of children recognize it, and are revolted by it, however ingeniously it may be disguised.

— *Leo Tolstoy, "Anna Karenina" (1873)*

1134 Trump Is Lying Again

— *New York Times, 5/10/17*

Man is practiced in disguise; / He cheats the most discerning eyes.

— *John Gay, "Introduction To Fables" (1727-38)*

1135 Washington Post Reporter: White House Playing Word Games

— *CNN, 5/16/17*

The most common sort of lie is the one uttered to one's self.
— *Nietzsche, "The Antichrist" (1888)*

_____

1136 Bernie Sanders Responds to Comey Testimony: 'Donald Trump Is a Blatant Liar'
— *Independent, 6/8/17*

The best liar is he who makes the smallest amount of lying go the longest way.
— *Samuel Butler, "Truth And Convenience," Note-Books (1903)*

_____

1137 The New York Times Used a Full Page to Print All of Trump's Lies Since Taking Office
— *Business Insider, 6/25/17*

A liar should have a good memory.
— *Quintilian, "Institutio Oratoria" (95 CE)*

_____

1138 Time Magazine Asks President to Remove Fake [Time] Covers From Display at [His] Golf Clubs
— *The Guardian, 6/28/17*

Any fool can tell the truth, but it requires a man of some sense to know how to tell a lie well.
— *Samuel Butler, "The Way Of All Flesh" (1903)*

_____

1139 CNN Taunts Trump on July 4 With Abraham Lincoln Quote on Facts
— *Independent, 7/4/17*

America will never be destroyed from the outside. If we falter and lose our freedoms, it will be because we destroyed ourselves.
— *Abraham Lincoln, Quote (1809-65)*

_____

1140 It's Not Just the Russia Scandal: Pence Lies About Health Care, Too

— *MSNBC, 7/17/17*

It always is the best policy to speak the truth, unless of course you are an exceptionally good liar.

— *Jerome K. Jerome, "The Idler" (1892)*

1141 Trump Has Made 836 False Or Misleading Claims Since January

— *Washington Post, 7/20/17*

All cruel people describe themselves as paragons of frankness.

— *Tennessee Williams, "The Milk Train Doesn't Stop Here Anymore" (1963)*

1142 Trump Personally Crafted Son's Misleading Account of Russia Meeting – Report

— *The Guardian, 7/31/17*

A family is but too often a commonwealth of malignants.

— *Alexander Pope, "Thoughts On Various Subjects" (1717)*

1143 Trump to Members Of His New Jersey Golf Club: 'The White House Is a Real Dump'

— *Business Insider, 8/1/17*

To make wail and lament for one's ill fortune when one will win a tear from the audience is well worth while.

— *Aeschylus, "Prometheus Bound" (478 BCE)*

1144 Trump Called New Hampshire a 'Drug Infested Den,' Drawing the Ire of Politicians

— *New York Times, 8/3/17*

The pettiness of a mind can be measured by the pettiness of its adoration or its blasphemy.

— *Andre Gide, Journals (1902)*

1145 Many Politicians Lie. But Trump Has Elevated the Art of Fabrication

— *New York Times, 8/7/17*

Words, as is well known, are the great foes of reality.

— *Joseph Conrad, Prologue To Part I, "Under Western Eyes" (1911)*

1146 On Radical Islam, Trump Has Lost His Focus

— *Wall Street Journal, 8/11/17 (Misconstrued)*

A man is usually more careful of his money than he is of his principles.

— *Edgar Watson Howe, "Ventures In Common Sense" (1919)*

1147 Trump Is Totally Wrong, Anti-Racist Protestors Actually Did Have Permits

— *LawNewz, 8/16/17*

Pure truth, like pure gold, has been found unfit for circulation, because men have discovered that it is far more convenient to adulterate the truth than to refine themselves.

— *Charles Caleb Colton, "Lacon" (1825)*

1148 Trump's Lies About James Comey Keep Unraveling

— *Foreign Policy, 8/19/17*

He will lie, sir, with such volubility that you would think truth were a fool.

— *Shakespeare, "All's Well That Ends Well" (1604 – 1605)*

1149 President Trump's List of False and Misleading Claims Tops 1000

— *Washington Post, 8/22/17*

Character is tested by true sentiments more than by conduct. A man is seldom better than his word.

— *Lord Acton, Postscript, Letter To Mandell Creighton (April, 1887)*

1150 Memo to Trump: There Is No Looming 'Retirement Crisis'

— *Wall Street Journal, 8/25/17 (Misconstrued)*

What hempen homespuns have we swaggering here?

— *Shakespeare, "A Midsummer's Night's Dream" (1595 - 1596)*

1151 President Trump Retweets False Facts About Obama Pardons

— *Daily News, 8/28/17*

Authorship of any sort is a fantastic indulgence of the ego.

— *John Kenneth Galbraith, "The Affluent Society" (1958)*

1152 Jeff Sessions' Rationale for Ending DACA Is a Gigantic Bucket of Horseshit

— *GQ, 9/5/17*

Man has such a predilection for systems and abstract deductions that he is ready to distort the truth intentionally; he is ready to deny the evidence of his senses only to justify his logic.

— *Dostoyevsky, "Notes From Underground" (1864)*

1153 Trump Continues to Falsely Claim America Is 'The Highest Taxed Nation in the World'

— *The Week, 9/6/17*

One of the most striking differences between a cat and a lie is that a cat has only nine lives.

— *Mark Twain, "Pudd'nhead Wilson's Calendar," Pudd'nhead Wilson (1894)*

———

1154 Jimmy Carter to Trump: 'Keep the Peace…Tell the Truth'

— *Washington Post, 9/12/17*

'Tis not enough to help the feeble [truth] up, / But to support him after.

— *Shakespeare, "Timon of Athens" (1607)*

———

1155 Mr. Trump Squanders the World's Trust

— *New York Times, 9/23/17*

We are all jellyfish, too pitiful and too afraid of being disliked to be honest.

— *May Sarton, "The House By The Sea: A Journal" (1977)*

———

1156 Trump Accused of Burying Research Showing Trickle-Down Tax Cuts Just 'Snake Oil' Scam

— *Common Dreams, 9/29/17*

Customary use of artifice is the sign of a small mind, and it almost always happens that he who uses it to cover one spot uncovers himself in another.

— *La Rochefoucauld, "Maxims" (1665)*

———

1157 Sad! President Trump Falsely Claims His Endorsement Helped Luther Strange at Alabama Polls

— *News Source, 9/30/17*

The unluckiest insolvent in the world is the man whose expenditure of speech is too great for his income of ideas.

— *Christopher Morley, "Inward, Ho!" (1923)*

1158 Lies, Lies, Lies, Lies, Lies, Lies, Lies, Lies, Lies, Lies
— *New York Times, 10/14/17*

Heaven truly knows, that thou art false as hell!
— *Shakespeare, "Othello" (1603)*

1159 Trump Falsely Claims Obama Didn't Contact Families of Fallen Troops
— *New York Times, 10/16/17*

How many actions most ridiculous hast thou been drawn to by thy fantasy?
— *Shakespeare, "As You Like It" (1599)*

1160 9 Things Donald Trump Didn't Tell the Truth About on Monday
— *CNN, 10/17/17*

Come, you are a tedious fool. To the purpose.
— *Shakespeare, "Measure For Measure" (1603 - 1604)*

1161 Trump Says He Called 'Every Family' of Soldiers Who Died. But Some Never Heard From Him
— *Time, 10/18/17*

A falsehood is, in one sense, a dead thing; but too often it moves about, galvanized by self-will, and pushes the living out of their seats.
— *Samuel Taylor Coleridge, "Aids To Reflection" (1825)*

1162 Sen. Corker: President Trump is 'Utterly Untruthful'
— *News Source, 10/24/17*

He's a most notable coward, an infinite and endless liar, an hourly promise-breaker, the owner of no one good quality.
— Shakespeare, "All's Well That Ends Well" (1604 - 1605)

1163 It's Not Just Trump, It's the Whole GOP That Calls 'Fake Things True and True Things Fake'
— Los Angeles Times, 10/27/17

A "penchant for telling the truth" can cripple a candidate's chances faster than being caught in flagrante dilecto with the governor's wife.
— Sydney J. Harris, "Clearing The Ground" (1986)

1164 Trump Falsely Tweets That Manafort Indictment Predates Campaign
— Bloomberg, 10/30/17

A liar goes in fine clothes, / A liar goes in rags. / A liar is a liar, clothes or no clothes.
— Carl Sandberg, "The Liars, " Complete Poems (1950)

1165 With Little Credibility and a New Crisis, Trump Reverts to Form With Fresh Untruths
— Huffington Post, 10/30/17

This above all: to thine own self be true, and it must follow, as the night the day, thou canst not then be false to any man.
— Shakespeare, "Hamlet" (1601)

1166 Carrier Plans More Layoffs at Plant Trump Vowed to Protect: Report
— The Hill, 11/9/17

The vow that binds too strictly snaps itself.

— Lord Tennyson, "The Last Tournament," Idylls Of The King (1871)

———————

1167 Trump Organization Worth One Tenth of Value Previously Reported

— Independent, 11/16/17

The smaller the mind the greater the conceit.

— Aesop, "The Gnat And The Bull," Fables (6th C. BCE)

———————

1168 In Transgender Ruling, Another Judge Finds Trump Credibility Gap [Regarding Professed Motives]

— Washington Post, 11/22/17

I'm sorry, what language are you speaking? It sounds like bullshit.

— Sarcasm Quotes And Sayings, #59, iEnglish Status.com

———————

1169 Trump Says He Passed on Being Time's 'Person of the Year' [Time Says He's Incorrect]

— News Source, 11/24/17

Weak people cannot be sincere.

— La Rochefoucauld, "Maxims" (1665)

———————

1170 [Campaign] 'Chaos' Is at the Heart of the Trump Camp's [Russian Investigation] Defense. But It Can Cut Both Ways

— NPR, 11/30/17

One unable to dance blames the unevenness of the floor.

— Malay Proverb

———————

1171 Trump Says Never Asked Comey to Stop Investigating Flynn

— Reuters. 12/3/17

Words, like, Nature, half reveal / And half conceal the Soul within.
— Lord Tennyson, "In Memorium A. H. H." (1850)

1172 Billy Bush: 'Of Course' It's Trump's Voice On 'Access Hollywood' Tape
— NPR, 12/4/17

What is actual is actual only for one time / And one place.
— T.S. Eliot, "Ash Wednesday" (1930)

1173 I Study Liars. I've Never Seen One Like President Trump
— Washington Post, 12/8/17

Lies, my dear boy can easily be recognized. There are two kinds of them: those with short legs and those with long noses. Your kind have long noses.
— Carlo Collidi, "The Adventures Of Pinocchio" (1880)

1174 Where the F* Is Trump's Infrastructure Plan?**
— Vice, 12/8/17

I can smell bullshit from a mile away, but it's so much harder to detect when it's around you all day.
— Dane Cook, Comedian, AZ Quotes (2012)

1175 Trump Thinks People Should Be Fired for Misrepresenting the Truth on Twitter
— New York Magazine, 12/9/17

The fact that human conscience remains partially infantile throughout life is the core of human tragedy.
— Erik. H. Erikson, "Childhood And Society" (1950)

1176 The Myth of Trump's Economic Populism, As Proven by the Tax Bill

— *NPR, 12/11/17*

There's a sucker born every minute.

— *Michael Cassius McDonald, Gambling House Operator (Late 1860s)*

1177 Trump's Voter Fraud Panel Has Gone Dark. Members Don't Know Why

— *NBC, 12/18/18*

Nothing more unqualifies a man to act with prudence than a misfortune [Voter Fraud Panel] that is attended by shame and guilt.

— *Jonathan Swift, "Thoughts On Various Subjects" (1711)*

1178 Donald Trump Accidently Admits Republican Tax Bill Was Deceptively Sold as Boost to the Middle Class

— *Independent, 12/20/17*

It is amazing what one ray of sunshine can do for a man!

— *Fyodor Dostoevsky, "The Insulted And Injured" (1861)*

1179 Trump's Credibility Is So Low That Americans Don't Believe They're Getting a Tax Cut

— *Huffington Post, 12/24/17*

Now you see it, now you don't.

— *Roland Kibbee, "Now You See It Now You Don't," Dialogue (1968)*

1180 Trump Boasts He's Signed More Laws Than Any President Since Truman. He's Actually Signed the Least

— *Slate, 12/27/17*

He misses not much. No; he doth but mistake the truth totally.

— *Shakespeare, "The Tempest" (1610 - 1611)*

1181 Trump Finally Gets the Honor He Deserves [Lie of the Year]

— *CNN, 12/28/17*

My tongue slipped over of my eye tooth and I couldn't see what I was saying.

— *Len Dudeck, Play Title (2005)*

1182 Trump Has Made, 1,950 False Claims in 347 Days

— *Washington Post, 1/2/18*

I'm forever blowing bubbles, / Pretty bubbles in the air, / They fly so high, nearly reach the sky, / Then like my dreams they fade and die...

— *Jaan Kenbrovin, "I'm Forever Blowing Bubbles" Lyrics (1919)*

1183 More Jobs Were Created in 2016 Than in 2017. Most Americans Don't Realize That

— *Huffington Post, 1/8/18*

Such is the irresistable nature of truth that all it asks, and all it wants, is the liberty of appearing.

— *Thomas Paine, "The Rights Of Man" (1791)*

CHAPTER 17

CALIFORNIA AGRICULTURAL INSTITUTE OF DRUPES AND KERNELS

TOPICS:
CONSERVATION AND REMEDIATION

California Agricultural Institute of Drupes and Kernels

1184 President Trump Takes Aim at the Environment
— *New York Times, 2/23/17*

A man will do more for his stubbornness than for his religion or his country.
— *Edgar Watson Howe, "Country Town Sayings" (1911)*

1185 Administration Seeks Deep Cuts for NOAA, a Leading Climate Science Agency
— *Washington Post, 3/4/17*

If there is anything more dangerous to the life of the mind than having no independent commitment to ideas, it is having an excess of commitment to some special and constricting idea.
— *Richard Hofstadter, "Anti-Intellectualism In American Life" (1963)*

1186 Donald Trump Is About to Undo Obama's Legacy on Climate Change
— *Huffington Post, 3/28/17*

Now Hatred is by far the longest pleasure; / Men love in haste, but they detest at leisure.
— *Byron, "Don Juan" (1819)*

1187 Trump Signs Order Undoing Policies to Fight Climate Change
— *New York Times, 3/29/17*

Who has enough credit in this world to pay for his mistakes?
— *Edward Dahlberg, "On Wisdom and Folly," Reasons of the Heart (1965)*

1188 The Planet Can't Stand This Presidency
— *New York Times, 4/21/17*

If there is a possibility of several things going wrong, the one that will cause the most damage will be the one to go wrong.
— *Arthur Bloch, "Murphology," Murphy's Law (1979)*

1189 23 Environmental Rules Rolled Back in Trump's First 100 Days
— *New York Times, 5/2/17*

Why, since we are always complaining of our ills, are we constantly employed in redoubling them?
— *Voltaire, "Whys," Philosophical Dictionary (1764)*

1190 By 2020, Every Chinese Coal Plant Will Be More Efficient Than Every U.S. Coal Plant
— *Vox, 5/18/17*

Neither a wise man nor a brave man lies down on the tracks of history to wait for the train of the future to run over him.
— *Dwight D. Eisenhower, Campaign Speech, Time (1952)*

1191 Sinkhole Forms in Front of Mar-a-Lago; Metaphors Pour in
— *Washington Post, 5/22/17*

Ask not for whom the bell tolls; it tolls for thee.
— *John Donne, "Devotions On Emergent Occasions," Meditation XVII (1624)*

1192 Leaders Issue G7 Declaration With U.S. a Holdout on Climate Change
— *Politico, 5/27/17*

We cannot tear out a single page from our life, but we can throw the whole book into the fire.

— *George Sand, "Mauprat" (1837)*

1193 The Top Five Worst Things Trump Has Done on Climate Change - So Far

— *The Guardian, 5/31/17*

A man's worst enemy can't wish him what he thinks up for himself.

— *Yiddish Proverb (1949)*

1194 Trump Likely to Withdraw U.S. From Paris Climate Deal

— *Wall Street Journal, 6/1/17 (Misconstrued)*

A way foolishness has of revenging itself is to excommunicate the world.

— *George Santayana, "The Life Of Reason: Reason In Art" (1905)*

1195 Trump's Pullout From the Paris Climate Agreement Is Biggest Failure of Leadership in American History

— *Citizens Climate Lobby, 6/1/17*

In a game, just losing is almost as satisfying as just winning... In life the loser's score is always zero.

— *W. H. Auden, "Postscript: The Frivolous/Earnest," The Dyer's Hand (1962)*

1196 U.S. Exit [From Climate Agreement] Draws Rebuke, Resolve From World Leaders

— *Wall Street Journal, 6/2/17 (Misconstrued)*

Freedom to differ is not limited to things that do not matter much. That would be a mere shadow of freedom. The test of its substance is the right to differ as to things that touch the heart of the existing order.

— *Justice Robert Jackson, West Virginia State Board v. Barnette (1943)*

1197 Abandoning Paris Climate Deal Marks Trump Return to Angry Populism

— *The Guardian, 6/2/17*

The efforts which we make to escape from our destiny only lead us into it.

— *Emerson, "Fate," The Conduct Of Life (1860)*

1198 The White House Still Won't Say If Trump Believes in Climate Change

— *Huffington Post, 6/2/17*

You will find that the truth is often unpopular and the contest between agreeable fancy and disagreeable fact is unequal. For, in the vernacular, we Americans are suckers for good news.

— *Adlai Stevenson, Commencement Address, Michigan State (1958)*

1199 How G.O.P Came to View Climate Change as Fake Science

— *New York Times, 6/3/17*

A conservative government is an organized hypocrisy.

— *Benjamin Disraeli Speech, "Agricultural Distress" (1845)*

1200 Trump Stomps Planet Earth

— *New York Times, 6/3/17*

He that fashions calamity for his neighbor, the instrument of his wounding is in his own head.

— *Berechiah Ben Natronai Ha-Nakdan, "Fables Of A Jewish Aesop" (1967)*

1201 EU Will Ignore White House and Work Directly With US States on Paris Agreement

— *IFLScience, 6/7/17*

Discord gives a relish for concord.

— *Publilius Syrus, "Moral Sayings," (1st C. BCE)*

1202 13 U.S. Cities Defy Trump by Posting Deleted Climate Data

— *Ecowatch, 6/12/17*

Disobedience, in the eyes of anyone who has read history, is man's original virtue. It is through disobedience that progress has been made, through disobedience and rebellion.

— *Oscar Wilde, "The Soul Of Man Under Socialism" (1891)*

1203 Trump Administration Scraps New Protection for Endangered Whales, Sea Turtles

— *Huffington Post, 6/13/17*

Morning comes whether you set the alarm or not.

— *Ursula K. Le Guin, "Dancing At the Edge Of The World" (1989)*

1204 Trump EPA Moves to Rescind Obama Clean Water Rule

— *Wall Street Journal, 6/27/17 (Misconstrued)*

We learn geology the morning after the earthquake.

— *Emerson, "Considerations by the Way," The Conduct of Life (1860)*

1205 Appeals Court Says Trump EPA Can't Suspend Obama-Era Emissions Standards

— *Washington Post, 7/3/17*

People live for the morrow, because the day-after-to-morrow is doubtful.

— *Neitschze, "The Will To Power" (1888)*

———————

1206 Senators to Trump: Hand's Off America's National Monuments

— *Huffington Post, 7/11/17*

I would feel more optimistic about a bright future for man if he spent less time proving he can outwit Nature and more time tasting her sweetness and respecting her seniority.

— *E. B. White, "Coon Tree," Essays Of E. B. White (1977)*

———————

1207 Tobacco Companies Tighten Hold on Washington Under Trump

— *The Guardian, 7/13/17*

The wind-footed steed is broken down in his speed, whilst the camel-driver [big tobacco] jogs on with his beast to the end of his journey.

— *SA'DI, "Gulistan" (1258)*

———————

1208 I'm a Scientist. I'm Blowing the Whistle on the Trump Administration

— *Washington Post, 7/19/17*

To an honest man, it is an honor to have remembered his duty.

— *Platus, "The Three-Penny Day" (194 BCE)*

———————

1209 Washington Governor on Donald Trump: 'Only Smallpox Has Done More to Unite Scientists'
— *IFL Science, 7/22/17*

Canst thou [Governor]not minister to a mind diseased, pluck from the memory a rooted sorrow, raise out the written troubles of the brain, and with some sweet oblivious antidote, cleanse the stuffed bosom of that perilous stuff, which weighs upon the heart?
— *Shakespeare, "Macbeth" (1605)*

1210 Top EPA Official Resigns Over Direction of Agency Under Trump
— *The Hill, 8/1/17*

There is no need to hang about waiting for the Last Judgment – it takes place every day.
— *Albert Camus, "The Fall" (1956)*

1211 Under Trump, Coal Mining Gets New Life on U.S. Lands
— *New York Times, 8/6/17*

When the last tree is cut, the last fish caught, and the last river is polluted; when to breathe air is sickening, you will realize too late that wealth is not in bank accounts and that you can't eat money.
— *Alanis Obomsawin, "Who Is The Chairman Of This Meeting?" Essay (1972)*

1212 Trump Is the Past. Clean Energy Is the Future for America and the Planet
— *The Guardian, 8/12/17*

We are not free to use today, or to promise tomorrow, because we are already mortgaged to yesterday.
— *Emerson, "Journals" (1858)*

1213 Campaigners Hope to Plant Enough Trees to Offset the Climate Impact of President Trump

— BBC, 8/15/17

The hierarchy of power is not the same as the hierarchy of value. A good human is higher than the animals on both scales; an evil human is high on the scale of power, but at the very bottom of the scale of values.

— Wendell Berry, "Poetry And Place," Standing By Words (1983)

———————

1214 Trump Signs Order Rolling Back Environmental Rules on Infrastructure

— New York Times, 8/15/17

Logic, n. The art of thinking and reasoning in strict accordance with the limitations and incapacities of human misunderstanding.

— Ambrose Bierce, "The Devil's Dictionary" (1881-1911)

———————

1215 Trump Cancels An Obama-Era Ban on the Sale of Plastic Water Bottles at National Parks

— Business Insider, 8/17/17

We are all passengers aboard one ship, the Earth, and we must not allow it to be wrecked. There will be no second Noah's Ark.

— Mikhail Gorbachev, "Perestroika" (1987)

———————

1216 The Trump Administration Just Disbanded a Federal Advisory Committee on Climate Change

— Washington Post, 8/20/17

Stupidity often saves a man from going mad.

— Oliver Wendell Holmes, Sr., "The Autocrat Of The Breakfast Table" (1858)

———————

1217 Trump Names Climate Science Denier to Run NASA
— *ThinkProgress, 9/2/17*

To never see a fool you lock yourself in your room and smash the looking-glass.
— *Carl Sandburg, "The People, Yes" (1936)*

1218 Scott Pruitt [EPA Administrator] Says It's Not the Time to Talk About Climate Change. For Him, It Never Is
— *Washington Post, 9/9/17*

Round about what is, lies a whole mysterious world of might be, a psychological romance of possibilities and things that do not happen.
— *Longfellow, "Table-Talk," Driftwood (1857)*

1219 What Could We Lose If a NASA Climate Mission Goes Dark [From Trump-Era Budget Cuts]?
— *New York Times, 9/12/17*

1220 The question is whether (suicide) is the way out or the way in.
— *Emerson, "Journals" (1839)*

1221 White House Denies Claim Trump Plans to Shift on Paris Climate Accord
— *News Source, 9/16/17*

Oh! let us never, never doubt / What nobody is sure about!
— *Hilaire Belloc, "The Microbe," More Beasts For Worse Children (1897)*

1222 Delingpole: Urgent Memo to Donald Trump – Biggest Threat to the Environment Are Environmentalists
— *News Source, 9/17/17*

Precisely in proportion to our own intellectual weakness will be our credulity as to those mysterious powers assumed by others [environmentalists].
— *Charles Caleb Colton, "Lacon" (1825)*

1223 Court Blocks Trump's 'Unlawful' Delay of Obama Methane Leak Rule
— *The Hill, 10/4/17*

The more featureless and commonplace a crime is, the more difficult it is to bring it home.
— *Sir Arthur Conan Doyle, "The Adventures Of Sherlock Holmes" (1891)*

1224 48 Environmental Rules on the Way Out Under Trump
— *New York Times, 10/5/17*

How true is it that our destinies are decided by nothings and that a small imprudence helped by some insignificant accident, as an acorn is fertilized by a drop of rain, may raise the trees on which perhaps we and others will be crucified.
— *Henri Frederic Amiel, Journal (Apr., 1856)*

1225 EPA Chief Scott Pruitt Tells Coal Miners He Will Repeal Power Plant Rule Tuesday: 'The War Against Coal Is Over'
— *New York Times, 10/9/17*

Lord, what fools these mortals be!
— *Shakespeare, "A Midsummer's Night Dream" (1595)*

1226 Trump to Nominate Climate Doubter as Environmental Adviser
— *AP, 10/13/17*

Let me say this: bein an idiot is no box of chocolates.
— Winston Groom, "Forest Gump" (1986)

———————

1227 'Blatant Censorship': Trump EPA Abruptly Muzzles Its Own Climate Scientists
— Common Dreams, 10/23/17

When nature exceeds culture we have the rustic. When culture exceeds nature, we have the pedant.
— Confucius, "Analects" (6th C. BCE)

———————

1228 Trump Should Tackle Climate If He Wants to Save Billions, Congressional Report Says
— Huffington Post, 10/24/17

Give me clean, beautiful and healthy air - not the same old climate change bullshit! I am tired of hearing this nonsense.
— Donald Trump, Statement (2014)

———————

1229 Exclusive: The Interior Department Scrubs Climate Change From Its Strategic Plan
— The Nation, 10/25/17

Thou sodden-witted lord, thou hast no more brain than I have in my elbows: an asinico [idiot] may tutor thee.
— Shakespeare, "Troilus And Cressida" (1602)

———————

1230 Loss of Federal Protections [Proposed by Trump Administration for Two National Marine Monuments] May Imperil Pacific Reefs, Scientists Warn
— New York Times, 10/31/17

We'll use this unwholesome humidity, this gross watery pumpion [pumpkin]; we'll teach him to know turtles from jays.
— *Shakespeare, "The Merry Wives Of Windsor" (1597 - 1601)*

1231 U.S. Report [of 13 Federal Agencies] Says Humans Cause Climate Change, Contradicting Top Trump Officials
— *New York Times, 11/3/17*

Truth - that long clean clear simple undeviable unchallengeable straight and shining line, on one side of which black is black and on the other white is white, now has become an angle, a point of view.
— *William Faulkner, "On Privacy," Essays, Speeches & Public Letters (1965)*

1232 Jerry Brown's Holy War on Donald Trump [Over Climate Change]
— *Politico, 11/5/17*

Praise, of course, is best: plain speech breeds hate. / But ah the Attic honey / Of telling a man exactly what you think of him!
— *Greek Anthology (7th C. BCE - 10th C. CE)*

1233 Syria Signs Paris Agreement - Leaving US Only Country in the World to Refuse Climate Change Deal
— *Independent, 11/7/17*

It is folly to drown on dry land.
— *English Proverb*

1234 US Groups Honouring Paris Climate Pledges Despite Trump
— *The Guardian, 11/11/17*

Let us replace sentimentalism by realism, and dare to uncover those simple and terrible laws which, be they seen or unseen, pervade and govern.
— *Emerson, "Worship, The Conduct Of Life" (1860)*

1235 Trump Administration Continues to Fight for Fossil Fuels at Global Climate Change Summit
— *News Source, 11/13/17*

The lights are on but nobody's home.
— *Idiom, "The Free Dictionary By Farlex," Online Dictionary (2017)*

1236 Trump's Environmental Rollbacks [on Water Use] Hit California Hard, Despite Sacramento's Resistance
— *Los Angeles Times, 11/16/17*

The earth we abuse and the living things we kill will, in the end, take their revenge; for in exploiting their presence we are diminishing our future.
— *Marya Mannes, "More In Anger" (1958)*

1237 A Civil Rights 'Emergency': Justice, Clean Water and Air in the Age of Trump
— *The Guardian, 11/20/17*

What men value in this world is not rights but privileges.
— *H. L. Mencken, "Minority Report" (1956)*

1238 EPA Drops Rule Requiring Mining Companies to Have Money to Clean Up Pollution
— *Chicago Tribune, 12/1/17*

Alack our life, so beautiful to see, / With how much ease life losest in a day, / What many years with pain and toil amassed!
— Petrarch, "Laura Dead," Canzoniere (1360)

———————

1239 Oceans Under Greatest Threat in History, Warns Sir David Attenborough
— The Guardian, 12/5/17

It is a curious situation that the sea, from which life arose, should now be threatened by the activities of one form of that life. But the sea, though changed in a sinister way, will continue to exist: the threat is rather to life itself.
— Rachel Carson, Preface, "The Sea Around Us" (1950)

———————

1240 Renewable Energy Is Surging. The G.O.P. Tax Bill Could Curtail That
— New York Times, 12/7/17

1241 It's one thing to shoot yourself in the foot. Just don't reload the gun.
— Lindsey Graham, U.S. Senator, Speech (Nov., 2012)

———————

1242 Macron [French President] to Award U.S. Climate Scientists With 'Make Our Planet Great Again' [Research] Grants
— The Hill, 12/11/17

Hold your head high, and your middle finger higher.
— Megan Fox, American Actress And Model, AZ Quotes (b. 1986)

———————

1243 EPA Consultant Is Investigating Anti-Trump 'Resistance' Within the Agency: Report
— The Hill, 12/16/17

Everyone loves a witch hunt as long as its someone else's witch being hunted.

— *Walter Kirn, American Novelist, Literary Critic And Essayist (2011)*

1244 The National Park Service Has Scrubbed 92 Documents About Climate Change From Its Website

— *New Republic, 12/22/17*

Sticking your head in the sand does not prevent the tide from coming in.

— *K. J., "Impaired Ocular Acuity And Other Demented Synapses" (2009)*

1245 Donald Trump Doesn't Know the Difference Between Climate and Weather

— *CNN, 12/28/17*

Would any but these boiled brains hunt this weather?

— *Shakespeare, "The Winter's Tale" (1609 - 1611)*

1246 U.S. to Roll Back Safety Rules Created After Deepwater Horizon Spill

— *The New York Times, 12/28/17*

Great crimes never come singly; they are linked / To sins that went before.

— *Racine, "Phaedra" (1677)*

1247 Vehicles Are Now America's Biggest CO2 Source but EPA Is Tearing Up Regulations

— *The Guardian, 12/31/17*

Our national flower is the concrete cloverleaf.

— *Lewis Mumford, Quote (Oct., 8, 1961)*

1248 Trump Plan to Shrink Ocean Monuments Threaten Ecosystems, Experts Warn
— *The Guardian, 1/2/18*

The peace of nature and of the innocent creatures of God seems to be secure and deep, only so long as the presence of man and his restless and unquiet spirit are not there to trouble its sanctity.
— *Thomas De Quincey, "Confessions Of An English Opium-Eater" (1821)*

1249 Trump Moves to Open Nearly All [U.S.] Offshore Waters to Drilling
— *New York Times, 1/4/18*

There exists among the intolerably degraded the perverse and powerful desire to force into the arena of the actual those fantastic crimes of which they have been accused, achieving their vengeance and their own destruction through making the nightmare real.
— *James Baldwin, "Many Thousands Gone" (1951)*

1250 Oceans Suffocating as Huge Dead Zones Quadruple Since 1950, Scientists Warn
— *The Guardian, 1/4/18*

To have your head in your ass means to ignore problems around you, usually by not wanting to see them. To get your head out of your ass means to start noticing those problems and stop ignoring them.
— *Rimmer, English Language Usage & Stack Exchange (Aug., 2012)*

CHAPTER 18

YEKATERINBURG CHLAMYDIA CONSERVATORY FOR SEXUAL PREFERENCES AND GENDER ORIENTATION

TOPICS:
ETHICS AND MORALITY

Yekaterinburg Chlamydia Conservatory for Sexual Preferences and Gender Orientation

1251 Trump Has Spent More Time Golfing Than at Intelligence Briefings

— *Reddit, 2/23/17*

The spirit is often most free when the body is satiated with pleasure, indeed, sometimes the stars shine more brightly seen from the gutter than from the hilltop.

— *W. Somerset Maugham, "The Summing Up" (1938)*

1252 Democrats Now Describe Trump's Unshared Tax Returns as a Matter of National Security

— *Reddit, 3/2/17*

Every vice has its excuse ready.

— *Publilius Syrus, "Moral Sayings" (1st C. BCE)*

1253 Don't Expect Leak to Expose Trump's Tax Returns

— *New York Times, 3/9/17*

The ceiling on taxation of capital gains reflects the national belief that speculation is a more worthwhile way to make a living than work.

— *Calvin Trillin, "Taxing Problems," Uncivil Liberties (1982)*

1254 No Trump Act: US Congressman Introduces Bill to Stop Taxpayer Funds From Going to President's Businesses

— *Reddit, 3/10/17*

Excess on occasion is exhilarating. It prevents moderation from acquiring the deadening effect of a habit.
— W. Somerset Maugham, "The Summing Up" (1938)

_____

1255 Less Than Two Months Into Trump's Presidency, There Is Still No End in Sight to His Conflicts of Interest
— Reddit, 3/14/17

A man should always consider how much he has more than he wants, and how much more unhappy he might be than he really is.
— Joseph Addison, "The Spectator" (1711)

_____

1256 Stephen Colbert to Be Investigated by FCC After 'Offensive' Trump Joke
— The Guardian, 5/6/17

A little fire is quickly trodden out, which, being suffered, rivers cannot quench.
— Shakespeare, "Henry VI, Part 3" (1591)

_____

1257 The President Has Now Made 33 Visits to Trump-Branded Properties Since His Inauguration
— Washington Post, 5/6/17

It's them as take advantage that get advantage i' this world.
— George Elliot, "Adam Bede" (1859)

_____

1258 Trump Pushes Back on Lawmakers' Attempt to Limit His Powers
— Politico, 5/8/17

Presidency, n. The greased pig in the field game of American politics.
— Ambrose Bierce, "The Devil's Dictionary" (1881-1911)

_____

1259 This is the Worst Abuse of Presidential Power Since Watergate

— *Reddit, 5/10/17*

Too many creatures / both insects and humans / estimate their own value / by the amount of minor irritation / they are able to cause / to greater personalities than themselves.

— *Don Marquis, "Pride," Archy Does His Part (1935)*

1260 Firing Comey Grotesque Abuse of Power

— *CNN, 5/10/17*

The benevolent despot who sees himself as the shepherd of the people still demands from others the submissiveness of sheep.

— *Eric Hoffer, "The Ordeal Of Change" (1964)*

1261 In a Private Dinner, Trump Demanded Loyalty, Comey Demurred

— *New York Times, 5/12/17*

Nothing so completely baffles one who is full of trick and duplicity himself, than straightforward and simple integrity in another.

— *Charles Caleb Colton, "Lacon" (1825)*

1262 Trump is Trying to Control the FBI, It's Time to Freak Out

— *New York Magazine, 5/12/17*

This is a sickness rooted and inherent / in the nature of a tyranny: / that he that holds it does not trust his friends.

— *Aeschylus, "Prometheus Bound" (478 BCE)*

1263 Trump's Voter Fraud Commission Is a Shameless White Power Grab

— *The Guardian, 5/14/17*

Any excuse will serve a tyrant.
— Aesop, "The Wolf And The Lamb" (6th C. BCE)

1264 Firing Comey Was a Grave Abuse of Power

— *The New Yorker, 5/14/17*

Power can corrupt, but absolute power is absolutely delightful.
— Anonymous

1265 Trump Asked Comey to End Flynn Probe, According to Memo

— *Wall Street Journal, 5/17/17 (Misconstrued)*

Men are too unstable to be just: they are crabbed because they have not passed water at the usual time, or testy because they have not been stroked or praised.
— Edward Dahlberg, "The Sorrows Of Priapus" (1957)

1266 Trump Considers Trying to Block Comey's Testimony

— *Wall Street Journal, 6/2/17 (Misconstrued)*

The man who is swimming against the stream knows the strength of it.
— Woodrow Wilson, Speech, "The New Freedom" (1913)

1267 It's Time to Demand Donald Trump's Resignation

— *Rolling Stone, 6/6/17*

Nothing has more strength than dire necessity.
— Euripides, "Helen" (412 BCE)

1268 Blocked by Trump on Twitter? Lawyers Say He Is Violating Your 1st Amendment Rights

— *L.A. Times, 6/7/17*

The hypocrite who always plays one and the same part ceases at last to be a hypocrite.

— *Nietzsche, "Human, All Too Human" (1878)*

1269 Democrats to Sue Trump Over Conflict of Interest

— *Politico, 6/7/17*

Do not confuse your vested interests with ethics. Do not identify the enemies of your privilege with the enemies of humanity.

— *Max Lerner, "Politics And Connective Tissue," Actions And Passions (1949)*

1270 Report: Trump Under Investigation for Possible Obstruction of Justice

— *NPR, 6/14/17*

A man had rather have a hundred lies told of him than one truth which he does not wish to be told.

— *Samuel Johnson, Quoted In Boswell's "Life of Samuel Johnson" (1773)*

1271 Mueller Just Shielded Himself Against Trump

— *USA Today, 6/16/17*

It isn't important to come out on top, what matters is to be the one that comes out alive.

— *Bertolt Brecht, "Jungle Of Cities" (1924)*

1272 Trump's Business Ties in the Gulf Raise Questions About His Allegiances

— *New York Times, 6/17/17*

Would that the simple maxim that honesty is the best policy, might be laid to heart; that a sense of the true aim of life might elevate the tone of politics and trade till public and private honor became identical.

— *Margaret Fuller, "Summer On The Lakes" (1844)*

1273 Trump to Host Trump Re-Election Fundraiser at Trump Hotel

— AP, 6/21/17

Human history is the sad result of each one looking out for himself.

— Julio Cortazar, "The Winners" (1960)

1274 Trump Sued for Allegedly Violating Presidential Records Act

— NPR, 6/22/17

A good man can be stupid and still be good. But a bad man must have brains - absolutely.

— Maxim Gorky, "The Lower Depths" (1903)

1275 [Carl] Bernstein: 'We Are in the Midst of a Malignant Presidency'

— CNN, 7/1/17

A belief in a supernatural source of evil is not necessary; men alone are quite capable of every wickedness.

— Joseph Conrad, "Under Western Eyes" (1911)

1276 Donald Trump and the Decline of the West: Ten Thousand Years of Civilization and We End Up With This Guy?

— Salon, 7/8/17

The test of civilization is, not the census, nor the size of cities, nor the crops - no, but the kind of man the country turns out.

— Emerson, "Civilization," Society And Solitude (1870)

1277 Get Off the Trump Train Before It Crashes

— Washington Post, 7/12/17

Those that fly, / may fight again, / Which he can never do that's slain. / Hence timely running's no mean part / Of conduct, in the martial art.

— *Samuel Butler, "Hudibras" (1663)*

1278 The Real Lesson of the Trump Family's Troubles? Nepotism Doesn't Pay

— *Washington Post, 7/14/17*

I have found the best way to give advice to your children is to find out what they want and then advise them to do it.

— *Harry S. Truman, Television Interview (1955)*

1279 Former US Prosecutor on Trump-Russia Investigation: 'People Will Be Going to Jail'

— *Independent, 7/16/17*

It's perfectly obvious that somebody's responsible and somebody's innocent. Otherwise it [justice] makes no sense at all.

— *Ugo Betti, "Landscape" (1936)*

1280 Donald Trump Will Have to Turn Over Mar-a-Lago Visitor Logs

— *Salon, 7/17/17*

What we fear comes to pass more speedily than what we hope.

— *Publilius Syrus, "Moral Sayings" (1st C. BCE)*

1281 Trump Takes Vacation From Mounting Scandals to Spend Entire Month of August Golfing

— *Shareblue Media, 7/21/17*

One really didn't believe till one saw it demonstrated that giving oneself up completely to art, to emotion, to enjoyment, without planning for the future or counting the cost, produced dreadful disabilities and bankruptcies later.
— Edmund Wilson, "The Forties" (1983)

_____

1282 Lindsey Graham: Firing Mueller Could Be 'Beginning of the End of the Trump Presidency'
— Huffington Post, 7/27/17

Very, very slowly, the dwarf remnants of what was once our mighty sun will cool and dim, until it embarks on its final metamorphosis, gradually solidifying into a crystal of extraordinary rigidity. Eventually it will fade out completely, merging quietly into the blackness of space.
— Paul Davies, "The Last Three Minutes" (1994)

_____

1283 With Trump It's Time to Go Beyond Mere Disgust
— The Guardian, 7/28/17

No notice is taken of a little evil, but when it increases it strikes the eye.
— Aristotle, "Politics" (4th C. BCE)

_____

1284 Trump's Luxury Vacation Costs Spiral Out of Control, Strain Taxpayers and National Security
— Shareblue Media, 7/29/17

When all other sins are old, avarice is still young.
— French Proverb

_____

1285 Senate Blocks Trump From Making Recess Appointments Over Break
— The Hill, 8/3/17

No wise man stands behind an ass when he kicks.
— Terence, "The Eunuch" (161 BCE)

1286 'Lazy Boy' Trump Has Taken More Vacation Than Obama Did in 8 Years
— *Independent Journal Review, 8/4/17*

It is better to have loafed and lost then never to have loafed at all.
— James Thurber, "Fables For Our Time" (1943)

1287 Judges Set Oct. 18 Arguments in Trump Foreign Emoluments Suit
— *Politico, 8/9/17*

I have a simple principle for the conduct of life – never to resist an adequate temptation.
— Max Lerner, "The Law Of Austere Hedonism," Unfinished Country (1959)

1288 Secret Service Director Says Agency Running Out of Money to Protect Trump
— *The Guardian, 8/21/17*

One of the most dangerously vicious circles menacing the continued existence of all mankind arises through that grim striving for the highest possible position within the ranked order, in other words, the reckless pursuit of power which combines with an insatiable greed of neurotic proportions that the results of acquired power confer.
— Konrad Lorenz, "The Waning Of Humaneness" (1983)

1289 The Ex-Sheriff Trump Wants to Pardon Ignored 400 Sex Crimes
— *Vice, 8/23/17*

Many among men are they who set high / the show of honor, yet break justice.
— Aeschylus, "Agamemnon" (458 BCE)

_____

1290 Donald Trump May Refuse to Leave the White House When His Term Ends
— Independent, 8/27/17

When we remember that we are all mad, the mysteries disappear and life stands explained.
— Mark Twain, "Notebook" (1935)

_____

1291 Donald Trump Is One of the Biggest Threats Facing Humankind: 50 Nobel Laureates on What Keeps Them Up at Night
— Salon, 8/31/17

In these times you have to be an optimist to open your eyes when you awake in the morning.
— Carl Sandburg, New York Post (Sept., 1960)

_____

1292 How An Obstruction of Justice Case May Be Shaping Up Against Donald Trump
— The Guardian, 9/2/17

How oft the sight of means to do ill deeds make deeds ill done!
— Shakespeare, "King John" (1594 -1596)

_____

1293 Trump's Secret Golf Club Membership Lists Reveal Lobbyists and CEO's Paying Millions, Giving Them Access to President
— Independent, 9/6/17

When the praying does no good, insurance does help.
— Bertolt Brecht, "The Mother" (1932)

1294 Trump Wades Into Legal Battle Over [Hurricane] Harvey Relief Funds for Churches
— *Politico, 9/8/17*

The garb of religion is the best cloak for power.
— *William Hazlitt, "On The Clerical Character," Political Essays (1819)*

1295 Trump FEMA Nominee Withdraws After NBC Questions on Falsified Records
— *NBC, 9/13/17*

The sower [Trump] may mistake and sow his peas crookedly: the peas make no mistake, but come up and show his line.
— *Emerson, "Journals" (1843)*

1296 Ex-Trump Staffer Says US President Has 'Hung Us Out to Dry' Over Spiraling Russia Probe Legal Costs
— *Independent, 9/16/17*

No man's pie is freed from your ambitious fingers.
— *Shakespeare, "Henry VIII" (1613)*

1297 Trump Tweets Doctored GIF of His Golf Ball Hitting Hillary Clinton
— *New York Times, 9/17/17*

Grinning like a Cheshire Cat.
— *Lewis Carroll, "Alice's Adventures In Wonderland" (1865)*

1298 Former Official 'Fought as Good a Fight as I Could' to Make Trump White House Follow Ethics Rules

— *The Texas Tribune, 9/23/17*

Acquisition means life to miserable mortals.

— *Hesiod, "Works And Days" (8th C. BCE)*

1299 Trump Slapped With Ethics Complaint Over Call to Fire NFL Players Who Protest Anthem (Exclusive)

— *Yahoo, 9/24/17*

The possession of unlimited power will make a despot of almost any man. There is a possible Nero in the gentlest human creature that walks.

— *Thomas Bailey Aldrich, "Ponkapog Papers" (1903)*

1300 The Trump Administration Is Waging An Unprecedented War on Governing

— *Washington Post, 9/28/17*

O me! for why is all around us here / As if some lesser God had made the world, / But had not force to shape it as he would?

— *Lord Tennyson, "The Passing Of Arthur," Idylls Of The King (1859-85)*

1301 Hill Democrats Demand Answers From Trump Admin on Obamacare 'Sabotage'

— *TPM, 9/29/17*

Delay always breeds danger and to protract a great design is often to ruin it.

— *Cervantes, "Don Quixote" (1605)*

1302 Dem Senator Compares Donald Trump to Marie Antoinette [For Lavish Spending and Aloofness]

— *The Hill, 9/30/17*

The drowning man is not troubled by rain.

— *Persian Proverb*

1303 Trump Still Hasn't Gotten Around to Appointing Someone to Protect Our Elections From Cyberattack

— *Mother Jones, 10/3/17*

What is life but a series of inspired follies? The difficulty is to find them to do.

— *George Bernard Shaw, "Pygmalion" (1913)*

1304 Pelosi: Trump 'Lacks Knowledge' About Our Responsibility as the Federal Government

— *News Source, 10/12/17*

He's out to lunch.

— *Slang, Webster's New World Dictionary, Third College Edition (1988)*

1305 Stupid Trump Tricks

— *New York Times, 10/13/17*

The central opposition between magic and science is the opposition between power and knowledge.

— *Jacob Bronowsky, "Magic, Science And Civilization" (1978)*

1306 Trump Nominees Showing Up for Work Without Waiting for Senate Approval

— *Politico, 10/20/17*

When you want to hurry something, that means you no longer care about it and want to get on to other things.

— *Robert M. Pirsig, "Zen And The Art Of Motorcycle Maintenance" (1974)*

1307 Breaching the Wall: Is the White House Encroaching on DOJ Independence?

— *NPR, 10/26/17*

In the first place, the Justice Department is prosecuting the seven [Watergate] defendants who broke into the Democratic National Committee headquarters last July. That's like having the fox watch the henhouse because the Justice Department is controlled by the national administration, which is generally believed to have been behind the spying on the Democrats.

— *Article, "Fox In The Henhouse," Miami News (Jan., 1973)*

1308 Trumps Set to Launch Two Real Estate Projects in India, Despite Conflict-of-Interest Concerns

— *Washington Post, 10/28/17*

None so deaf as he who will not hear.

— *Thomas Fuller, M.D. "Gnomologia" (1732)*

1309 US Court Bars Trump From Changing Military Policy on Service by Transgender People

— *Washington Post, 10/30/17*

Thou dar'st not, fool, thou canst not, thou art feeble.

— *Shakespeare, "The Two Noble Kinsmen" (1612 - 1614)*

1310 Trump and His Allies Are Laying the Groundwork for a Saturday Night Massacre

— *Washington Post, 10/31/17*

Said a fervent young lady of Hammels, / "I object to humanity's trammels! / I want to be free! / Like a bird! / Like a bee! / Oh, why am I classed with the mammals?"
— *Morris Bishop, "A Subtreasury Of American Humor" (1941)*

1311 Donald Trump: Bowe Bergdahl Verdict 'Complete And Total Disgrace'
— *News Source, 11/3/17*

The highest possible stage in moral culture is when we recognize we ought to control our thoughts.
— *Charles Darwin, "The Descent Of Man" (1871)*

1312 Trump Voter Fraud Commission Sued By One of Its Own Members, Alleging Democrats Are Being Kept in the Dark
— *Washington Post, 11/9/17*

When angry, count four; when very angry, swear.
— *Mark Twain, "Pudd'nhead Wilson's Calendar," Pudd'nhead Wilson (1894)*

1313 Gaby Gifford's Gun Group Sues Trump Administration [for Failing to Turn Over NRA Documents]
— *Huffington Post, 11/9/17*

Woe to him who doesn't know how to wear his mask, be he king or Pope!
— *Luigi Pirandello, "Henry IV" (1922)*

1314 Trump Judge Nominee, 36, Who Has Never Tried a Case [and Practiced Law Only Three Years] Wins Approval of [GOP Majority] Senate Panel
— *Los Angeles Times, 11/10/17*

All tragedies are finished by a death, / All comedies are ended by a marriage

— Byron, "Don Juan" (1819)

1315 Trump Is Using DOJ Lawyers to Defend His Right to Profit From Presidency

— New York Magazine, 11/16/17

O' it is excellent to have a giant's strength; but it is tyrannous to use it like a giant.

— Shakespeare, "Measure For Measure" (1604 - 1605)

1316 Who Pays for Trump's Contempt for Ethics? USA. USA. USA.

— USA Today, 11/16/17

Without civic morality communities perish; without personal morality their survival has no value.

— Bertrand Russell, "Authority And The Individual" (1949)

1317 Donald Trump Begins Vacation, but Controversies Extend to Mar-a-Lago

— Wall Street Journal, 11/22/17 (Misconstrued)

You can run but you can't hide.

— Girl Thing, "You Can Run But You Can't Hide," Song Title (2001)

1318 Consumer Agency Official Sues Trump Administration Over Agency Leadership [Two Acting Directors]

— Wall Street Journal, 11/26/17 (Misconstrued)

If we must accept Fate, we are not less compelled to affirm liberty, the significance of the individual, the grandeur of duty, the power of character.

— Emerson, "Fate," The Conduct Of Life (1860)

1319 We Will All Pay a Price for Trump's Nihilism
— *Washington Post, 11/27/17*

Because democratic institutions do not renew themselves as effortlessly as flowering trees, they demand the ceaseless tinkering of people who possess both the courage and the honesty to admit their mistakes and to accept responsibility for even the most inglorious acts.

— *Lewis Lapham, "Imperial Masquerade" (1990)*

1320 Trump Claims 'Rigged System' Has 'Destroyed' Flynn's Life, Let Hillary Off the Hook
— *The Hill, 12/2/17*

A dream is always simmering below the conventional surface of speech and reflection.

— *George Santayana, "Life Of Reason: Reason In Common Sense" (1905)*

1321 What Is Trump So Desperate to Cover Up?
— *The Washington Post, 12/4/17*

Fate leads the willing, and drags along the reluctant.

— *Seneca, "Letter To Lucillius" (1st C. CE)*

1322 Trump's Accuser's Lawyer: If He Has Time to Golf, He Can Defend Himself in Court
— *New York Post, 12/5/17*

Time is a great legalizer, even in the field of morals.

— *H. L. Mencken, "A Book Of Preferences" (1917)*

1323 'Abetting a Cover-Up': Watergate Reporter [Carl Bernstein] Says Fox News is Complicit in Trump Misconduct

— *Shareblue Media, 12/10/17*

8 Warning Signs That You Are in a Relationship of Benign Neglect

— *Collen Sheehy Orme, "How Great Thou Part" (Posted On Facebook)*

———————

1324 If Trump Fires Mueller, We Must Impeach

— *The Nation, 12/15/17*

There's life alone in duty done. / And rest alone in striving.

— *John Greenleaf Whittier, "The Drovers" (1847)*

———————

1325 President Trump Spent Nearly One-Third of First Year in Office at Trump-Owned Properties

— *Wall Street Journal, 12/25/17 (Misconstrued)*

The ache for our home lives in all of us, the safe place where we can go as we are and not be questioned.

— *Maya Angelou, "All God's Children Need Traveling Shoes" (1986)*

———————

1326 Former Federal Judge: Trump is Packing the Courts With Unqualified Conservative Extremists

— *Democracy Now, 12/27/17*

A sympathetic friend can be quite as dear as a brother.

— *Homer, "Odyssey" (9th C. BCE)*

———————

1327 Trump Looks to Cash in From Lavish NYE Party at Mar-a-Lago – But Is it Ethical?

— *The Guardian, 12/31/17*

A curious and eager soul was imprisoned in all this lard, but by dint of never refusing himself a pheasant or a goose or his daily procession of Roman wines, he was his own bitter jailer.
— *Thornton Wilder, "The Bridge Of San Luis Rey" (1927)*

1328 Trump Reportedly Starts His Days Later Because He Wants More 'Executive Time' to Watch TV and Tweet
— *Business Insider, 1/7/18*

Work! Work! Work! Work! Work! Work! Work!
— *Andrew Bergman, Mel Brooks, et. al., "Blazing Saddles," Dialogue (1974)*

1329 Trump's First Year: President Spent 38 Weekends at His Own Properties
— *USA Today, 1/19/18*

Give me the luxuries of life and I will willingly do without the necessities.
— *Frank Lloyd Wright, Quoted In His Obituary (April, 1959)*

CHAPTER 19

ALCATRAZ JUNIOR COLLEGE AND RECIDIVIST TRAINING CENTER

TOPICS:
SANITY AND STABILITY

Alcatraz Junior College and Recidivist Training Center

1330 The Abnormal Presidency of Donald Trump

— *New York Times, 1/31/17*

If you be mad, be gone; if you have reason, be brief.

— *Shakespeare, "Twelfth Night" (1601 – 1602)*

1331 Mental Health Professionals Warn About Trump

— *New York Times, 2/13/17*

Dangers, by being despised, grow great.

— *Edmund Burke, Speech "On the Petition of the Unitarians" (1792)*

1332 Is It Time to Call Trump Mentally Ill?

— *New York Times, 2/17/17*

We are all born mad. Some remain so.

— *Samuel Beckett, "Waiting For Godot" (1952)*

1333 President Trump's Island Mentality

— *New York Times, 3/5/17*

Minds that have nothing to confer, find little to perceive.

— *William Wordsworth, "Yes! Thou Art Fair, But Be Not Moved" (1845)*

1334 Trump's Alpha Male Foreign Policy

— *Politico, 3/8/17*

Men love war because it allows them to look serious: because it is the one thing that stops women from laughing at them.

— *John Fowles, "The Magus" (1965)*

1335 Trump Can't Stop Obsessing About the Clintons
— *Politico, 3/29/17*

They must needs go whom the Devil drives.
— *Cervantes, "Don Quixote" (1605)*

1336 Is Donald Losing His Mind?
— *Huffington Post, 4/1/17*

They [eccentrics] are explosive mixtures. Some of them are as sensitive as those fulminates which can be detonated by a falling leaf.
— *Gilbert Highet, "The Art of Teaching" (1950)*

1337 It's Time to Seriously Consider That Trump Is Unfit to Be President
— *CNBC, 4/3/17*

The worse the carpenter, the more the chips.
— *Dutch Proverb*

1338 Trump Says U.S. Will Act Alone on North Korea If China Fails to Help
— *The Guardian, 4/3/17*

A wise man does not try to hurry history. Many wars have been avoided by patience and many have been precipitated by reckless haste.
— *Adlai Stevenson, Speech, San Francisco (1952)*

1339 Nader: Trump Is a Freeloading, Pontificating Empty Suit Who Has Cheated at Everything He's Done
— *Reddit, 4/10/17*

There is no there there.

— *Gertrude Stein, "Everybody's Autobiography" (1937)*

1340 Trump Getting Hot and Bothered by Protesters

— *Politico, 4/18/17*

This is, I think, very much the Age of Anxiety, the age of the neurosis, because along with so much that weighs in our minds there is perhaps even more that grates on our nerves.

— *Louis Kronenberger, "The Spirit Of The Age," Company Manners (1954)*

1341 Trump Has Dangerous Disability

— *Washington Post, 5/4/17*

The world is so full of simpletons and madmen, that one need not seek them in a madhouse.

— *Goethe, Quoted in Eckermann's, "Conversations with Goethe" (1830)*

1342 Donald Trump Is 'Worse than Any Horror Story I've Written,' Says Stephen KIng

— *Independent, 5/5/17*

There are more things in heaven and earth, Horatio, than are dreamt of in your philosophy.

— *Shakespeare, "Hamlet" (1600)*

1343 Trump Once Again Invites Questions About His Stability

— *Huffington Post, 5/11/17*

The wily lunatic is lost if through the narrowest crack he allows a sane eye to peer into his locked universe and thus profane it.

— *Colette, "Freedom," Earthly Paradise (1966)*

1344 Trump Doesn't Want to Be President, He Wants to Be Emperor

— *Los Angeles Times, 5/15/17*

But who can speak to God, or rather who can't? The question is, who can get an answer.

— *William Saroyan, "Chance Meetings" (1978)*

1345 Imagining Trump's Downfall: A Greek Tragedy in Five Acts

— *The Guardian, 5/16/17*

Men fall from great fortune because of the same shortcomings that led to their rise.

— *La Bruyere, "Characters" (1688)*

1346 Experts: Trump's Speaking Style 'Raises Questions About His Brain Health'

— *Vanity Fair, 5/24/17*

'Twas brillig, and the slithy toves / Did gyre and gimbal in the wabe; All mimsy were the borogoves, / And the mome raths outgrabe…

— *Lewis Carroll, "Jabberwocky" (1871)*

1347 Donald Trump Behaves Like a Toddler During Memorial Day National Anthem

— *Metro News, 5/30/17*

"Well, I guess the children have left for school by this time - I might as well go home."

— *F. Scott Fitzgerald, Letter from Ring Lardner, "The Crack Up" (1945)*

1348 Donald Trump Is Stressed Out, Isolated and Gaining Weight, Says New Report

— *Independent, 5/31/17*

The torture of being the unseen object, and the constantly observed subject.
— LeRoi Jones, "The System Of Dante's Hell" (1963)

1349 Trump Just Cemented His Legacy as America's Worst-Ever President
— The Guardian, 6/1/17

One longs for the presence of a leader like Lincoln, who openly admitted his doubts and as openly preserved his commitment.
— Rollo May, "The Courage To Create" (1975)

1350 Trump, Furious and Frustrated, Gears Up to Punch Back at Comey Testimony
— Washington Post, 6/6/17

Wars of opinion, as they have been the most destructive, are also the most disgraceful of conflicts, being appeals from right to might and from argument to artillery.
— Charles Caleb Colton, "Lacon" (1825)

1351 Can Trump Govern?
— Wall Street Journal, 6/7/17 (Misconstrued)

Mystery magnifies danger as the fog the sun.
— Charles Caleb Colton, "Lacon," (1825)

1352 Donald Trump Is a Profoundly Incompetent President
— Chicago Tribune, 6/12/17

Folly often goes beyond her bounds, but impudence knows none.
— Ben Johnson, "Explorata," Timber (1640)

1353 Trump Is So Mentally Ill That the White House Used a Cabinet Meeting to Treat His Depression

— *Politicususa 6/12/17*

The melancholy days are come, the saddest of the year, / Of wailing winds, and naked woods, and meadows brown and sere.

— *William Cullen Bryant, "The Death of The Flowers" (1825)*

1354 Friend Says Trump Is Considering Firing Mueller as Special Counsel

— *New York Times, 6/13/17*

The scapegoat has always had the mysterious power of unleashing man's ferocious pleasure in torturing, corrupting, and befouling.

— *Francois Mauriac, "Child Martyrs," Second Thoughts (1961)*

1355 White House Meetings Add to Tech's Awkward Dance With Trump

— *Politico, 6/18/17*

We love flattery, even though we are not deceived by it, because it shows that we are of importance enough to be courted [by Tech].

— *Emerson, "Gifts," Essays: Second Series (1844)*

1356 U.S. Shakespeare Theaters Report Abuse Amid Uproar Over Trump-Like Caesar

— *The Guardian, 6/19/17*

Mobs in their emotions are much like children, / subject to the same tantrums and fits of fury.

— *Euripides, "Orestes" (408 BCE)*

1357 Trump In Free Fall After Only Five Months

— *Washington Post, 6/20/17*

In the long run, failure was the only thing that worked predictably. All else was accidental.

— Joseph Heller, "Good As Gold" (1979)

1358 Trump Not Ready for a Crisis

— Politico, 6/20/17

We are like thistle-down blown about by the wind – up and down, here and there – but not one in a thousand ever getting beyond seed-hood.

— Samuel Butler, "Lord, What Is Man?" Note-Books (1912)

1359 'Donald Trump Is Greatest Threat to International Security,' Says Former MI6 Head

— Independent, 6/23/17

If God created us in his own image, we have more than reciprocated.

— Voltaire, "Le Sottisier," 32

1360 Few Overseas Have Faith in Trump's Leadership, Survey Finds

— New York Times, 6/26/17

An ass may bray a good while before he shakes the stars down.

— George Eliot, "Romola" (1863)

1361 Senate GOP Seethes at Trump's Impulsiveness

— Politico. 6/27/17

Too much improvisation leaves the mind stupidly void.

— Victor Hugo, "Fantine," Les Miserables (1862)

1362 Trump's Obama Obsession

— New York Times, 6/29/17

The mistake which is commonly made about neurotics is to suppose that they are interesting. It is not interesting to be always unhappy, engrossed with oneself, ungrateful and malignant, and never quite in touch with reality.
— Cyril Connolly, "The Unquiet Grave" (1945)

———————

1363 Dem Proposes Panel to Remove President If Unfit to Lead
— CNN, 6/30/17

Extreme remedies are very appropriate for extreme diseases.
— Hippocrates, "Aphorisms" (4th C. BCE)

———————

1364 Commentary: Donald Trump, the Most Insecure Man in America
— Chicago Tribune, 7/3/17

How can a man learn navigation / Where there's no rudder.
— Christopher Fry, "A Sleep of Prisoners" (1951)

———————

1365 Julia Gillard: Former Australian PM Claims There Is 'Genuine Concern' Over Donald Trump's Mental Health
— Independent, 7/4/17

The "sensibility" claimed by neurotics is matched by their egotism; they cannot abide the flaunting by others of the sufferings to which they pay an ever increasing attention in themselves.
— Marcel Proust, "Remembrance of Things Past" (1913)

———————

1366 Podesta Hits Back at 'Whack Job' Trump Over Server Tweet: 'Get a Grip Man'
—TPM, 7/6/17

Sell when you can, you are not for all markets.
— Shakespeare, "As You Like It" (1599)

1367 Trump Reiterates Plans for Steel-Import Curbs
— *Wall Street Journal, 7/13/17 (Misconstrued)*

As any action or posture, long continued, will distort and disfigure the limbs, so the mind likewise is crippled and contracted by perpetual application to the same set of ideas.
— *Samuel Johnson, "The Rambler" (1750)*

1368 Don't Compare Trump to Nixon. It's Unfair to Nixon
— *Politico, 7/17/17*

To create an unfavorable impression, it is not necessary that certain things should be true, but that they have been said.
— *William Hazlitt, "Characteristics" (1823)*

1369 President Trump Has the Work Ethic of a Bored, Lazy Child
— *Newsweek, 7/19/17*

Children, after being limbs of Satan in traditional theology and mystically illuminated angels in the minds of educational reformers, have reverted to being little devils - not theological demons inspired by the Evil One, but scientific Freudian abominations inspired by the Unconscious.
— *Bertrand Russell, "Virtue Of The Oppressed," Unpopular Essays (1950)*

1370 Trump's Coming Saturday Night Massacre [at Justice Department]
— *Huffington Post, 7/30/17*

It's like a little boy whistling in the dark...This is a purely hyper casual reaction indicative of cold panic.
— *Navy Commodore Rex Robles, Quote HD (PMA Class 1965)*

1371 Donald Trump: A 71-Year Old Man Who Needs a Military General to Manage His Twitter Use
— *Newsweek, 8/5/17*

All children find chaos congenial. Any unruliness, even by nature, advances the child's program of subverting authority.
— *George Will, "Suddenly: The American Idea Abroad and At Home" (1990)*

———————

1372 Trump Threatens N.K. [North Korea] With Fire, Fury
— *Huffington Post, 8/8/17*

The greater the power, the more dangerous the abuse.
— *Edmund Burke, Speech "On The Middlesex Election" (1771)*

———————

1373 North Korea Calls Donald Trump 'Senile' and 'Bereft Of Reason'
— *Independent, 8/10/17*

Now I know the things I know, / And do the things I do; / And if you do not like me so, / To hell, my love, with you!
— *Dorothy Parker, "Indian Summer," Enough Rope (1926)*

———————

1374 Republicans, Remove This Madman From Power
— *New Republic, 8/11/17*

Spare me the sight / of this thankless breed, these politicians / who cringe for favors from a screaming mob / and do not care what harm they do their friends, / providing they can please a crowd!
— *Euripides, "Hecuba" (425 BCE)*

———————

1375 When Aides Worry Their President Is Unhinged
— *Politico, 8/15/17*

It is better to lose the saddle than the horse.
— *Italian Proverb*

1376 Trump To Congress: Fund the Wall Or I'll Shut the Government
— *New York Times, 8/23/17*

Poor little men! Poor little strutting peacocks! They spread out their tails as conquerors almost as soon as they are able to walk.
— *Jean Anouilh, "Cecile" (1949)*

1377 Ex-Intelligence Chief: Trump's Access to Nuclear Codes Is 'Pretty Damn Scary'
— *The Guardian, 8/23/17*

God Himself is not secure, having given man dominion over his Works.
— *Helen Keller, "Let Us Have Faith" (1940)*

1378 Republicans Are Asking a Horrific Question: Is Our President Insane?
— *Los Angeles Times, 8/2817*

Man, in good earnest, is a marvelous vain, fickle, and unstable subject, and on whom it is very hard to form any certain and uniform judgement.
— *Montaigne, "Men by Various Ways Arrive At Same End," Essays (1580)*

1379 John le Carre on Trump: 'Something Seriously Bad Is Happening'
— *The Guardian, 9/7/17*

I would rather worry without need than live without heed.
— *Beaumarchais, "The Barber of Seville" (1775)*

1380 Time to Restrict the President's Power to Wage Nuclear War
— *New York Times, 9/12/17*

An atom tossed in a chaos made / Of yeasting worlds, which bubble and foam. / Whence have I come? / What would be home? / I hear no answer. I am afraid!
— *Amy Lowell, "Sword Blades And Poppy Seeds" (1914)*

1381 The Loneliest President
— *Politico, 9/15/17*

In solitude the lonely man is eaten up by himself, among crowds by the many.
— *Nietzsche, "Miscellaneous Maxims and Opinions" (1879)*

1382 Trump Threatens to Exterminate 25 Million People on the Floor of UN
— *ThinkProgress, 9/19/17*

The great proof of madness is the disproportion of one's designs to one's means.
— *Napoleon I, "Maxims" (1804)*

1383 Kim Jong-un, the NFL and 'Screaming at Senators': Donald Trump's Strange Night in Alabama
— *The Guardian, 9/22/17*

Beware lest you lose the substance by grasping at the shadow.
— *Aesop, "The Dog And The Shadow," Fables (6th C. BCE)*

1384 Trump Called White Supremacists 'Very Fine People.' But An Athlete Who Protests Is a 'Son Of A Bitch'
— *Huffington Post, 9/23/17*

A disputant no more cares for the truth than the sportsman for the hare.

— Alexander Pope, "Thoughts On Various Subjects" (1727)

———————

1385 Trump's Iran Derangement

— New York Times, 10/11/17

There is a pleasure sure / In being mad which none but madmen know.

— John Dryden, "The Spanish Fryer" (1681)

———————

1386 Former Republican Member of Congress: 'Trump Is Unhinged. We Are Waiting to Get Tax Bill Through Before Impeachment'

— Independent, 10/12/17

He's nutty as a fruitcake.

— Adjective Phrase, The Dictionary Of American Slang, 4th Edition (1935+)

———————

1387 Waters: GOP Needs To 'Confront The Fact' That Trump 'Appears To Be Unstable,' We Should 'Be Moving On Impeachment'

— News Source, 10/12/17

The wise man in the storm prays God, not for safety from danger, but for deliverance from fear.

— Emerson, Journals (1833)

———————

1388 'He Is Failing': Trump Strikes Out Solo as Friends Worry and Enemies Circle

— The Guardian, 10/14/17

There are some solitary wretches who seem to have left the rest of mankind, only, as Eve left Adam, to meet the devil in private.

— Alexander Pope, "Thoughts On Various Subjects" (1727)

1389 Multiple NFL Owners Believe Trump is Waging a Personal Vendetta Against the NFL Because He Was Prevented From Buying a Team

— *Business Insider, 10/19/17*

Small minds are much distressed by little things [slights]. Great minds see them all but are not upset by them.

— *La Rochefoucauld, "Maxims" (1665)*

1390 Antiquities Act / Trump and Congress Could Wreck America's National Parks

— *The Guardian, 10/21/17*

Lovers and madmen have such seething brains, such shaping fantasies.

— *Shakespeare, "A Midsummer's Night's Dream" (1595 - 1596)*

1391 Health Premiums to Rise, Trump Administration Says

— *Wall Street Journal, 10/30/17 (Misconstrued)*

Men of cold passions have quick eyes.

— *Nathaniel Hawthorne, Journals (1837)*

1392 Judith Miller: Who Worries [South] Korea's Leader the Most – Trump Or Kim?

— *News Source, 11/7/17*

A Hobson's choice.

— *Samuel Fisher, "A Rustic Alarm To The Rabbies" (1660)*

1393 Corker Announces Senate Hearing to Examine Trump's 'Authority to Use Nuclear Weapons'

— *CNBC, 11/9/17*

The lunatics have taken over the asylum.
— Fun Boy Three, "The Lunatics Have Taken Over The Asylum" (1981)

_____

1394 How Trump Is Slowly Destroying America's National Security Agencies
— The Guardian, 11/25/17

One minute gives invention to destroy; / What to rebuild, will a whole age employ.
— William Congreve, "The Double-Dealer" (1694)

_____

1395 Diplomats Sound Alarm as They Are Pushed Out in Droves
— New York Times, 11/26/17

Rashness succeeds often, still more often fails.
— Napolean I, "Maxims" (1804)

_____

1396 Churchill 'in the Year of Trump': Darkest Hour Feeds America's Love For Winston
— The Guardian, 11/26/17

The deeper the nostalgia and the more complete the fear, the purer, the richer the word and the secret.
— Elie Wiesel, "Legends Of Our Times" (1968)

_____

1397 New Reports Suggest Trump Might Not Be a Liar at All, But Truly Delusional
— New York Magazine, 11/28/17

Imagination, that dost so abstract us / That we are not aware, not even when / A thousand trumpets sound about our ears!
— Dante, "Purgatorio," 17, The Divine Comedy (1300)

_____

1398 Donald Trump's TV Habits Would 'Get Most American's Sacked'
— Independent, 12/10/17

The charm of television entertainment is its ability to bridge the chasm between dinner and bedtime without mental distraction.
— Russell Baker, "On With Mindlessness," All Things Considered (1962)

1399 Interior Secretary Pushing Controversial Road Project [Through National Wildlife Refuge]
— CNN, 12/10/17

What is man, when you come to think upon him, but a minutely set, ingenious machine for turning, with infinite artfulness, the red wine of Shiraz into urine?
— Isak Dinesen, "The Dreamers, " Seven Gothic Tales (1934)

1400 John Kelly Must Be Exhausted
— Washington Post, 12/11/17

Wise parents know that fighting a teenager, like fighting a riptide, is inviting doom.
— Haim G. Ginott, "Between Parent & Teacher" (1969)

1401 Alabama Election Result Seen as 'Miracle' in a Europe Horrified by Trump
— Washington Post, 12/13/17

Take all away from me, but leave me Ecstasy, / And I am richer than all my Fellow Men –
— Emily Dickenson, Poem (1885)

1402 Trump Predicts Exoneration in Russia Investigation as Allies Fear a Meltdown

— *CNN, 12/18/17*

What a curious creature is man! With what a variety of powers and faculties is he endued! Yet how easily is he disturbed and put out of order!

— *James Boswell, "London Journal" (Mar., 1763)*

1403 Donald Trump Shows 'Qualities' Usually Found In 'Narcissistic, Vengeful Autocrats', Says Former CIA Director

— *Independent, 12/22/17*

Your face is as a book, where men may read strange matters.

— *Shakespeare, "Macbeth" (1606)*

1404 Kasich: US Should be Working With Allies on North Korea, Not Threatening War

— *The Hill, 12/26/17*

A body seriously out of equilibrium, either with itself or with its environment, perishes outright. Not so a mind. Madness and suffering can set themselves no limit.

— *George Santayana, " Life In Reason/Reason In Common Sense" (1905)*

1405 Donald Trump Is a Dangerously Weak President

— *Vox, 12/27/17*

There is nothing so imperious as feebleness which feels itself supported by force.

— *Napolean I, "Maxims" (1804)*

1406 President Trump Included on List of Top Nuclear Threats

— *MSNBC, 12/30/17*

Praise is always pleasing, let it come from whom, or upon what account it will.

— Montaigne, "Of Vanity," Essays (1580)

———————

1407 Trump Says His 'Nuclear Button' Is 'Much Bigger' Than North Korea's

— *New York Times, 1/2/18*

An example I often use to illustrate the reality of vanity is this: look at the peacock; it's beautiful if you look at it from the front. But if you look at it from behind, you discover the truth…Whoever gives in to such self-absorbed vanity has huge misery hiding inside of them.

— Pope Francis, National Catholic Reporter (Mar., 2013)

———————

1408 Yale Psychiatrist Briefed Members of Congress on Trump's Mental Fitness

— *CNN, 1/4/18*

Let us not seek our disease out of ourselves; 'tis in us, and planted in our bowels; and the mere fact we do not perceive ourselves to be sick, renders us more hard to be cured.

— Seneca, "Letters To Lucilius" (63 – 65 CE)

———————

1409 Trump On Questions About Mental Stability: I'm a 'Very Stable Genius'

— *The Hill. 1/6/18*

All those happy confusions of himself with God, those identifications with divinity and genius, and that supreme self-confidence - all of them were as lost as the smoke of Gettysburg, the tears of Gethsemane.

— John O'Hara, "The Instrument" (1967)

———————

1410 [Rep. Adam] Schiff Believes Most of Congress Sees Trump as Mentally Unfit

— *New York Daily News, 1/8/18*

How should men know what is coming to pass within them, when there are no words to grasp it? How could the drops of water know themselves to be in a river? Yet the river flows on.

— *Saint-Exupery, "The Wisdom Of The Sands" (1948)*

1411 What Happens When Americans Try to Psychoanalyze Their Leaders?

— *Politico, 1/13/17*

Ask, and it shall be given you; seek, and ye shall find; knock, and it shall be opened to you.

— *Bible, Matthew 7:7*

1412 Ex-Obama Defense Official on Hawaii [Ballistic Missile] False Alarm: 'Thank God The President Was Playing Golf'

— *The Hill, 1/13/18*

In our play we reveal what kind of people we are.

— *Ovid, "The Art Of Love" (81 CE)*

1413 The Man-Child in the White House Reels Wildly Out of Control

— *Washington Post, 1/18/18*

He hath been five thousand years a boy.

— *Shakespeare, "Love's Labour's Lost" (Early 1590s)*

CHAPTER 20

FLORIDA NONDENOMINATIONAL SEMINARY OF THE SOUTHWEST EVERGLADES

TOPICS:
CARING AND COMPASSION

Florida Nondenominational Seminary of the Southwest Everglades

1414 Trump Rescinds Protections for Transgender Students
— *New York Times, 1/23/17*

Pleasure is sweetest, when 'tis paid for by another's pain.
— *Ovid, "The Art Of Love" (81 CE)*

1415 Trump's Next Target: People Living With HIV/AIDS
— *New York Times, 2/2/17*

Happiness, n. An agreeable sensation arising from the misery of another.
— *Ambrose Bierce, "The Devil's Dictionary" (1881 – 1906)*

1416 Trumpcare and the GOP: Legislating Cruelty
— *Washington Post, 2/8/17*

Cruelty is, perhaps, the worst kind of sin. Intellectual cruelty is certainly the worst kind of cruelty.
— *G. K. Chesterton, "Conceit And Caricature," All Things Considered (1908)*

1417 'A Sense of Dread' for Civil Servants Shaken by Trump Transition
— *New York Times, 2/11/17*

After all, it's not where a man lands that marks his punishment. It's how far he falls.
— *Tip O'Neill, "Man Of The House" (1987)*

1418 Trading Health Care for the Poor for Tax Cuts for the Rich

— *New York Times, 3/14/17*

Extreme avarice misapprehends itself almost always; there is no passion which more often misses its aim, nor upon which the present has so much influence to the prejudice of the future.

— *La Rochefoucauld, "Maxims" (1665)*

———————

1419 Entire Homelessness Agency Could be Eliminated by Trump's Budget Cuts

— *The Guardian, 3/17/17*

Man's inhumanity to man / Makes countless thousands mourn.

— *Robert Burns, "Man Was Made To Mourn" (1784)*

———————

1420 The Innocent Lives Lost Amid Trump's War on Terror

— *Washington Post, 3/27/17*

Pity is a thing often avowed, seldom felt; hatred is a thing often felt, seldom avowed.

— *Charles Caleb Colton, "Lacon" (1825)*

———————

1421 'Torture Memo' Author Spotted at Trump's White House

— *Huffington Post, 3/31/17*

During war, we imprison the 'rights of man.'

— *Jean Giraudoux, "Tiger At The Gates" (1935)*

———————

1422 The Struggle to Give a Soul to a Soulless Presidency

— *Washington Post, 4/11/17*

You cannot teach an old dog new tricks.

— *Joseph Chamberlain, British Politician, BrainyQuotes (b. 1836)*

———————

1423 It Looks Like Donald Trump Is Trying to Bomb His Way to Popularity

— *Reddit, 4/14/17*

If ambitious fantasies make people blush, and sexual fantasies make people blush and feel guilty, fantasies of violence and death may make people blush and feel guilty – and frightened too.

— Judith Virost, "Necessary" (1986)

1424 Warren Buffet: Obama Care Repeal Bill 'A Huge Tax Cut for Guys Like Me'

— *The Hill, 5/7/17*

Verily the kindness that gazes upon itself in a mirror turns to stone, / And a good deed that calls itself by tender names, becomes the parent to a curse.

— Kahlil Gibran, "The Farewell," The Prophet (1923)

1425 The Trump News You Missed: He Asked Comey to Jail Journalists

— *The Guardian, 5/17/17*

The press exerts the pressure of dissent on officials otherwise inclined to rest content with the congratulations of their retainers.

— Lewis Lapham, "Imperial Masquerade" (1990)

1426 Donald Trump Budget: $800 Billion in Medicaid Cuts

— *CNN, 5/22/17*

The worst sin towards our fellow creatures is not to hate them, but to be indifferent to them: that's the essence of inhumanity.

— George Bernard Shaw, "The Devil's Disciple' (1897)

1427 CBO Releases New Estimates on Obamacare Repeal; 23 Million Would Lose Insurance Coverage

— *CNBC, 5/24/17*

O! many a shaft, at random sent / Finds mark the archer little meant!

— *Sir Walter Scott, "The Lord Of The Isles" (1815)*

1428 Concerns Rise Over Trump's Veterans Affairs Budget

— *Wall Street Journal, 5/30/17 (Misconstrued)*

We cannot be kind to each other here for an hour: / We whisper, and hint, and chuckle, and grin at a brother's shame; / However we brave it out, we men are a little breed.

— *Lord Tennyson, "Maud; A Monodrama" (1856)*

1429 Trump Is Abdicating All the Country's Moral Power

— *Washington Post, 6/1/17*

If there is one thing worse than the modern weakening of major morals it is the modern strengthening of minor morals.

— *G. K. Chesterton, "On Lying In Bed," Tremendous Trifles (1909)*

1430 Trump Sends Tone-Deaf Travel Ban Tweet Amid London Bridge Terror

— *New York Daily News, 6/3/17*

What makes people hard-hearted is this, that each man has, or fancies he has, as much as he can bear in his own troubles.

— *Schopenhauer, "Psychological Observations," Parega/Paralipomena (1851)*

1431 Trumpcare is a Dangerous Gamble. The Prognosis Isn't Good

— *The Guardian, 6/22/17*

The best throw of the dice is to throw them away.
— *English Proverb*

1432 Breaking With Tradition, Trump White House Forgoes Ramadan Dinner
— *CNN, 6/24/17*

In the end, as any successful teacher will tell you, you can only teach the things that you are. If we practice racism, then it is racism that we teach.
— *Max Lerner, "We Teach What We Are," Actions And Passions (1949)*

1433 As Health Care Repeal Bill Heads into Ditch, Trump Complains About Amazon
— *Huffington Post, 6/28/17*

Fools rush in where angels fear to tread.
— *Alexander Pope, "An Essay On Criticism" (1711)*

1434 As California Burns, Trump's Proposed Cuts to Forest Service Loom
— *Huffington Post, 7/10/17*

Truth lies within a little and certain compass, but error is immense.
— *Henry St. John, "Reflections Upon Exile" (1716)*

1435 Trump Administration Scraps Obamacare Signup Assistance in 18 Cities
— *CNBC, 7/20/17*

One likes people much better when they are battered down by a prodigious siege of misfortune than when they triumph.
— *Virginia Woolf, "A Writer's Diary" (1921)*

1436 CBO Says Revised Senate [Health] Plan Would Increase Uninsured by 22 Million
— *Wall Street Journal, 7/20/17 (Misconstrued)*

What really raises one's indignation against suffering is not suffering intrinsically, but the senselessness of suffering.
— *Nietzche, "The Genealogy of Morals" (1887)*

———

1437 Trump Does Not Acknowledge Or Respect (Or Support] DOJ's Independence. That Can't End Well
— *Huffington Post, 7/21/17*

Those who expect to reap the blessings of freedom must, like men, undergo the fatigue of supporting it.
— *Thomas Paine, "The American Crises" (1776)*

———

1438 Schumer Blasts Trumps Threat to End Obamacare's Payments: Start 'Acting Presidential,'
— *The Hill, 7/29/17*

The president we get is the country we get. With each new president the nation is conformed spiritually.
— *E. L. Doctorow, "Jack London, Hemingway, And The Constitution" (1993)*

———

1439 Conway: Trump to Decide 'This Week' Whether to Let Obamacare Implode
— *Politico, 7/30/17*

This is a hard and precarious world, where every mistake and infirmity must be paid for in full.
— *Clarence Day, "This Simian World" (1920)*

———

1440 Trump's Treatment of Sessions Is No Class Act
— *Wall Street Journal, 8/5/17 (Misconstrued)*

Accusing is proving, where Malice and Force sit judges.
— *Thomas Fuller, M.D., "Gnomologia" (1732)*

1441 Chicago to Sue Trump Over Sanctuary Funding Threat
— *Huffington Post, 8/6/17*

Tyranny is tyranny no matter what its form; the free man will resist it if his courage serves.
— *Learned Hand, "The Spirit Of Liberty" (1959)*

1442 Have a Heart, Mister President, and Defend Those Immigrants in Court
— *Wall Street Journal, 8/8/17 (Misconstrued)*

There is no more mercy in him than there is milk in a male tiger.
— *Shakespeare, "Coriolanus" (1605 – 1608)*

1443 Study Says Trump Moves Trigger Health Premium Jumps for 2018
— *Associated Press, 8/10/17*

Sacrificers are not the ones to pity. The ones to pity are those they sacrifice.
— *Elizabeth Bowen, "The Death of The Heart" (1938)*

1444 Trump Tweets on Trade, Military, Alabama, But Not Charlottesville
— *The Hill, 8/14/17*

Life's but a walking shadow, a poor player that struts and frets his hour upon the stage and then is heard no more. It is a tale told by an idiot, full of sound and fury, signifying nothing.
— *Shakespeare, "MacBeth" (1606)*

1445 Donald Trump's Administration 'Closes State Department Office That Investigates War Crimes and Genocide'

— *Independent, 8/18/17*

The heart can ne'er a transport know, / That never feels a pain.

— *George Lyttleton, "Song" (1751)*

———————

1446 Trump Officials Renew Effort to Expand Use of Prison at Guantanamo

— *New York Times, 8/18/17*

Pity is not natural to man. Children are always cruel. Savages are always cruel.

— *Samuel Johnson, Quoted In Boswell's "Life of Samuel Johnson" (1763)*

———————

1447 Under Trump Rule, Nursing Home Residents May Not Be Able to Sue After Abuse

— *NPR, 8/21/17*

For the good that I would do I do not: but the evil which I would not, that I do.

— *Bible, Romans 7:19*

———————

1448 Ivanka Backs Trump Administration's Plan to Scrap Obama Rules Preventing Pay Discrimination

— *Newsweek, 8/30/17*

Tis e'er the wont of simple folk to prize the deed and o'erlook the motive, and of learned folk to discount the deed and lay open the soul of the doer.

— *John Barth, "The Sot-Weed Factor" (1960)*

———————

1449 Trump Steered Clear of Storm Victims During Texas Visit

— *MSNBC, 8/30/17*

He that has no charity deserves no mercy.

— *English Proverb*

_____

1450 Trump to End DACA Program Affecting 800K Dreamers

— *CBS Miami, 9/3/17*

There is only one way to achieve happiness on this terrestrial ball, / And that is to have either a clear conscience, or none at all.

— *Ogden Nash, "I'm A Stranger Here Myself" (1938)*

_____

1451 Trump Has Decided to End DACA – With 6-Month Delay

— *Politico, 9/3/17*

There is a time where the word "eventually" has the soothing effect of a promise, and a time when the word evokes in us bitterness and scorn.

— *Eric Hoffer, "The Passionate State Of Mind" (1954)*

_____

1452 Donald Trump 'Wasn't Aware What Scraping DACA Would Mean' Before Deciding Fate of 800,000 People

— *Independent, 9/6/17*

Wisdom is prevented by ignorance, and delusion is the result.

— *Bhagavadgita, 5 (2nd C. BCE)*

_____

1453 Trump Is Assembling the Most Male-Dominated Government In Decades

— *The Guardian, 9/21/17*

Male, n. A member of the unconsidered or negligible sex. The male of the human race is commonly known (to the female) as Mere Man. The genus has two varieties: good providers and bad providers.

— *Ambrose Bierce, "The Devil's Dictionary" (1881 – 1911)*

_____

1454 Singer Marc Anthony to Trump: 'Shut the F___ Up About NFL' and Do Something About Puerto Rico

— *The Hill, 9/25/17*

Nature has, herself, I fear, imprinted in man a kind of instinct to inhumanity.

— *Montaigne, "Of Cruelty," Essays (1580)*

———————

1455 There Should Be 'Great Anger' Over Trump's Puerto Rico Response

— *Esquire, 9/26/17*

A man's behavior is the index of the man, and his discourse is the index of his understanding.

— *Ali Ibn-Ab-Talib, "Sentences" (7th C. CE)*

———————

1456 Donald Trump Refuses to Send More Aid to Puerto Rico, Citing Business Interests [Protecting Shipping Industry]

— *Newsweek, 9/27/17*

We all have enough strength to bear the misfortunes of others.

— *La Rochefoucauld, "Maxims" (1665)*

———————

1457 Trump Has Some New Ideas About How to Sabotage Obamacare

— *Huffington Post, 9/27/17*

The necessity of saying something, the embarrassment produced by the consciousness of having nothing to say, and the desire to exhibit ability, are three things sufficient to render even a great man ridiculous.

— *Voltaire, "Society Of London, And Academies" (1764)*

———————

1458 Donald Trump Spends 67th Day at His Golf Resort While Puerto Rico Struggles With Hurricane Devastation
— *Independent, 9/30/17*

Men first feel necessity, then look for utility, still better amuse themselves with pleasure, thence grow dissolute in luxury, and finally go mad and waste their substance.
— *Giambattista Vico, "The New Science" (1725)*

———————

1459 Trump Hails 'Incredible' Response in 'Lovely' Trip to Storm-Torn Puerto Rico
— *Washington Post, 10/3/17*

Money talks. Bullshit walks.
— *Urban Dictionary, Online Dictionary Of Slang Words And Phrases (1999)*

———————

1460 Trump Signs Order Expected to Weaken Health-Care Law
— *Wall Street Journal, 10/12/17 (Misconstrued)*

The curse of modern times is the preponderance of male hormones in places where they can do long-term damage. Even if we're not talking about wars between nations or assaults on nature, there's still that aggressiveness that keeps us apart from each other and the problems we need to be working on.
— *Robert James Waller, "The Bridges Of Madison County" (1992)*

———————

1461 Collins: Trump is Hurting 'Vulnerable' Americans, His Acts 'Destabilize the Insurance Market'
— *News Source, 10/15/17*

Now, what a thing it is to be an ass!
— *Shakespeare, "Titus Andronicus" (1588)*

———————

1462 Republicans Want to Make It Harder for You to Pay Off Student Loans

— *Vice, 11/3/17*

Finding a 'sacrificial lamb' on whom to tag blame for complicated problems is an important instrument in the toolkit of politicians, because it deflects blame for the nation's economic woes away from their own regulatory lapses, economic mismanagement and coddling to labor unions.

— *Clayton M. Christensen, Author Of "The Innovator's Dilemma" (1997)*

———————

1463 [GOP] House Tax Plan Would Mean Higher Borrowing Costs for Hospitals, Schools, Affordable Housing

— *Los Angeles Times, 11/17/17*

Pray that success will not come any faster than you are able to endure it.

— *Elbert Hubbard, "The Note Book" (1927)*

———————

1464 Federal Judge Blocks Trump's Executive Order on Denying Funding to Sanctuary Cities

— *Washington Post, 11/21/17*

All virtue is summed up in dealing justly.

— *Aristotle, "Nicomachean Ethics" (4th C. BCE)*

———————

1465 How Trump's Hands-Off Approach to Policing [Rebuilding Community Trust] Is Frustrating Some Chiefs

— *New York Times, 11/21/17*

No man is an island, entire of itself; every man is a piece of the continent.

— *John Donne, "Devotions" (1624)*

———————

1466 Donald Trump: Egyptian Terror Attack Proves We Need Border Wall

— *News Source, 11/24/17*

If it's important to you, you will find a way. If not, you'll find an excuse.

— *Kim Murray, "2015 By Kmurray 0423," Pinterest.com*

1467 Kellyanne Conway Has Zero Experience in Drug Policy But Is Running the White House Opioid Response

— *Mother Jones, 11/29/17*

What trick, what device, what starting-hole canst thou [Trump] now find out, to hide thee from this open and apparent shame?

— *Shakespeare, "Henry IV, Part 1" (1597)*

1468 Trump Slashes Size of Bears Ears and Grand Staircase National Monuments in Utah

— *The Guardian, 12/4/17*

It is those people who know that they are right because some outside or higher power [unrestrained capitalism] conveys the conviction to them, who do the great damage in the world.

— *Maxwell Perkins, "Editor To Author: The Letters Of Maxwell Perkins" (1950)*

1469 Trump Ends Homeless Vets Program as Their Numbers Rise for First Time in 7 Years

— *Shareblue Media. 12/6/17*

A penny saved is a penny to squander.

— *Ambrose Bierce, "Saw," The Devil's Dictionary (1881 - 1911)*

1470 16 of Trump's [Sexual Misconduct] Accusers to Demand Congressional Investigation on Monday

— *The Week, 12/11/17*

There is safety in numbers.

— *Euripides, Greek Tragedian (480 - 406 BCE)*

———————

1471 Thanks to Trump's Tax Plan, Victims of Disasters Large and Small Are About to Get Scrooged [By Limits on Deductability of Uninsured Casualty Losses]

— *Los Angeles Times, 12/18/17*

In thy need such comfort come to thee, as now I reap at thy too cruel hand!

— *Shakespeare, "Henry VI, Part 3" (1591)*

———————

1472 Bit By Bit, Trump Is Taking Apart New Deal's Glorious Legacy

— *The Guardian, 12/23/17*

No man at bottom means injustice; it is always for some distorted image of a right that he contends: an obscure image diffracted, exaggerated, in the wonderfulest way, by natural dimness and selfishness; getting tenfold more diffracted by exasperation of contest, till at length it becomes all but irrecognisable.

— *Thomas Carlyle, "Chartism" (1839)*

———————

1473 Trump Administration Rolls Back Regulations for Nursing Homes

— *Democracy Now, 12/28/17*

Let them eat cake.

— *Marie Antoinette, Rousseau's "Confessions" (1765)*

———————

1474 Trump Fires HIV/AIDS Council in Its Entirety by FedEx Letter, Report Claims
— *Newsweek, 12/29/17*

No sadder proof can be given by a man of his own littleness than disbelief in great men.
— *Thomas Carlyle, 'Hero Worship & The Heroic In History" (1841)*

———————

1475 With Their Fate in the Trump Administration's Hands, 260,000 Salvadoran Immigrants Wait and Worry
— *Los Angeles Times, 1/7/18*

A thin reed indeed.
— *Matt Welch, "McCain: The Myth Of A Maverick" (2007)*

———————

1476 Trump Administration Opens Door to Let States Impose Medicaid Work Requirements
— *Washington Post, 1/11/18*

Now that another is suffering pain at your hand, trust not that thy heart shall be exempt from affliction.
— *Sa'Di, "Gulistan" (1258)*

———————

1477 UN Calls Donald Trump's ***hole Immigrants Comments 'Racist'
— *Independent, 1/12/18*

What you see is but the smallest part and least proportion of humanity.
— *Shakespeare, "Henry VI, Part 1" (1591)*

———————

1478 Number of Uninsured Americans [for Health Care] Increased by Over 3M in Trump's First Year: Gallup
— *The Hill, 1/16/18*

For the poor of this world, two major ways of expiring are available: either by the absolute indifference of your fellow-men in peace-time, or by the homicidal passion of these same when war breaks out.

— *Louis-Ferdinand Celine, "Voyage Au Bout De La Nuit" (1932)*

———————

1479 Trump Denies Changing His Position on Border Wall

— *New York Times, 1/18/18*

What is so tedious as a twice-told tale?

— *Homer, "Odyssey" (9th C. BCE)*

———————

1480 Trump Official Trivializes the Holocaust, Misuses MLK, All to Support Bigotry

— *Salon, 1/19/17*

It is certain that when he makes water, his urine is congealed ice.

— *Shakespeare, "Measure For Measure" (1604)*

CHAPTER 21

CANNELLONI SCHOOL OF MUSIC, DANCE AND THE CASUAL ARTS

TOPICS:
FOREIGN AFFAIRS AND DIPLOMACY

Cannelloni School of Music, Dance and the Casual Arts

1481 Trump Abandons Trans-Pacific Partnership, Obama's Signature Trade Deal
— *New York Times, 1/23/17*

Radicalism ceases to be radical when absorbed mainly in preserving its control over a society or an economy.
— *Eric Hoffer, "The Passionate State Of Mind" (1954)*

1482 Emboldened by Trump, Israel Approves a Wave of West Bank Settlement Expansion
— *New York Times, 1/24/17*

Fools rush in where angels fear to tread.
— *Edmund Burke, "Reflections On The Revolution In France" (1790)*

1483 Trump Prepares Orders Aiming at Global Funding and Treaties
— *New York Times, 1/25/17*

It is as though nature must needs make men narrow in order to give them force.
— *W. E. B. DuBois, "The Souls Of Black Folk" (1903)*

1484 Nicki Haley Puts U.N. on Notice: U.S. Is Taking Names
— *New York Times, 1/27/17*

How different the new order would be if we could consult the veteran instead of the politician.
— *Henry Miller "The Alcoholic Veteran With The Washboard Cranium" (1941)*

1485 For Leaders of U.S. Allies, Getting Close to Trump Can Sting
— *New York Times, 1/30/17*

Here's an object more of dread / Than aught the grave contains - / A human form with reason fled, / While wretched life remains.
— *Abraham Lincoln, "Letter To Andrew Johnson" (1846)*

———————

1486 State Dept. Officials Should Quit If They Disagree With Trump, White House Warns
— *New York Times, 1/31/17*

He who knows only his own side of the case, knows little of that.
— *John Stuart Mill, "On Liberty" (1859)*

———————

1487 State Dept. Dissent Cable on Trump's [Travel] Ban Draws 1,000 Signatures
— *New York Times, 1/31/17*

God grant me to contend with those that understand me.
— *Thomas Fuller, M.D., "Gnomologia" (1732)*

———————

1488 Iran's Supreme Leader Thanks Trump for Showing America's 'True Face'
— *New York Times, 2/7/17*

The most shocking fact about war is that its victims and its instruments are individual human beings, and that these individual beings are condemned by the monstrous conventions of politics to murder or be murdered in quarrels not their own.
— *Aldous Huxley, "The Olive Tree" (1937)*

———————

1489 Worried Europe Finds Scant Reassurances on Trump's Plans
— *New York Times, 2/19/17*

Patriotism is a lively sense of responsibility. Nationalism is a silly cock crowing on its own dunghill.

— Richard Arlington, "The Colonel's Daughter" (1931)

1490 Trump's Jabs at Mexico Are Stirring Nationalism South of the Border

— Washington Post, 2/25/17

When we come to judge others it is not by ourselves as we really are that we judge them, but by an image that we have formed of ourselves from which we have left out everything that offends our vanity or would discredit us in the eyes of the world.

— W. Somerset Maugham, "The Summing Up" (1938)

1491 Donald Trump Branded 'International Embarrassment' After Handing Made-Up NATO Invoice to Angela Merkle

— Reddit, 3/27/17

Better to trip with the feet than with the tongue.

— Zeno of Citium, "Lives And Opinions of Eminent Philosophers" (3rd C. CE)

1492 Trump Gives U.S. Forces More Freedom to Strike in Somalia

— Wall Street Journal, 3/31/17 (Misconstrued)

Let him who hath no power of patience retire within himself, though even there he will have to put up with himself.

— Baltasar Gracian, "The Art Of Worldly Wisdom" (1647)

1493 North Korea Tests Missile Ahead of Trump-Xi Meeting

— Politico, 4/5/17

Men more quickly learn and more gladly recall what they deride than what they approve and esteem.

— Horace, "Epistles" (65 BCE – 8 BCE)

1494 Trump, China and the Art of Easy Promises
— *Wall Street Journal. 4/10/17 (Misconstrued)*

People often overdo the matter when they attempt deception.
— *Charles Dudley Warner, "My Summer In A Garden" (1871)*

1495 Trump Meet's With Australia's Turnbull in Effort to Reset
— *Wall Street Journal, 5/5/17 Misconstrued)*

Men are always sincere. They change sincerities, that's all.
— *Tristan Bernard, "Ce Que L'on Dit Aux Femmes" (1923)*

1496 Foreign Leaders Have Realized That Trump Is a Pushover
— *The Atlantic, 5/16/17*

He that makes himself an ass must not take it ill if men ride him.
— *Thomas Fuller, M.D., "Gnomologia" (1732)*

1497 Dumped by Trump, Remaining TPP Nations Vow to Forge Ahead
— *Wall Street Journal, 5/20/17 (Misconstrued)*

A broken friendship may be soldered, but will never be sound.
— *Thomas Fuller, M.D. "Gnomologia" (1732)*

1498 Donald Trump Cancels Speech to Israeli Parliament Because He Did Not Want to Be Heckled
— *Independent, 5/26/17*

No person loving or admiring himself is alone.
— *Theodore Reik, "Of Love And Lust" (1957)*

1499 Donald Trump's Isolationism Is His First Great Export, and Italy Could Be First in Line

— *Huffington Post, 5/26/17*

When the world has once begun to use us ill, it afterwards continues the same treatment with less scruple or ceremony, as men do a whore.

— *Jonathan Swift, "Thoughts On Various Subjects" (1711)*

———————

1500 Trump's Trip Was a Catastrophe for U.S.-Europe Relations

— *The Atlantic, 5/28/17*

They say if you get bored enough with calamity you can learn to laugh.

— *Lawrence Durrell, "Monsieur" (1974)*

———————

1501 US Officials Scramble to Limit Trump's Diplomatic Damage Over Qatar Tweets

— *The Guardian, 6/6/17*

I asked Tom if countries always apologized when they had done wrong, and he says; "Yes; the little ones does."

— *Mark Twain, "Tom Sawyer Abroad" (1894)*

———————

1502 Jeremy Corbin Welcomes 'Cancellation' of Donald Trump State Visit

— *Independent, 6/11/17*

A healthy male adult bore consumes each year one and a half times his weight in other people's patience.

— *John Updike, "Confessions Of A Wild Bore," Assorted Prose (1965)*

———————

1503 Trump to Issue Directive Narrowing Obama's Cuban Opening

— *Wall Street Journal, 6/16/17 (Misconstrued)*

Malice swallows the greater part of its own venom.

— *Publilius Syrus, "Moral Sayings" (1st C. BCE)*

———————

1504 Canada's Trump Strategy: Go Around Him

— *New York Times, 6/22/17*

The chief difference between mankind and the cockroach is that one continuously bitches over his fate while the other [Canada] stoically plods on, uncomplaining, with never a glance backward nor a sigh for what might have been.

— *Jean Shepherd, "Fun City," The Ferrari In The Bedroom (1972)*

———————

1505 State's Afghanistan–Pakistan Unit Dissolved as Trump Weighs More Troops

— *Politico, 6/23/17*

We shall be judged more by what we do at home than what we preach abroad.

— *John F. Kennedy, State Of The Union Message (1963)*

———————

1506 Trump – and Merkel's Response to Him – Is Issue in German Election

— *Wall Street Journal, 6/25/17 (Misconstrued)*

Great hatred can be concealed in the countenance, and much in a kiss.

— *Publilius Syrus, "Moral Sayings" (1st C. BCE)*

———————

1507 Poll: American's Have More Confidence in Merkel than Trump
— *The Hill, 7/5/17*

Uneasy lies the head that wears the crown.
— *Shakespeare, "Henry IV, Part 2" (1597 - 1599)*

————————

1508 As Trump Sounds Dire Warnings for G-20, His Peers Sound Optimistic
— *Washington Post, 7/6/17*

The vision of an entire world becoming just like us is at least as discomfiting as the thought that most of it won't.
— *Eva Hoffman, "Exit Into History" (1933)*

————————

1509 Trump Clashes With Global Leaders Over Trade
— *Wall Street Journal, 7/6/17 (Misconstrued)*

The same reason that makes us wrangle with a neighbor causes a war between princes.
— *Montaigne, "Apology For Raymond De Sebonde," Essays (1580)*

————————

1510 Trump's Foreign Policy: the Conservatives' Report Card
— *New York Times, 7/21/17*

Some of the more fatuous flag-waving Americans are in danger of forgetting that you can't extract gratitude as you would extract a tooth; that unless friendship is freely given, it means nothing and less than nothing.
— *Max Lerner, "How Grateful Should Europe Be," Actions/Passions (1949)*

————————

1511 Scotland Blocks Trump From Expanding His Golf Empire There
— *Washington Post, 7/30/17*

This is the devilish thing about foreign affairs; they are foreign and will not always conform to our whim.

— James Reston, The New York Times, (Dec. 1964)

1512 Transcripts Show How Contentious Trump's Calls Were with Mexican and Australian Leaders

— New York Times, 8/3/17

A big man knows he don't have to fight, but whin a man is little an' knows he's little an' is thinkin' all th' time he's little an' feels that iverybody else is thinkin' he's little, look out f'r him.

— Finley Peter Dunne, "The Japanese Scare," Mr. Dooley Says (1910)

1513 Diplomats Laughing at Trump Over Leaked Mexico Transcripts

— McClatchy DC Bureau, 8/3/17

Oh Lord, give us a sense of humor with courage to manifest it forth, so that we may laugh to shame the pomps, the vanities, the sense of self-importance of the Big Fellows that the world sometimes sends among us, and who try to take our peace away.

— Sean O'Casey, "The Power Of Laughter," The Green Crow (1956)

1514 European Diplomats Reportedly Consider Trump a 'Laughing Stock' Who Is 'Obsessed With Obama'

— Business Insider, 8/9/17

A laugh's the wisest, easiest answer to all that's queer.

— Herman Melville, "Moby-Dick" (1851)

1515 Top European Diplomats Just Revealed Trump's Sinister Obsession With Obama

— Washington Journal, 8/9/17

Living with golden fantasies of an endless nurtured infancy can be a neurotic refusal to grow up.
— Judith Viorst, "Necessary Losses" (1986)

———————

1516 Trump's Shift [More Troops] Boost Afghans, Risks Pushing Pakistan to China
— Wall Street Journal, 8/23/17 (Misconstrued)

Do I contradict myself? / Very well then I contradict myself, / (I am large, I contain multitudes).
— Walt Whitman, "Song of Myself," 51, Leaves Of Grass (1855)

———————

1517 'The President Speaks For Himself': Rex Tillerson Distances Himself from Trump
— The Guardian, 8/27/17

All the mind's activity is easy if it is not subjected to reality.
— Marcel Proust, "Remembrance Of Things Past: Cities Of The Plain" (1913)

———————

1518 Trump Says He Will Not Talk to North Korea. Experts Fear He Will
— New York Times, 8/30/17

Man is Nature's sole mistake!
— W.S. Gilbert, "Princess Ida" (1884)

———————

1519 Trump Looks to Rally World Leaders on North Korea
— Wall Street Journal, 9/16/17 (Misconstrued)

A fantasy can be equivalent to a paradise and if the fantasy passes, better yet, because eternal paradise would be very boring.
— Juan Ramon Jimenez, "To Burn Completely," Selected Writings (1957)

———————

1520 Trump's 'Rocket Man' Tweet Claims Korea Sanctions Biting, But Experts Unsure
— *The Guardian, 9/17/17*

The greatest deception men suffer is from their own opinions.
— *Leonardo da Vinci, Notebooks (1500 CE)*

———————

1521 Trump to Push Nationalist Policy in First U.N. Address
— *Wall Street Journal, 9/19/17 Misconstrued)*

Nationalism has two fatal charms for its devotees; it presupposes local self-sufficiency, which is a pleasant and desirable condition, and it suggests, very subtly, a certain personal superiority by reason of one's belonging to a place which is definable and familiar, as against a place which is strange, remote.
— *E.B. White, "Intimations," One Man's Meat (1944)*

———————

1522 Trump's First Speech to the United Nations Was a Disastrous, Nationalistic Flop
— *Washington Post, 9/19/17*

Men, unlike mocking birds, have the capacity for systematic self-delusion. We echo each other with equal precision, equal eloquence, equal assurance.
— *Robert Ardrey, "The Territorial Imperative" (1966)*

———————

1523 The Contradiction Buried In Trump's Iran and North Korea Policies
— *New York Times, 9/20/17*

Man never knows what he wants; he aspires to penetrate mysteries and as soon as he has, wants to re-establish them. Ignorance irritates him and knowledge cloys.
— *Henri Frederic Amiel, Journal (1882)*

———————

389

1524 Trump Imposes New Sanctions on North Korea; Kim Says He Will 'Tame the Mentally Deranged US Dotard With Fire'
— *Washington Post, 9/21/17*

Solemnity is the shield of idiots.
— *Montesquieu, "Pensees Et Jugements" (1899)*

———————

1525 Trump Can't Handle North Korea Responsibly, Majority Say in New Poll
— *Newsweek, 9/24/17*

No man is wise enough nor good enough to be trusted with unlimited power.
— *Charles Caleb Colton, "Lacon" (1825)*

———————

1526 Trump Talks Tough on China and Mexico, But Trade Actions Hit Canada
— *New York Times, 9/27/17*

Thy have been at a great feast of languages, and stolen the scraps.
— *Shakespeare, "Love's Labour's Lost" (Mid – 1590s)*

———————

1527 Iran's Foreign Minister Has Some Things He Wants to Say to Donald Trump
— *Politico, 10/2/17*

There is no being so poor and so contemptible, who does not think there is somebody still poorer, and still more contemptible.
— *Samuel Johnson, Quoted In Boswell's "Life Of Samuel Johnson" (1766)*

———————

1528 Tillerson News Conference Only Highlights Strains With Trump
— *New York Times, 10/4/17*

A diplomat should be yielding as a liana that can be bent but not broken.

— *Maylay Proverb*

_____

1529 'Calm Before the Storm': Trump Remark [About North Korea] Sparks Foreign Policy Speculation

— *News Source, 10/6/17*

Clumsy jesting is no joke.

— *Aesop, "The Ass And The Lapdog," Fables (6th C. BCE)*

_____

1530 Trump on North Korea: 'Sorry, But Only One Thing Will Work!'

— *Washington Post, 10/7/17*

To delight in war is a merit in the soldier, a dangerous quality in the captain, and a positive crime in the statesman.

— *George Santayana, "The Life Of Reason: Reason In Society" (1905)*

_____

1531 Trump Wants to Weaken NAFTA'S Influence, Power

— *Wall Street Journal, 10/11/17 (Misconstrued)*

At any street corner the feeling of absurdity can strike any man in the face. As it is, in its distressing nudity, in its light without effulgence, it is elusive.

— *Albert Camus, "The Myth Of Sisyphus" (1955)*

_____

1532 Trump Vows to End Iran Deal Himself If Congress Won't Act

— *Wall Street Journal, 10/13/17 (Misconstrued)*

Kings stand more in need of the company of the intelligent than the intelligent do of the society of kings.

— *Sa'Di, "Gulistan" (1258)*

_____

1533 Thanks to Trump, America's Word Is Now Worthless
— *Washington Post, 10/16/17*

The world is an old woman, and mistakes any gilt farthing for a gold coin; whereby being often cheated, she will thenceforth trust nothing but the common copper.
— *Thomas Carlyle, "Sartor Resartus" (1833)*

1534 President Trump: The World Has a Drug Problem
— *News Source. 10/17/17*

He bids fair to grow wise who has discovered he is not so.
— *Publilius Syrus, "Moral Sayings" (1st C. BCE)*

1535 Iran's Khamenei Threatens to 'Shred' Nuclear Deal, Blasts 'Foul-Mouthed' Trump
— *News Source, 10/18/17*

Out of the mouths of babes.
— *Bible, Derived From Psalms 8:2 and Matthew 21:16*

1536 George W. Bush Emerges to Bash Trump, 'Nativism': 'We Cannot Wish Globalism Away'
— *News Source, 10/19/17*

Innocence dwells with Wisdom, but never with Ignorance.
— *William Blake, Annotations, "The Four Zoas" (1795)*

1537 President Trump: United Nations Has Tremendous Potential
— *News Source, 10/20/17*

Is insincerity such a terrible thing? I think not. It is merely a method by which we can multiply our personalities.
— *Oscar Wilde, "The Picture Of Dorian Grey" (1891)*

1538 White House in Damage Control Over Niger Ambush
— *News Source, 10/20/17*

Public-relations specialists make flower arrangements of the facts, placing them so that the wilted and less attractive petals are hidden by sturdy blooms.
— *Alan Harrington, "Public Relations," Life In The Crystal Palace (1959)*

———

1539 Under Trump, U.S. Passport Value for Global Travel Is Plummeting
— *Newsweek, 10/25/17*

Injuries may be forgiven, but not forgotten.
— *Aesop, "The Man And The Serpent," Fables (6th C. BCE)*

———

1540 Emails Reveal [English] Foreign Office Alarm at Trump Travel Ban
— *BBC, 10/26/17*

Suspense - is Hostiler than Death - / Death - tho'soever Broad, / Is just Death, and cannot increase - / Suspense - does not conclude - .
— *Emily Dickenson, Poem (1863)*

———

1541 Trump Admin to Defend Cuba Embargo at UN, Reversing Obama
— *News Source, 10/31/17*

Revenge proves its own executioner.
— *John Ford, "The Broken Heart" (1633)*

———

1542 An Emboldened Xi Will Greet a Troubled Trump in China
— *Wall Street Journal, 11/7/17 (Misconstrued)*

He was oppressed, and he was afflicted, yet he opened not his mouth; he is brought as a lamb to the slaughter, and as a sheep before her shearers is dumb, so he openeth not his mouth.
— *King James Bible, Isaiah 53:7*

1543 After a Year of Trump, Good News for Europe - He Doesn't Care About Us
— *The Guardian, 11/11/17*

Pleasure is the object, the duty, and the goal of all rational creatures.
— *Voltaire, "Epitre A Madame De G." (1716)*

1544 China's Rise Didn't Have to Mean America's Fall. Then Came Trump
— *Washington Post, 11/15/17*

Now I am become Death, the destroyer of worlds.
— *Vishnu, "Bhagavad Gita" (400 BCE - 200 CE)*

1545 Jerry Brown Trashes Donald Trump to Chinese Officials in Europe
— *News Source, 11/16/17*

Try the Lamentations of Jeremiah. They always pick me up.
— *Peter De Vries, Letter To Paul Theroux, Quoted In The New York Times (1993)*

1546 Amid Growing Tensions With White House, Tillerson's State Dept to Skip Ivanka's India Trip
— *News Source, 11/24/17*

The Original Amateur Hour.
— *Major Edward Bowes, Creator, Radio And Television Program (1934 - 1970)*

1547 Critics Fear Trump's Asia Trip Served to Cede Power to China
— *News Source, 11/28/17*

Like shooting fish in a barrel.
— *Adjective Phrase, The Dictionary Of American Slang, 4th Ed. (2007)*

———————

1548 The Peril of Trump's Populist Foreign Policy
— *Wall Street Journal, 11/28/17 (Misconstrued)*

A nation can be no stronger abroad than she is at home. Only an America which practices what it preaches about equal rights and social justice will be respected by those whose choice affects our future.
— *John F. Kennedy, Undelivered Address, Dallas TX (November 22, 1963)*

———————

1549 Trump Isn't Welcome in UK After Sharing Far-Right [Anti-Muslim] Videos, London Mayor Says
— *CNBC, 11/30/17*

You are not worth another word, else I'd call you a knave.
— *Shakespeare, "All's Well That Ends Well" (1604 - 1605)*

———————

1550 White House Considering Recognizing Jerusalem as Israel's Capital Soon
— *CNN, 11/30/17*

Out of the frying pan and into the fire.
— *English Idiom (Early 16th C.)*

———————

1551 'This Will Be Bad': Clashes Break Out in West Bank Over Trump Jerusalem Speech
— *Washington Post, 12/7/16*

Revolutions are not made by fate but by men.
— *Jacob Bronowski, "The Ascent Of Man" (1973)*

1552 Jerusalem Status: World Condemns Trump's Announcement
— *BBC, 12/8/17*

Lost in the solitude of his immense power, he began to lose direction.
— *Gabrial Garcia Marquez, "One Hundred Years Of Solitude" (1970)*

1553 White House Contradicts Tillerson and Says Not Right Time for North Korea Talks
— *The Guardian, 12/13/17*

Even after a bad harvest there must be sowing.
— *Seneca, "Letters To Lucilius" (63 - 65 CE))*

1554 Madeleine Albright: It's Time for Congress to Override Trump's Foreign Policy Powers
— *CNN, 12/14/17*

He that is everywhere is nowhere.
— *Thomas Fuller, M. D., "Gnomologia" (1732)*

1555 Trump's Tough Talk Can't Hide the Incoherence of His Foreign Policy
— *Washington Post, 12/19/17*

F**ked up beyond all recognition. [FUBAR]
— *Lawrence Paros, 'The Erotic Tongue" (1984)*

1556 Appeals Court Rules That Trump's Third Travel Ban Is Illegal
— *ThinkProgress, 12/22/17*

A just cause needs no interpreting. / It carries it's own case. But the unjust argument / since it is sick, needs clever medicine.
— Euripides, "The Phoenician Women" (411 BCE)

———————

1557 Trump Claims He Is Boosting U.S. Influence, But Many Foreign Leaders See America in Retreat
— Los Angeles Times, 12/26/17

So, my good window of lattice, fare thee well; thy casement I need not open, for I look through thee.
— Shakespeare, "All's Well That Ends Well" (1604 - 1605)

———————

1558 How Can Trump Help Iran Protesters? Be Quiet
— New York Times, 12/30/17

Nothing is often a good thing to say, and always a clever thing to say.
— Will Durant, "New York World-Telegram & Sun" (June, 1958)

———————

1559 Trump Starts 2018 With Tweets Criticizing Pakistan, Iran and Former U.S. Leaders
— Politico, 1/1/18

If you once understand an author's character, the comprehension of his writings becomes easy.
— Longfellow, "Hyperion" (1839)

———————

1560 Trump's Twitter Threats Put American Credibility on the Line [More Mouth Than Fist]
— New York Times, 1/7/18

If you keep your mouth shut you will never put your foot in it.
— Austin O'Malley, American Physicist, QuoteHD (1858 - 1932)

———————

1561 Tillerson and Mattis Are Reportedly Trying to Hold Trump Back From Striking North Korea

— *Business Insider, 1/9/18*

Where no wood is, there the fire goeth out: so where there is no tale Bearer, the strife ceaseth.

— *Bible, Proverbs 26:20*

1562 US Ambassador to Panama Says He Cannot Serve Trump

— *BBC, 1/12/18*

Life as we find it is too hard for us; it entails too much pain, too many disappointments, impossible tasks. We cannot do without palliative remedies.

— *Sigmund Freud, "Civilization And Its Discontents" (1930)*

1563 South Africa Summons US Diplomat to Explain Trump ["Shithole"] Comment

— *Washington Post, 1/15/1814.*

Amity itself can only be maintained by reciprocal respect, and true friends, are punctilious equals.

— *Herman Melville, "Battlepieces And Aspects Of The War" (1866)*

1564 Trumplomacy: Has Trump Made the World More Dangerous?

— *BBC, 1/16/18*

Does a bear shit in the woods?

— *Dana Marie Bell, "Bear Necessities" (2010)*

CHAPTER 22

COMMAND AND GENERAL STAFF COLLEGE FOR STAR FLEET AIR, LAND AND SEA FORCES

TOPICS:
INTELLIGENCE AND PERCEPTION

Command and General Staff College for Star Fleet Air, Land and Sea Forces

1565 President Trump Has No Idea How the Trade Deficit Works

— *Reddit, 1/22/17*

If I cannot brag of knowing something, then I brag of not knowing it.

— *Emerson, "Journals" (1866)*

1566 President Rejects Intelligence Report on Travel Ban

— *Wall Street Journal, 1/25/17 (Misconstrued)*

Stubbornness and stupidity are twins.

— *Sophocles, "Antigone" (441 BCE)*

1567 Building a Wall of Ignorance

— *New York Times, 1/30/17*

The spirit of our American radicalism is destructive and aimless: it is not loving, it has no ulterior and divine ends; but is destructive only out of hatred and selfishness.

— *Emerson, "Politics," Essays: Second Series (1844)*

1568 Trump Pick for Army Secretary: Citizens Should Have the Same Weapons as the Government

— *Huffington Post, 2/5/17*

Anarchy is the stepping-stone to absolute power.

— *Napoleon I, "Maxims" (1804-15)*

1569 President Trump, White House Apprentice

— *New York Times, 2/18/17*

A man has no ears for that to which experience has given him no access.

— *Nietzsche, "Ecco Homo" (1888)*

───────────

1570 Trump Says 'He Can't Find a Country Where We Actually Do Well' With Trade

— *Washington Post, 2/24/17*

The obstinacy of human beings is exceeded only by the obstinacy of inanimate objects.

— *Alexander Chase, "Perspectives" (1966)*

───────────

1571 Cabinet Members Keep Scrambling to Clean Up After Trump Speaks

— *Washington Post, 2/26/17*

Either thou art most ignorant by age, or thou wert born a fool.

— *Shakespeare, "The Winter's Tale" (1609 – 1611)*

───────────

1572 Trump's Wiretap Rant Betrays Ignorance of the Law

— *Reddit, 3/5/17*

A reading machine always wound up and going, he mastered whatever was not worth knowing.

— *James Russell Lowell, "A Fable For Critics" (1848)*

───────────

1573 While Trump Is So Ignorant We Cannot be Free

— *Huffington Post, 3/5/17*

If the blind lead the blind, both shall fall into the ditch.

— *Bible, Matthew 15:14*

───────────

1574 Billionaire Mark Cuban: Trump Too Clueless to Collude With Russia
— *Huffington Post, 4/2/17*

The ignorance of the world leaves one at the mercy of its malice.
— *William Hazlitt, "On The Disadvantages Of Intellectual Superiority" (1821)*

1575 Ten Weeks in, Trump Has Racked Up Few Victories
— *Wall Street Journal, 4/2/17 (Misconstrued)*

It's not the tragedies that kill us, it's the messes.
— *Dorothy Parker, Interview, "Writers At Work: First Series" (1958)*

1576 Trump's Idiocracy: The New Paradigm of Fools
— *Huffington Post, 4/3/17*

Political extremism involves two prime ingredients: an excessively simple diagnosis of the world's ills and a conviction that there are identifiable villains back of it all.
— *John W. Gardner, "No Easy Victories" (1968)*

1577 The Coming Incompetence Crises
— *New York Times, 4/7/17*

I hate all bungling like sin, but most of all bungling in state affairs, which produces nothing but mischief to thousands and millions.
— *Goethe, Quoted In "Conversations With Goethe" (1832)*

1578 As Trump Plays the Global Strongman, What Happened to 'America First?'
— *The Guardian, 4/16/17*

The less justified a man is in claiming excellence for his own self, the more ready is he to claim all excellence for his nation, his religion, his race or his holy cause.
— Eric Hoffer, "The True Believer" (1951)

1579 National Monuments Could Soon Be on the Chopping Block
— Wall Street Journal, 5/1/17 (Misconstrued)

The smell of profit is clean / And sweet, whatever the source.
— Juvenal, "Satires" (2d C. CE)

1580 Trump Administration Defends Inviting [Philippine] President Who Admitted Murdering People to Washington
— Huffington Post, 5/1/17

One man's wickedness may easily become all men's curse.
— Publilius Syrus, "Moral Sayings" (1st. C. BCE)

1581 Most of Trump's Voters Don't Think He's Changed Since Taking Office
— Huffington Post, 5/2/17

Obstinacy / standing alone is the weakest of all things / in one whose mind is not possessed by wisdom.
— Aeschylus, "Prometheus Bound" (478 BCE)

1582 Half a Million People Sign Petition to Take Away Donald Trump's Ability to Launch Nuclear Weapons
— Independent, 5/5/17

The real menace in dealing with a five-year old is that in no time at all you begin to sound like a five-year old.
— Jean Kerr, "Please Don't Eat The Daisies" (1957)

1583 'What is Wrong With You?' Michelle Obama Savages Trump's Gutting of Her Legacy

— *The Guardian, 5/13/17*

To be able to destroy with good conscience, to be able to behave badly and call your bad behavior 'righteous indignation' - this is the height of psychological luxury, the most delicious of moral treats.

— *Aldous Huxley, "Chrome Yellow" (1921)*

1584 Trump Is Dangerously Incompetent

— *Washington Post, 5/15/17*

Oh thrice unhappy home / whose master doesn't know the difference between a watt and an ohm!

— *Ogden Nash, "I'm A Stranger Here Myself" (1938)*

1585 Despite Campaign Boasts, Trump Has No Idea How to Handle Classified Material

— *Huffington Post, 5/17/17*

A good many men and women want to get possession of secrets just as spendthrifts want to get money - for circulation.

— *George Dennison Prentice, "Prenticeana" (1860)*

1586 The 'I'm Really Smart' President Faces Crises of Ignorance

— *Huffington Post, 5/17/17*

Folly pursues us at all periods of our lives. If someone seems wise it is only because his follies are proportionate to his age and fortune.

— *La Rochefoucauld, "Maxims" (1665)*

1587 Someone Needs to Explain to Donald Trump That His Own Administration Appointed the Special Counsel

— *New York Magazine, 5/19/17*

If his IQ slips any lower, we'll have to water him twice a day.

— *Molly Ivans, "Molly Ivans Can't Say That, Can She?" (1991)*

1588 Analysis: Trump Just Gave Billions of Dollars of Sophisticated Weapons to a State He Said Masterminded 9/11

— *Haaretz, 5/21/17*

'Tis time to fear when tyrants seem to kiss.

— *Shakespeare, "Pericles" (1606 -1608)*

1589 Trump Proposes Selling Off Half the U.S. Strategic Oil Reserve

— *Bloomberg, 5/22/17*

No man sees far; the most see no farther than their noses.

— *Thomas Carlyle, "Count Cagliostro" (1833)*

1590 Trump Budget Based on $2 Trillion Math Error

— *New York Magazine, 5/23/17*

Any man can make mistakes, but only an idiot persists in his error.

— *Cicero, "Philippics" (44-43 BCE)*

1591 Trump Might be the Dimmest President Ever

— *Washington Post, 5/31/17*

The hardest thing to cope with is not selfishness or vanity or deceitfulness, but sheer stupidity.

— *Eric Hoffer, "The Passionate State Of Mind" (1954)*

1592 Naomi Klein: Trump Is An Idiot, But Don't Underestimate How Good He Is at That

— *The Guardian, 6/11/17*

The fool has one great advantage over a man of sense – he is always satisfied with himself.

— *Napoleon I, "Maxims" (1804-1815)*

1593 Trump Era Ignorance Triumphs Over Shakespeare

— *Huffington Post, 6/12/17*

Ignorance and incuriosity are two very soft pillows.

— *French Proverb*

1594 Report: Trump Administration Has Done Next to Nothing to Prevent Future Election Hacking

— *New York Magazine, 6/23/17*

We are not certain, we are never certain. If we were, we would reach some conclusions, and we could, at last, make others take us seriously.

— *Albert Camus, "The Fall" (1956)*

1595 Are Donald Trump Supporters Idiots?

— *New Republic, 6/29/17*

One great mistake by intelligent people is to refuse to believe that the world is as stupid as it is.

— *Mme De Tencin, Quoted In Chamfort's "Caracteres Et Anecdotes" (1771)*

1596 Trump Has Wasted the Major Advantage He Had Coming Into Office

— *Washington Post, 7/2/17*

Every President reconstructs the Presidency to meet his own psychological needs.

— *Arthur M. Schlesinger, "The Imperial Presidency" (1973)*

―――――――

1597 'Close to the Stupidest Idea': Critics Lash Trump-Russia Cyber Security Plan

— *The Guardian, 7/9/17*

Whenever a man does a thoroughly stupid thing it is always from the noblest motive.

— *Oscar Wilde, "The Picture Of Dorian Grey" (1891)*

―――――――

1598 Trump's Biggest Political Asset Is Supporters Who Believe Any Negative News Is Fake

— *New York Magazine, 7/11/17*

All that is necessary to raise imbecility into what the crowd regards as profundity is to lift it off the floor and put it on a platform.

— *George Jean Nathan, "Profundity," American Mercury (1929)*

―――――――

1599 Donald Trump's Views on Britain Show Him Up for the Narcissist He Is

— *The Guardian, 8/2/17*

He who is in love with himself has at least this advantage – he won't encounter many rivals.

— *Georg Christophe Lichtenberg, "Aphorisms" (1764)*

―――――――

1600 It's Not a Coup. The President Is Just Incompetent

— *Washington Monthly, 8/6/17*

Nature, in her blind thirst for life, has filled every possible cranny of the rotting earth with some sort of fantastic creature.

— *Joseph Wood Krutch, "Genesis Of A Mood," The Modern Temper (1929)*

1601 Trump Is Wrong: A Weak Dollar Doesn't Make a Strong Economy
— *Wall Street Journal, 8/9/17 (Misconstrued)*

Thinking is hard work. One can't bear burdens and ideas at the same time.
— *Remi De Gourmont, "Promenades Philosophiques" (1905)*

1602 Trump's Tangles of Rhetorical Inadequacy
— *Wall Street Journal, 8/19/17 (Misconstrued)*

Despite the constant negative press covfefe.
— *Donald Trump, Tweet (May 31, 2017)*

1603 Trump Set to Roll Back Limits on Military Gear for Police
— *Washington Post, 8/28/17*

We get into the habit of living before acquiring the habit of thinking. In that race, which daily hastens us toward death, the body maintains its irreparable lead.
— *Albert Camus, "The Myth Of Sisyphus" (1955)*

1604 Donald Trump Confused Hopes and Facts in Fighter Jet Sale Announcement, Says Finland
— *Newsweek, 8/30/17*

Everything is a dangerous drug except reality, which is unendurable.
— *Cyril Connolly, "The Unquiet Grave" (1945)*

1605 'We Don't Answer to Him': McCain Calls Trump 'Poorly Informed,' 'Impulsive' in Blistering Op-Ed
— *Business Insider, 9/1/17*

A child should always say what's true, / And speak when he is spoken to, / And behave mannerly at table: / At least as far as he is able.
— *Robert Lewis Stevenson, "A Child's Garden Of Verses" (1885)*

1606 Bannon Calls Comey Firing the Biggest Mistake in 'Modern Political History'
— *New York Times, 9/10/17*

Each believes easily what he fears and what he desires.
— *La Fontaine, "The Wolf And The Fox," Fables (1668)*

1607 Twitter Founder: Trump Presidency Is the Product of Short Attention Spans
— *The Guardian, 9/13/17*

This won't hurt, did it?
— *Michael J. Weinstock, "Aphorisms" (1975)*

1608 Trump Claims Graham-Cassidy [Repealing Obamacare] Covers Pre-existing Conditions. It Doesn't
— *Huffington Post, 9/21/17*

It takes a long time to understand nothing.
— *Edward Dahlberg, "On Wisdom And Folly," Reasons Of The Heart (1965)*

1609 It Was Candidate Trump's Best Trick [Not Sweating the Details]. Now It's Stalling President Trump's Agenda
— *Washington Post, 9/28/17*

He that knows little often repeats it.
— *Thomas Fuller, M.D., "Gnomologia" (1732)*

1610 Nobel Peace Prize Winner Calls Donald Trump a Moron
— *News Source, 10/6/17*

The dumbness in the eyes of animals is more touching than the speech of men, but the dumbness in the speech of men is more agonizing than the eyes of animals.

— *Hindustani Proverb*

1611 In Embarrassing Display, Trump Flubs Test on How Money Works

— *MSNBC, 10/12/17*

The length of the sky is just about the size of my ignorance. Pure and wide.

— *Louise Erdrich, "Saint Marie," Love Medicine (1984)*

1612 Did Trump's Tweet Make It Safer for NFL Players to Kneel for the Anthem?

— *Washington Post, 10/15/17*

Have I lived to stand at the taunt of one that makes fritters of English?

— *Shakespeare, "The Merry Wives Of Windsor" (1597)*

1613 The Great Dealmaker? Lawmakers Find Trump to Be An Untrustworthy Negotiator

— *Washington Post, 10/23/17*

Suspicion is a thing very few people can entertain without letting the hypothesis turn, in their minds, into fact.

— *David Cort, "Social Astonishments" (1963)*

1614 Where Donald Trump's Unpredictability Could Hurt Him

— *Wall Street Journal, 10/23/17 (Misconstrued)*

If he has no other burden, he'll take up a load of stones.

— *Malay Proverb*

1615 Poll: Voters See Trump as Reckless, Not Honest

— *Politico, 10/25/17*

Power, like a desolating pestilence, pollutes whate'er it touches.
— *Shelley, " Queen Mab" (1813)*

1616 One Year Later, Trump Voters Blame the President's Tweets for His Troubles

— *USA Today, 11/5/17*

His words are a very fantastical banquet, just so many strange dishes.
— *Shakespeare, "Much Ado About Nothing" (1598 - 1599)*

1617 Will Virginia Teach Trump Fans a Lesson?

— *Wall Street Journal, 11/9/17 (Misconstrued)*

Herein lies the tragedy of the age: not that men are poor, - all men know something of poverty; not that men are wicked, - who is good? not that men are ignorant, - what is truth? Nay, but that men know so little of men.
— *W. E. B. Dubois, "The Souls Of Black Folk" (1903)*

1618 Trump Says Putin 'Means It' About Not Meddling [in Presidential Election]

— *New York Times, 11/11/17*

Simple Simon met a pieman, Going to the fair. Says Simple Simon to the pieman, Let me taste your ware…
— *Popular English Nursery Rhyme, Roud Folk Song Index (No. 19777)*

1619 John Oliver on Trump: 'An iPhone Would Be a More Coherent President'

— *The Guardian, 11/13/17*

Give me your hand. I can tell your fortune. You are a fool.
— *Shakespeare, "The Two Noble Kinsmen" (1612 - 1614)*

1620 China Could Sell Trump the Brooklyn Bridge
— *New York Times, 11/14/17*

Our credulity is greatest concerning the things we know least about. And since we know least about ourselves, we are ready to believe all that is said about us. Hence the mysterious power of both flattery and calumny.
— *Eric Hoffer, "The Passionate State Of Mind" (1955)*

1621 Aides Have Given Up Trying to Control Trump's Tweets
— *Politico, 11/17/17*

Futility: playing a harp before a buffalo.
— *Burmese Proverbs (1962)*

1622 Donald Trump Jokes About 'Pocahontas' Elizabeth Warren During Navajo Code Talkers Event
— *News Source, 11/18/17*

People ask what I am really trying to do with humor. The answer is, "I'm getting even."
— *Art Buchwald, "Leaving Home: A Memoir" (1993)*

1623 Report: Trump Revealed Israeli Commando and Mossad Operation in Syria to Putin
— *Haaretz, 11/23/17*

Many complain of their looks, but none of their brains.
— *Yiddish Proverbs (1949)*

1624 Donald Trump Tweeted A Woman With Six Followers Thinking She Was the Leader of Britain

— *Newsweek, 11/30/17*

There's many a man hath more hair than wit.

— *Shakespeare, "A Comedy Of Errors" (1594)*

1625 Reagan Advisor Bruce Bartlett: 'Trump is Clearly the Most Incompetent President We've Ever Had'

— *Salon, 12/2/17*

You rise to play, and go to bed to work.

— *Shakespeare, "Othello" (1603)*

1626 Trump Didn't Seem to Have Complete Understanding of Jerusalem Decision: Report

— *The Hill, 12/7/17*

Clueless – completely or hopelessly bewildered, unaware, ignorant, or foolish.

— *Definition, Mirriam-Webster Dictionary (Since 1828)*

1627 Kansas's Ravaged Economy a Cautionary Tale as Trump Plans Huge Tax Cuts for the Rich

— *The Guardian, 12/10/17*

Those who cannot remember the past are doomed to repeat it.

— *George Santayana, "The Life Of Reason" (1905)*

1628 Trump Believes That Democrats and Republicans Will Come Together to Craft a New Health Plan. He's Also an Idiot

— *The Root, 12/26/17*

A delusion is something people believe despite a total lack of evidence.

— *Richard Dawkins, Evolutionary Biologist And Author (b. 1941)*

———————

1629 Merkel's Efforts to Teach Trump About Diplomacy Didn't Go Well

— *New York Magazine, 12/29/17*

He that knows least commonly presumes most.

— *Thomas Fuller, M. D., "Gnomologia" (1732)*

———————

1630 Trump Did Not Know What Brexit Was Two Weeks Before EU Referendum, Author of Explosive Book Claims

— *Independent, 1/6/18*

Far more crucial than what we know or do not know is what we do not want to know.

— *Eric Hoffer, "The Passionate State Of Mind" (1954)*

———————

1631 White House Caught Censoring Transcript to Cover Up Trump's Bungling His Own Basic Policy [on Immigration]

— *Shareblue Media, 1/10/18*

The surest way of concealing from others the boundaries of one's own knowledge, is not to over step them.

— *Giacomo Leopardi, "Pensiere" (1834)*

———————

1632 [Former Mexican President] Vicente Fox: Trump's 'Mouth is the Foulest S---hole in the World'

— *The Hill, 1/11/18*

He has not so much brain as ear wax.

— *Shakespeare, "Troilus And Cressida" (1602)*

———————

1633 German Magazine Der Spiegel Shows Trump as Devolved Man in 'March of Progress' Spoof

— The Hill, 1/14/18

I believe our Heavenly Father invented man because he was disappointed in the monkey.

— Mark Twain, ""Mark Twain In Eruption" (1940)

ABOUT THE EDITOR

Mr. Penname's first incarnation was as a ferret during the Jurassic Period. In eras subsequent to that, he was a gerbil, a stoat, a sloth, an Airedale and an orangutan until finally manifesting himself in human form as Ethelred the Unready, King of England, in 978. Subsequent to that he was Peter the Great, Juan the Offensive, Jimmy the Toad and Paul the Prurient before joining the literary world as both Oscar Wilde and Ambrose Bierce. He received his bachelor's degree in literature from Stankey Junior College, his master's degree in obfuscation from the Crapstone Institute of Technology, and his doctoral degree in philology from The School Of Hard Knocks. He divides his time between his wife and three children near Baffin Bay, Canada, and his other wife and four children in Villa O'Higgins, Chile. When asked if he believes in reincarnation, he said, "No, and I didn't believe in it the last time around."

www.ingramcontent.com/pod-product-compliance
Lightning Source LLC
Chambersburg PA
CBHW060808030726
47503CB00002B/400